C0-AMZ-810

Coping with Poverty

Coping with Poverty

The Social Contexts of
Neighborhood, Work, and Family
in the African-American Community

Edited by

Sheldon Danziger and Ann Chih Lin

CABRINI COLLEGE LIBRARY
610 KING OF PRUSSIA ROAD
RADNOR, PA 19087

Ann Arbor

THE UNIVERSITY OF MICHIGAN PRESS

#43333537

Copyright © by the University of Michigan 2000
All rights reserved
Published in the United States of America by
The University of Michigan Press
Manufactured in the United States of America
♾ Printed on acid-free paper

2003   2002   2001   2000   4   3   2   1

No part of this publication may be reproduced, stored in a retrieval system, or transmitted in any form or by any means, electronic, mechanical, or otherwise, without the written permission of the publisher.

A CIP catalog record for this book is available from the British Library.

Library of Congress Cataloging-in-Publication Data

Coping with poverty : the social contexts of neighborhood, work, and family in the African-American community / edited by Sheldon Danziger and Ann Chih Lin.
       p.   cm.
    Includes bibliographical references and index.
     ISBN 0-472-11145-0 (acid-free paper) — ISBN 0-472-08697-9 (pbk. : acid-free paper)
     1. Afro-Americans—Social conditions—1975–   2. Urban poor—United States.   3. Afro-Americans—Economic conditions.   4. Afro-Americans—Employment.   5. Urban policy—United States.   6. Afro-American families—Social conditions.   7. Inner cities—United States.   I. Danziger, Sheldon. II. Lin, Ann Chih.

E185.86 .C58213   2000
305.896073—dc21

                                                                    00-020956

To the memory of Dr. Andrew L. Reaves:
Colleague, Friend, and Role Model

For Andy, a doctorate and a university professorship were never just a career: they were a lifelong dream. At the age of forty-two, a successful businessman and a survivor of lung cancer, Andy dared to start a new life, entering a doctoral program in social psychology at the University of Michigan. He earned his Ph.D. in 1992 and an M.P.H. in 1993. Andy's education and subsequent work as an Assistant Professor of Psychology at the University of Alabama were his victories in the face of death. Illness could not kill his passion for helping others cope with and overcome poverty. His great kindness and compassion, his deep dedication, and his gallant courage will always be an inspiration to us.

Contents

Preface

The disproportionate rate of poverty among African-Americans often leads policymakers, researchers, and advocates for the poor to focus on their plight. In 1997, 26.5 percent of all black persons lived below the official poverty line. The comparable figure for whites was 11 percent. In fact, the 1997 rate for African-Americans was higher than the 1959 rate for whites. The poverty rate for African-Americans living in female-headed households was 42.8 percent, compared with 30.7 percent for similar whites. Even among married couples, who have relatively low poverty rates, the black rate, 8 percent, is substantially higher than the 4.8 percent white rate.

The persistence of poverty is also greater for minorities. That is, once an African-American becomes poor, she or he is likely to remain poor for more years than whites (Gottschalk, McLanahan, and Sandefur 1994). The probability that a poor child will be poor as an adult is also higher for African-Americans than for whites (Corcoran 1995; Corcoran and Chaudry 1997).

Poverty among African-Americans is geographically concentrated in a way that is not true for whites. Between 1970 and 1990, the number of poor persons living in high-poverty census tracts (tracts where at least 40 percent of all persons are poor) increased by 98 percent, even as the total number of poor persons increased by only 37 percent. In 1990, one-third of poor blacks resided in these high-poverty areas, compared with only 6 percent of poor whites (Jargowsky 1997). Thus, poor African-Americans struggle not only with insufficient incomes but also with the added disadvantages of poor neighborhoods. Concentrated poverty, unemployment, and crime combine with persistent residential segregation and labor market discrimination to generate a social context that makes socioeconomic advancement more difficult.

Focusing primarily on African-American poverty, however, can be problematic. The history of racial hostility in America lends a racial cast to behaviors associated with long-term poverty, even though whites account for a substantial percentage of all poor persons. Condemnations of out-of-wedlock births evoke images of black promiscuity, lamentation over sporadic employment draws on historical accusations of unwillingness to take available jobs, and public distress over crime is fueled by a racist tradition of fear of black men. This history makes it hard to objectively analyze the higher-than-average rates of out-of-wedlock births and teen pregnancies (Moore 1995) and rates of joblessness and incarceration (Sampson and Wilson 1995; Wilson 1996) among African-Americans. The challenge is to investigate the social and structural causes of behaviors that are associated with poverty and that violate mainstream norms, without relying on racist stereotypes.

The studies in this volume rise to this challenge. They do not flinch from describing behaviors that many African-Americans—poor or non-poor—would consider undesirable. But they reject both the liberal view that the poor are forced into adopting undesirable behaviors, and the conservative view that such behaviors are evidence that the poor choose to make bad choices. Instead, the authors focus on the social context and analyze the ways that neighborhoods, family relationships, and workplaces influence beliefs and behaviors in the African-American community. They document how individual outcomes are shaped by multiple aspects of the relationships among individuals, their families, and the environments in which they live and work.

This approach helps us understand that a distinctive aspect of coping with poverty in the African-American community involves numerous undesirable options. A young African-American man who voluntarily leaves job after job is not acquiring the stable work record necessary for promotion. But he may be leaving these jobs to avoid racial harassment and discrimination, not only because such workplaces are hard to endure but also because he realizes that the opportunity for advancement in these jobs is limited. A mother who keeps her children inside where she can supervise them and isolates herself from her neighbors is protecting her children from the problems of a high-crime neighborhood in the best way she can. But her actions may keep her from developing close interpersonal ties with her neighbors and may decrease her ability to coalesce with other neighborhood parents on strategies to keep their children out of trouble. The social isolation may also prevent her from learning about an available job that might eventually provide the resources needed to move her family to a safer community. These behaviors would not represent wise choices in the American mainstream, but the chapters here show that they do make "sense" within the social context of urban poverty.

The chapters thus offer a more-sophisticated understanding of poverty in the lives of those who cope with it that is relevant both for poverty research and for the development of antipoverty policies. Knowledge of the social contexts of poverty can help policymakers to anticipate some of the obstacles that policies might face, and to address the main problems that the poor themselves say they face.

Intellectual Context of Recent Research on Urban Poverty

Over the past decade, the intellectual foundations for this task have been laid by William Julius Wilson, first in *The Truly Disadvantaged* (1987) and its analysis of the development of an urban "underclass" of concentrated African-American poverty, and then in *When Work Disappears* (1996). In these books, Wilson brought race and space back into poverty research. Noting that economic trends since the early 1970s have negatively affected the employment and earnings prospects of all low-skilled workers, Wilson emphasizes that the labor market consequences were especially pernicious for African-Americans. Persistent residential segregation concentrated poor minorities in the inner cities at the same time that the civil rights revolution made it easier for middle-class minorities to move out of these neighborhoods. The result was an increased concentration of poverty in areas where residents are socially isolated, both from the economic mainstream and from middle-class peers.

Wilson argues that the disappearance of employment opportunities in racially segregated high-poverty neighborhoods is at the core of a set of interrelated economic and social problems. Structural changes in the labor market—decreases in unionization, reductions in the manufacturing sector, increased global competition and the consequent expansion of the import and export sectors—all lowered the wages of less-skilled workers. As automation and other technological innovations continue to increase the demand for skilled personnel who can run sophisticated equipment, less-skilled workers are either displaced by automated systems or in direct competition with overseas workers producing the rise in imports (Danziger and Gottschalk 1995). Because African-Americans have historically had less access to education and training and fewer completed years of schooling than whites, the decline in the fortunes of all less-skilled workers falls heavily on them (Holzer 1994; Mincy 1994).

Racial discrimination also matters, according to Wilson, because it exacerbates the decline in employment opportunities caused by economic restructuring. For example, he documents that many employers discourage black applicants by advertising job openings only in Chicago's white ethnic newspapers and not in the major dailies or newspapers that serve the black community. Many firms do not advertise entry-level jobs in Chicago's major dailies; others reported recruiting workers from Chicago's Catholic high schools, but not from public schools, welfare programs, or state employment agencies.

Widespread joblessness fosters changes in attitudes and behaviors: high levels of single-parent families, antisocial behavior, social networks that do not extend beyond the confines of the ghetto, and a lack of informal social control over the behavior and activities of children and adults. Most important, the poor children who remain in the ghetto not only receive an inferior education in troubled public school systems but also grow up in an environment that is harmful to healthy child development and intellectual growth. Absent policy interventions, this environment, according to Wilson (1996), will contribute to higher levels of joblessness, violence, hopelessness, welfare dependency, and nonmarital childbearing in the next generation.

Wilson does not deny the existence of negative "ghetto-related" behaviors that make some inner-city residents unattractive to potential employers. But his research suggests that most inner-city residents adhere to mainstream values and behaviors and that those deviating from the mainstream are reacting primarily to their environment, especially prior experiences with employers. "Inner-city black men grow bitter and resentful in the face of their employment prospects and often manifest or express these feelings in their harsh, often dehumanizing, low-wage work settings" (1996, 144). This leads employers to "make assumptions about the inner-city black workers in general" so that many qualified "black inner-city applicants are never given the chance to prove their qualifications on an individual level because they are systematically screened out by the selective recruitment process" (1996, 137).

Wilson's hypotheses have motivated many studies that emphasize the nexus between individual behavioral choices, the social contexts of the inner city, and the opportunity structure. Such studies have focused on the relationships among family structure, neighborhood effects, racial discrimination, and poverty (e.g., Jencks 1992; Jencks and Peterson 1991; Kotlowitz 1991; Massey and Denton 1993; Yinger 1995). These researchers, along with Wilson and other poverty researchers (e.g., Blank 1997, and Danziger and Gottschalk 1995), have advocated policies designed to increase educational attainment, employment, and training programs to make work more available; more rigorous enforcement of antidiscrimination laws in the labor and housing markets; and tax-based policies to raise the incomes of the working poor.

These studies and policy prescriptions, however, do not adequately address many of the issues that the respondents in the chapters in this volume name as those they must cope with as they seek economic sufficiency. Most poverty researchers assume that employment is central to the ability of the poor to fulfill their responsibilities as parents, role models, and neighbors, as well as to respect themselves and their obligations to others. But the chapters demonstrate that the poor are already and simultaneously parents, relatives, neighbors, and role models, as well as individuals with self-respect and with obligations. The influence of all of these factors means that work opportunities may not be the primary factor that shapes the behavior of the poor. It also means that policy prescriptions that emphasize only employment, housing, and transportation—work and its correlates—will not address all of the barriers that keep the poor from fully participating in the economic and social mainstream.

The chapters in this volume emphasize the social contexts of poverty that are typically missing from poverty studies and the public policy debate that view the poor as individuals and seek mechanisms for influencing their individual work and family behaviors. They present a more-detailed account of how the social contexts of neighborhoods, work, and family relationships shape people's lives and how they navigate within them. They examine how poor people develop mechanisms for coping with poverty: strategies that are motivated by values such as parental care and worry, obligation toward relatives and neighbors, support from and trust toward authority figures, peer relationships, and self-respect, and that draw upon the available knowledge, social support, and resources in their communities.

These strategies will not disappear simply because employment or housing opportunities become available, even though such opportunities are vitally important. Policies must be constructed, therefore, that recognize and value the coping strategies the poor have developed, if those policies are to address the decisions that affect self-sufficiency.

Origins of This Volume

Realizing that antipoverty policies are implemented in complex social environments, James Hyman, then Associate Director for Income, Opportunity and Work at the Annie E. Casey Foundation, and Ronald Mincy, Senior Program Officer at the Ford Foundation, turned their attention to sponsoring research that would investigate how African-Americans cope with urban poverty. In 1995, they asked me to combine this substantive research goal with the training mission of the Program on Poverty, the Underclass and Public Policy, which I have directed at the University of Michigan since 1989. This program brings together faculty, graduate students, and postdoctoral fellows from all of the social sciences and professions. It seeks to train a new generation of scholars, particularly those from underrepresented groups, who can influence both social science research and social policy practices in the pursuit of equal opportunity and social justice.

With generous grants from the Casey and Ford Foundations, I commissioned papers from a group of promising young scholars, who were at the time either postdoctoral fellows in this program or assistant professors at the University of Michigan. With the twin goals of generating new research by new researchers, we began the project with a series of visits by distinguished urban ethnographers—Elijah Anderson, Katherine Newman, Carol Stack, and Mercer Sullivan. Each author/professor presented seminars on his/her research and consulted with the chapter authors. As the chapter drafts evolved, we received feedback from them and also from Linda Burton, Kathryn Edin, Donna Franklin, Robinson Hollister, and Lois Weis. It quickly became apparent that I needed the help of a trained qualitative researcher, so I enlisted my colleague, Ann Chih Lin, Assistant Professor of Public Policy and Political Science, to serve as volume coeditor and to prepare the introductory and concluding chapters. After the volume was prepared, we benefited enormously from the superb editorial assistance of Elena Delbanco.

As this volume goes to press in late 1999, the economic context of urban poverty differs from that of the previous decade in that rates of urban joblessness have been falling. The good news is that the robust economic recovery of the 1990s has raised average living standards and seems to have stopped the quarter century trend toward rising inequality. The bad news is that poverty and joblessness in the African-American community remain very high, and the economic prospects of many poor families remain dim. The continuing decline in employer demand for less-skilled workers means that many welfare mothers and many other less-skilled workers continue to fare badly in the labor market, even when aggregate unemployment rates are low. This economic context suggests that, if we are to significantly reduce inner-city poverty, we must do more not only to expand work opportunities but also to carry out antipoverty policies in ways that consider the social contexts of the neighborhoods, workplaces, and families in which the poor live. For example, the 1996 welfare reform demands that welfare recipients take personal responsibility for seeking employment. The studies in this volume suggest that the agencies charged with enforcing these work requirements need to consider more than just the individual when implementing the new policies.

Academics, the public, and policymakers all tend to simplify complex social problems. Conservatives, for example, often assume that jobs are available to anyone who is willing to work and that the high rate of inner-city joblessness is due primarily to cultural factors, expressed via attitudes and behaviors that are not conducive to employment in today's labor market. Liberals, on the other hand, assume that joblessness is due primarily to racism in the public school system and in the housing and labor markets that makes employment inaccessible and unattainable. The chapters in this book tell us to avoid embracing simple solutions. They ask us to consider the everyday processes and relationships that shape the lives of the poor. If we did, they suggest that it would increase the likelihood that the programs and policies undertaken on behalf of the poor would be accepted and supported by the poor themselves.

Sheldon Danziger

REFERENCES

Blank, Rebecca M. 1997. *It Takes a Nation: A New Agenda for Fighting Poverty.* Princeton, NJ: Princeton University Press.

Corcoran, Mary. 1995. "Rags to Rags: Poverty and Mobility in the United States." *Annual Review of Sociology* 21:237–67.

Corcoran, Mary, and Ajay Chaudry. 1997. "The Dynamics of Childhood Poverty." *Children and Poverty* 7 (2): 40–54.

Danziger, Sheldon, and Peter Gottschalk. 1995. *America Unequal.* Cambridge: Harvard University Press.

Gottschalk, Peter, Sara McLanahan, and Gary Sandefur. 1994. "The Dynamics and Intergenerational Transmission of Poverty and Welfare Participation." In *Confronting Poverty: Prescriptions for Change,* ed. Sheldon Danziger, Gary Sandefur, and Daniel Weinberg, 85–103. Cambridge: Harvard University Press.

Holzer, Harry. 1994. "Black Employment Problems: New Evidence, Old Questions." *Journal of Policy Analysis and Management* 13:699–722.

Jargowsky, Paul. 1997. *Poverty and Place: Ghettos, Barrios, and the American City.* New York: Russell Sage Foundation.

Jencks, Christopher. 1992. *Rethinking Social Policy: Race, Poverty, and the Underclass.* Cambridge: Harvard University Press.

Jencks, Christopher, and Paul E. Peterson, eds. 1991. *The Urban Underclass.* Washington, DC: The Brookings Institute.

Kotlowitz, Alex. 1991. *There Are No Children Here: The Story of Two Boys Growing Up in the Other America.* New York: Doubleday.

Massey, Douglas, and Nancy Denton. 1993. *American Apartheid: Segregation and the Making of the Underclass.* Cambridge: Harvard University Press.

Mincy, Ronald. 1994. "The Underclass: Concept, Controversy, and Evidence." In *Confronting Poverty: Prescriptions for Change,* ed. Sheldon Danziger, Gary Sandefur, and Daniel Weinberg, 109–46. Cambridge: Harvard University Press.

Moore, Kristin. 1995. "Nonmarital Childbearing in the United States." In *Report to Congress on Out-of-Wedlock Childbearing,* v–xxii. Washington, DC: Department of Health and Human Services.

Sampson, Robert, and William Julius Wilson. 1995. "Toward a Theory of Race, Crime, and Urban Inequality." In *Crime and Inequality,* ed. John Hagan and Ruth Peterson, 37–54. Stanford, CA: Stanford University Press.

Wilson, William Julius. 1987. *The Truly Disadvantaged: The Inner-City, the Underclass and Public Policy.* Chicago: University of Chicago Press.

———. 1996. *When Work Disappears: The World of the New Urban Poor.* New York: Knopf.

Yinger, John. 1995. *Closed Doors, Opportunities Lost: The Continuing Costs of Housing Discrimination.* New York: Russell Sage Foundation.

CHAPTER 1

Interpretive Research for Public Policy

Ann Chih Lin

One of the strengths of research and policy-making for poverty policy is the availability of data sources that span long time periods. Panel surveys like the Panel Study of Income Dynamics and the National Longitudinal Study of Youth, cross-sectional data collected by the U.S. Bureau of the Census, and evaluations performed by universities and nonprofit research groups all provide rich information about the observed behavior of the poor. As a result, researchers have learned much about the incidence and scope of behaviors associated with poverty and have assessed numerous hypotheses about its causes and consequences. Researchers have also proposed policy tools based on this knowledge: for instance, to mandate participation, rather than rely on voluntary enrollment, in programs for teenage mothers (Maynard 1997), or to move toward a system of work supports and time-limited, transitional cash assistance for welfare recipients (Bane and Ellwood 1994).

But the leap from observed behavior to policy tools meant to change behavior is much more precarious than the availability of data might suggest. Survey responses about income, hours worked, family structure or residential location and evaluations describing changes over time or in comparison to a control group are all observations of behavior. But while observations can serve as a basis for inferring causes or explanations for behavior, they are not explanations themselves.

For example, documenting an association between long-term welfare receipt and teenage childbirth does not establish why teenage childbirth is associated with long-term welfare receipt. The association might signal a lack of interest or desire to work, the lack of opportunity to acquire skills, a default position as the family baby-sitter for sisters and cousins who have children after they begin working, or numerous other possibilities. Of course, some of these explanations could be evaluated by complementary observations; for example, the hypothesis that teenage mothers fail to acquire skills could be tested if high school graduation rates and test scores were also collected in the survey. But others, such as the family baby-sitter hypothesis, require information that surveys do not or cannot collect. Moreover, which explanations merit investigation depends on the investigator's background and interests. If a researcher is not acquainted with a social milieu in which extended families pool incomes and provide services for each other, she is unlikely to even consider this explanation.

The policy implications of these problems are significant. Policy solutions based on inferences from observed behavior, as gathered in surveys and evaluations alone, will neglect dimensions that were not included in the data gathering. This can result in policies that fail or that have unanticipated consequences. Similarly, if explanations of behavior reflect the investigator's notions of plausibility, their "goodness of fit" depends on the investigator's knowledge of the groups in question. When this knowledge is incomplete, biased by class and racial assumptions, or overly schematic, policy solutions based on the investigator's explanations will be mystifying at best, destructive at worst.

For these reasons, the design of policy tools requires multiple kinds of research: in particular, research that allows interpretations of behavior to emerge from detailed interviewing, participant observation, or both. Because respondents' answers, not preset response categories or outcome measures, determine the scope of the research, researchers are more likely to uncover nonobvious connections between problems. Because respondents' interpretations of their own behavior, rather than researchers' hypotheses about the world, are the subject of research, policy tools that result from research are more likely to employ concepts, motivations, and reasons that are plausible to the people being studied.

These methods have limitations as well. For instance, the small samples in most interpretive studies raise questions of representativeness. Nonetheless, interpretive research can illuminate the meaning of results presented by surveys and evaluations. Interpretive research places context at the center of the study of policy, shows how seemingly disparate problems are connected, and clarifies both potential obstacles and potential alternatives to policy solutions. At the same time, it redefines policy problems in ways that the people most affected by policy can recognize and accept.

The Distinctive Contributions
of Interpretive Policy Research

The extensive, open-ended interview and participant observation techniques used in this book differ fundamentally in approach from research that primarily seeks to test hypotheses. While researchers always enter the field with a specific focus and often with specific questions, in interpretive research those questions are a point of entry, not the content of the inquiry. In other words, interpretive researchers ask questions to discover what is salient to their respondents. Their answers generate further questions and investigations, allowing the researchers' discoveries, not their prior beliefs, to shape the study. Someone interested in employment issues, for instance, might begin by asking about work history. But rather than collecting job titles, salaries, and time in job from multiple respondents, as might a survey researcher, the interpretive researcher would listen to his informants describe what they considered work, take note of how they organized their descriptions, and examine recurring evaluative standards or beliefs. He would then seek to understand those descriptions, methods of organization, or underlying value systems. Work histories might still matter, but so might efforts to cope with racism, stories about supervisor-employee relationships, or beliefs about children's well-being.

This kind of research requires familiarity with both specific phenomena and their context. For example, an interpretive study of employment might move from a set of opening questions about work histories to an in-depth discussion of racial expectations, authority relationships, or family composition. The researcher would not restrict discussion to the aspects of race or authority or family that concern employment; she would also be prepared to discuss these parallel conditions. Thus interpretive analysis tends to be syncretic, drawing together multiple relationships and illuminating the connections among them.

Researchers used to testing hypotheses on large data sets or through quasi-experiments might find this method unfocused or even ad hoc. Such researchers use statistical techniques or experimental designs to "hold the world constant" so that one particular relationship can be isolated. For interpretive researchers, however, this approach lacks realism: in the world, relationships never operate in isolation. They forgo estimates of effect size and strength in favor of multifaceted description and fidelity to respondents' experience.

It is important, however, not to see the work of interpretive researchers as creating a snapshot of life, much less contending that that snapshot represents a society or a phenomenon in microcosm. Rather, interpretivists take features of a phenomenon that are particularly salient within the context they study and look for explanations of that significance. Thus, if workers' understanding of a "good" job has less to do with pay and more to do with camaraderie and respect in the workplace, interpretive research attempts to explain why that might be and what implications that might have, and then compares that understanding with one that emphasizes pay scales, or family provision, or other guiding values. This concern with perspective distinguishes it from research based on objective measures, in which the amount of a paycheck matters, regardless of context. Such objective measures might also be important for interpretivists, but only if they carry or do not carry meaning in a particular context.

Interpretive work is an accepted category of research in anthropology, sociology, and history and is gaining more recognition in political science and economics. But its utility for policy-making is more problematic. Policies are often conceptualized in mechanistic terms: intervention x within an existing situation should increase or decrease y. Hypothesis testing on survey data or as part of program evaluations fits this model of cause-and-effect relationships. For instance, if a job retention policy is set up in an experimental or quasi-experimental fashion, researchers can claim to have a direct test of the marginal impact of that policy initiative. Hypothesis testing can also provide a measure of the scope of a policy problem. If a significant relationship between tenure in a first job and future employment stability is documented in a large representative survey, researchers can both suggest a manipulable factor—tenure in first jobs—and make a case for its significance to the general population.

By contrast, interpretive work does not analyze isolated causal relationships, which makes it hard to identify specific policy tools. The contextual, multidimensional character of interpretive work is antithetical to the creation of specific policy initiatives: the interrelationships described imply that every problem must be solved, in a coordinated fashion, before anything can improve. Thus, early interpretive studies of poverty that illuminated the behavior and the perspectives of the urban poor (Hannerz 1969; Liebow 1967; Stack 1974) often concluded that wholesale restructuring of an unfair economic system, the creation of new cultural models, and/or the political mobilization of ghetto communities would be required to improve the condition of the poor. As diagnoses of the problems afflicting these communities, their vision may have been accurate. But even if it were, the gap between restructuring an economic system and specific policies to this end remains deep and wide.

More recent interpretive work (Anderson 1990; Bourgois 1995) tends not to advocate fundamental economic or social changes, but to propose a list of specific needs—better schools, better child care, better job training, better job opportunities—culled from detailed analysis of how the absence of such resources has harmed the poor. Having assessed the total impact of all of these problems, scholars conducting interpretive research also think about all of the policy changes they recommend as a package. But this raises difficulty in policy design, because policy tools are usually subject-specific and policy initiatives are seldom coordinated. The marginal impact of any incremental change, rather than the possibilities of a coordinated flow of new programs, is what policymakers must usually consider. The more interpretivists call for coordinated policy solutions, the less likely their solutions are to be adopted.

But this characteristic of interpretive work is advantageous when one evaluates how a discrete policy might work in context. Hypothesis testing generates policy proposals by analyzing causal relationships in isolation from each other. The resulting estimates of marginal impacts allow researchers to compare the relative advantages of different policies. But while useful as a conceptual exercise, actual policies rarely function in isolation. Instead, they operate in a world where other simultaneous causal processes can overwhelm, or intensify, the process induced by any particular policy. Interpretive work can chart those other causal processes and explain how they interact with the particular initiative in question. Its concern for context means that otherwise peripheral issues are investigated if research participants consider them important. Thus consequences that might be unanticipated by more directed researchers, and possible obstacles to policy success, may be identified through interpretive research.

Interpretive research can also explore how those targeted by policies are likely to understand them and respond. Those targeted by policy often understand it differently than policymakers intend. The belief that AIDS results from government experiments or that the spread of crack cocaine is a CIA conspiracy are some recent, dramatic instances of miscommunication and mistrust between citizens and government. The combination of this mistrust and policymakers' stereotypes—for instance, that most welfare recipients prefer welfare to work—often undermine the acceptance and effectiveness of policy. Interpretive work may help to change beliefs on both sides of the policy divide. Its emphasis on understanding and then explaining the perspectives of its participants may contribute to problem definitions that are more responsive to the experience of target groups, framed in ways they understand. Target groups are more likely to buy into policies when they understand them, and in cases where they do not, their familiarity with the language and images of policy might help to empower them to challenge its provisions.[1]

Understood on its own terms, interpretive policy research is neither a substitute for nor an inferior imitation of hypothesis testing. Rather, by situating causal relationships in their context, and anticipating some problems that bedevil the implementation of policy proposals, interpretive research complements hypothesis testing. This is best illustrated by example. As the following sections show, research of the kind presented in this book can further our understanding of parenting, employment, and community support among the poor. It can explain why some popular policy initiatives may be more complicated than they seem. And it can chart a different course for policy, one that might eventually gain more acceptance and cooperation from the poor themselves.

Neighborhood: Family and Community as Supports

The common understanding of poor communities is that of families living fearfully and aimlessly in dilapidated buildings, neither able nor willing to overcome their isolation from each other and the larger society. This understanding is bolstered by research on high levels of racial segregation and concentrated poverty (Jargowsky 1997; Massey and Denton 1993), by accounts of job loss and black middle-class flight from central cities (Wilson 1987), and by journalistic reports of individuals imprisoned by poverty and lack of exposure to mainstream opportunities and standards (Auletta 1982; Dash 1996; Kotlowitz 1991). Yet though striking and well founded, this focus on absence and isolation can encourage policymakers to believe that poor communities have no structure left to build on, no interactions to be preserved, and no points of contact between their neighborhoods and the wider world.

The chapters on community context in this book show that this is not the case. Instead, they depict communities in which impoverished residents create networks for resource sharing and mutual support, networks that also extend, with varying degrees of success, into other less poor communities. These networks can affect policy success. For example, policy change that negatively affects some members of a support network—welfare recipients, absent fathers, the unemployed, the elderly—will ripple through the lives of others, resulting in a multitude of obstacles and unanticipated consequences. Policies that impose costs on some individuals may result in costs being passed on to others in the support network. And policies that offer benefits to a particular individual may inflict a cost upon her support network, thus making those benefits less valuable.

Individuals, of course, have the option of refusing to provide support when the cost is too high or the demands too importunate. But this option, while logical, is difficult when one has few resources of one's own. The knowledge that one may need—or that one currently depends on—a costly relationship makes it hard to break. And ties of affection and family obligation add a moral and emotional cost to refusals of support. Understanding the centrality of support networks within even impoverished, isolated communities allows policymakers to evaluate policy with the context, and not just the individual recipient, in mind. And it also provides insight into the values that individuals in these communities hold dear, allowing policymakers to understand actions that are incomprehensible if viewed solely from an individual perspective.

These points are emphasized in Sharon Hicks-Bartlett's exploration of the coping strategies prevalent in one impoverished, African-American suburb. In this community, a minimal tax base and a shortage of compensatory intergovernmental funding mean that neither afterschool care nor elder care, nor even effective police and fire protection, are provided by government. The lack of jobs in the neighborhood, and the lack of transportation to jobs outside the neighborhood, means that most families have too little income to purchase these services from the market. As a result, creating safe spaces, responding to immediate needs, and nurturing kin-based networks of reciprocal obligation and shared resources become the context for policy changes.

Hicks-Bartlett's chapter shows how danger, scarcity, and obligation impose upon parental choices. When violence is common, mothers place great emphasis on knowing that their children are safe, even keeping them under constant adult supervision well past the age where children could, in safer environments, care for themselves. When mothers depend on others for transportation or baby-sitting, they are unwilling to take jobs that might require them to ask for even more help. When the most reliable resource families have is their sense of mutual responsibility, they see decisions about paid work or nonpaid caretaking in terms of their effects on the family support system, rather than only on individual well-being.

Getting some policy changes, like welfare-to-work programs, to succeed in such neighborhoods will inflict serious practical costs. Work requirements take away one option for family survival: the division of labor among different members of a support system. By requiring that unpaid care be abandoned in favor of paid work, such reforms prevent residents from exchanging time and personal attention for a sense of safety, or to support someone else's wage earning. If wages are not high enough to allow families to purchase what they have lost, then paid employment will decrease their standard of living and increase their sense of vulnerability.

Many of the women interviewed by Hicks-Bartlett understand that only paid employment will improve their situation in the long run, even if it requires increased expenditures for transportation, clothing, and child care. Beyond the calculation of individual and family costs and benefits, however, lies another problem: the fear that policy change will dismantle the coping strategies that have been their only sure means of survival. Family and neighborly ties are not perfect, but they are precious. Policy change that ignores them misses the opportunity to harness the creativity and the coping skills already present in these communities.

The vulnerability of poor communities, and their ability to survive, is also a key focus of Gina Barclay-McLaughlin's chapter on long-term residents of a housing project in the inner city. Barclay-McLaughlin's interviewees speak about ways in which a sense of responsibility for one's neighbors can nurture children's dreams and aspirations. Communal support from neighbors, teachers, and adult mentors, who watched out for one another and helped to raise one another's children, was as much a part of the housing project of their childhood as the poverty they experienced. Although the lack of resources and knowledge about opportunities certainly affected their life choices, these adults also remember that poverty was not accompanied by isolation in the same ways that it is now.

Barclay-McLaughlin's respondents identify the prevalence of crime and drugs in the housing project, and the security measures used to combat crime, as central factors in the weakening of communal support today. Fear of what kids will do if neighbors try to correct their behavior; fear of adults who may be on drugs; the loss of shared space for neighbors to build camaraderie and make their presence felt in the neighborhood, all inhibit the interpersonal relationships at the heart of communal support. At the same time, residents contemplate moving to higher-quality scattered-site public housing elsewhere with regret. While such moves may be necessary to avoid the crime and fear that rules the projects, they do not allow residents to re-create the community interaction and the interdependence that nurtured early residents of Skylan.

Barclay-McLaughlin's chapter suggests that problem definition is central to policy formulation. Thinking about crime as a problem that hurts individual victims, versus one that prevents community interactions, can lead to different solutions. In the first case, punishing criminals and/or ensuring individual safety is the right response. A strong and intimidating police presence, subsidies that allow individuals to move to safer neighborhoods, or expanded search and seizure permission would be possible solutions. In the second case, strengthening communal support would be a parallel goal. As a result, even effective strategies against crime—an intimidating police presence, greater latitude for police searches and arrests, and outmigration—might be undesirable because they diminish community trust. Instead, training residents to monitor behavior in the project, subsidizing pushcart vendors to bring more legitimate activity onto the streets, or encouraging police to lead community activities might enhance safety while encouraging the rebirth of communal support.

Barclay-McLaughlin's piece also has implications for researchers looking for indicators of isolation. Research on neighborhood effects typically defines isolation as the concentration of the poor—for instance, as any census tract in which 40 percent or more of the residents have incomes below the poverty line (Brooks-Gunn, Duncan, and Aber 1997; Wilson 1987). But for these respondents, the key component of isolation is not income, but rather separation and alienation. Taking account of both these perspectives opens a new avenue for research: What effect does acute, concentrated poverty have on the quality of interaction within a neighborhood? Are there ways to prevent poverty from leading inexorably to isolation, and situations in which interaction can buffer a neighborhood against the effects of concentrated poverty? Answering questions like these would address important policy problems and make them relevant to the concerns expressed by residents of these neighborhoods.

Of course, the intertwining of kin with kin and neighbor with neighbor has negative aspects as well. The gangs that Barclay-McLaughlin's respondents fear are made up of neighborhood youth; the relatives who support Hicks-Bartlett's respondents make reciprocal demands. This mix of influences is highlighted in Mary Pattillo-McCoy's chapter on adolescents growing up in a lower-middle-class African-American neighborhood. The teenagers she profiles all have parents who are educated and employed; they attend magnet or parochial schools and have career ambitions their families support. Community and extended family support have been important for all of them: one teenager has multiple "parents" supervising her through her involvement with a local church; another's early role model was his uncle; a third moved in with her boyfriend and his grandmother after she became pregnant. But all also have been drawn, through neighborhood friends, into less positive relationships: one teen's mother depends on the drug income of her daughter's boyfriend to supplement the earnings she brings home; one teen has a crush on a boy who is in and out of prison; and a third was a gang member before setting off for college.

As Pattillo-McCoy points out, within the same family, and even within the same person, "street" and "decent" lifestyles coexist. The middle-class background of these adolescents gives them opportunities that are unavailable to many residents of the neighborhoods profiled by Hicks-Bartlett and Barclay-McLaughlin. Resources and expectations, both from within the family and from institutions like churches and schools, matter. But neither is enough to buffer these teenagers from the friendships and the sense of identification that both they and their immediate families have with their less fortunate kin and neighbors. Friendships do not stop when one friend has a child out of wedlock; income shared with others is not less necessary because it is earned from drug dealing; a son's friend is not unworthy one day because he belongs to a gang, but worthy the next when he begins college.

The policy context illuminated by this research is complex. In some ways, helping lower-middle-class parents isolate themselves from their less successful friends and relatives might enhance their control over their children's acquaintances and choices. A greater range of school choices, increased drug enforcement, and attacks on the racial segregation that limits their housing choices could all facilitate this separation. But these policies would collide with another feature of the context: those who provide less positive models for children are often also siblings, cousins or neighbors, who play an important emotional, and sometimes an important economic, role in "decent" families.

This context provides one explanation for the paradox that African-Americans, who suffer the most from crime, seldom demand "tougher" crime policy. They are not merely reacting to beliefs about a racist criminal justice system, although this is part of their ambivalence (DiIulio 1996). Instead, they also recognize and, without approving it, take responsibility for the fact that those who commit crimes are also part of their community. The same is true for behavior that is not criminal, but often considered undesirable: having children out of wedlock, separating from a spouse. Policy solutions need to respect both the practical consequences and the emotional commitments of this perspective.

The central place of support networks, as documented in these chapters, shows how context can play a critical role in compliance with and acceptance of social policy. However, the way to understand support networks, or any contextual influence on policy, is not as a variable with a particular causal effect. It is not that people with larger or smaller support networks will be more likely to work rather than receive welfare, to move into scattered-site housing rather than stay in a housing project, or support tougher crime legislation. Rather, context changes the causal process that operates: people isolated from support networks are more likely to base their decisions to work or receive welfare on individual calculations, rather than on how their decision will affect others. Understanding context is thus particularly appropriate for predicting which obstacles and frames will be encountered by policy changes, and which are most likely to matter.

Viewed from this perspective, the context of policy includes, but is much more than, "place": it also incorporates the beliefs and practices that people carry with them and that structure their response to policy. A good way to examine context from this perspective is by looking at employment. As the following sections show, the interpretations created out of common experiences and histories matter a great deal.

Employment: From Removing Barriers to Coping with Obstacles

Jobs mean much more than earnings in American culture: they are also markers of one's social position, self-respect, sense of contribution, and aspirations and dreams. Job loss in the inner city, racism on the job, and restricted opportunities to pursue one's vocational ambitions thus hurt African-Americans in multiple ways. The inability to earn a living not only keeps families in poverty but attacks one's sense of self; it underscores racist messages that tell African-Americans that they are incapable, unintelligent, or unmotivated. Because work is often the prerequisite for social legitimacy, the jobless or underemployed garner little attention from the more fortunate regarding the social conditions that undergird their unemployment.

Statistical studies of employment miss many of these dimensions. They can show how the loss or unavailability of work is correlated with the absence of educational opportunities in schools, with race and neighborhood, or with stress and depression (Conger and Elder 1994; McLoyd 1998). But they tend to overlook subtle problems that are associated with these correlations: the ways in which families and schools support or discourage career ambitions; the persistence of beliefs about jobs that no longer fit a changing job market; the ways in which employment ambitions are thwarted and advancement constrained even for the successfully employed.

Interpretive work illuminates this aspect of employment policy. Opportunities—education, job openings, promotion potential—are important and, as the chapters in Part 2 show, too often lacking for low-income African-Americans. But individuals also need empowerment and support from numerous places to make use of opportunity: from a teacher who helps a student negotiate obstacles, from a friend who helps an unemployed man make sense of the work world, from a supervisor who understands how subtle racism and unjust working conditions isolate and discourage her black employees. Without this support, many low-income workers can find it impossible to take advantage of their few available opportunities.

Carla O'Connor's chapter details the ways in which the aspirations of ambitious young women growing up in the midst of inner-city poverty are supported or derailed. All of her respondents dream of careers that would enable them to live better lives. But only two of the six young women have access to people who can give them the information and the assistance to reach their goals and overcome obstacles, and who encourage their efforts. The others are stymied in their ambitions when teachers, caretakers, and extended family communicate more modest expectations and are unable to provide academic tutoring or information about problems like paying for school or applying to college. Their ambitions remain dreams that they do not expect to attain.

O'Connor's portrait does not suggest that these ambitions would be fulfilled if only families and teachers paid more attention to children. As she points out, the neglect of these young women's ambitions is a social product of families who have not had experience or education enough to make them knowledgeable about how to help children, and of schools that are too overburdened to give special tutoring and assistance to more than a few of the most prepared students. The problem is one of the distribution of human capital and material resources, not merely of personal will. At the same time, O'Connor's work shows that resources alone might not suffice: resources delivered outside of the supportive relationship with family or trusted teachers might not give students the self-confidence, the self-esteem, or optimism they need to use them.

That link between the material and the emotional aspects of social problems is another indicator of the importance of context. Researchers have long documented the connections between family background, school quality, and future achievement (Corcoran 1995). But an understanding of the processes that influence those connections—mutual reinforcement between family and schools, information conveyed as part of an ongoing relationship between the student and people who care about her—suggests that policy initiatives cannot identify a single missing piece and try to replace it.

The problems that arise when policymakers do not understand the context of employment are evident in Alford A. Young Jr.'s chapter on low-income, unemployed black men. These young men do not have the benefit of support for their ambitions or information about how to achieve them: some ten years older than the high school students O'Connor interviewed, they face a working world that they do not understand. Without families to provide academic help or access to job networks, friends with consistent records of employment, or a school experience that prepared them for employment, these men make inferences from information that is often outdated, taken out of context, or barely comprehensible. Thus they value their manual skills and base their job aspirations on finding this kind of work; they dream of owning a business that would allow them to escape the disrespect and dependence they experienced in the few jobs they found; and they cannot think of viable strategies to obtain employment other than being out in the street, hoping an opportunity will find them.

Young's chapter shows how context shapes beliefs and guides individual action. Because men "know" that unionized, semi- or unskilled labor once provided stable factory work for their neighborhoods and families, they base their evaluations of the "good job" on this history, even though economic changes have made such evaluations obsolete. Similarly, having grown up in a world where exposure to new technologies was limited, these young men have no way of understanding the educational or credentialing demands of a high-tech workplace. Instead, they talk about meeting its demands by having an eager and aggressive work attitude. As Young suggests, such misreadings of the labor market will affect how these men respond to work or training opportunities, even if such opportunities become available.

Would changing the opportunity structure also change their beliefs? After all, their sense of the "good job" is based on a historical abundance of skilled and unskilled jobs, jobs that have now mostly disappeared from their inner-city neighborhoods. Perhaps if more jobs were available, more friends and relatives employed in them, the expectations, beliefs, and practices of the unemployed would change too. This hope is reflected in comprehensive employment policy proposals targeted at disadvantaged communities (Wilson, 1996). But relying simply on the availability of jobs to effect such changes may not be enough. As Young points out, "not only must low-income black men learn to relate better to a white-collar service sector, but . . . that sector must learn to relate better to them." The men Young interviewed are looking for particular kinds of work. They want to start in a stable job with benefits, because their comparison job is profitable, but unstable and dangerous, illegitimate work. They look for wages high enough to support a family because, for many of them, the birth of a child has motivated them to find work. Thus, it is not clear how these men would respond to increased opportunities for work that did not satisfy these conditions.

From one perspective, this is certainly an unreasonable attitude. Most of these men do not have skills that would merit stable, well-paid jobs with benefits. Other workers who lack skills accept less desirable jobs until they acquire the skills or experience necessary to get a better one; these men should be able to do the same. But this perspective only makes sense if one believes that one can be promoted from inferior jobs to better ones. If workers doubt that an "inferior" job will increase their skills or improve their promotion prospects, the rationale for accepting the job becomes much weaker.

Doubts about whether job ladders will work for them find some justification in the African-American experience. As Andrew L. Reaves's chapter shows, even successfully employed African-American men experience working conditions that restrict their chances for promotion and limit their job satisfaction. The men he interviewed did not give up working in response to multiple examples of discrimination. But they moved from job to job seeking fair treatment. They restrict their own efforts when they feel that employers take advantage of their willingness to work hard. They feel isolated from co-workers of a different race or gender, which makes their work experience unhappy and hinders the formation of networks. They face so much abuse from managers that they sometimes pass up a chance for promotion. Because they have more labor market contact than the men in Young's chapter, the workers Reaves interviews know enough to see that improving their skills might allow them to move to a less discriminatory line of work; others have union jobs that provide at least some stability. They have more reason to persevere, but the difference between the labor market difficulties faced by these two groups of men is one of degree and not of kind.

The strategies adopted by the workers in Reaves's chapter underscore the importance of the employment context. Glaring instances of racism—denial of employment, for instance—are easier to measure than the subtle denials of opportunity and self-limiting adaptations that Reaves describes. But subtle or, as Reaves terms it, aversive racism is no less damaging, especially when coping with it requires confronting one's second-class status and accommodating to it. When policymakers make employment policy without recognizing the full range of workplace injustices, they risk blaming African-Americans for not trying hard enough at work after they are hired, seeing isolation on the job as a choice rather than a response, or dismissing the unwillingness to try for a promotion as lack of ambition.

The wider perspective presented in these chapters shows how interpretive research leads not only to a better understanding of the policy context in general, but also to improvement in the design and implementation of specific policies. In the chapters on parenting, we see what an interpretive approach can add to the evaluation of one policy in particular: the welfare reform legislation of 1996.

Parenting: From Enforcing Responsibility to Enabling Care

The passage of the Personal Responsibility and Work Opportunity Reconciliation Act (PRWORA) in 1996 enshrined in law a vision of parenting that focuses primarily on economic provision. Time limits were placed on the receipt of cash assistance by caretaking parents, and increasing percentages of the caseload were required to work or to enroll in work-related programs. Child support enforcement efforts were increased. Such efforts, Congress stated, were necessary because "promotion of responsible fatherhood and motherhood is integral to successful child rearing and the well-being of children" (PRWORA, Title I, Sec. 101 [3]).

The legislation also targeted other areas of parenting—for instance, grants to states for programs to encourage visitation and access to children for noncustodial parents who pay child support, and grants for the prevention of teenage pregnancy. But neither the legislation nor the political rhetoric that accompanied it acknowledged that parenting decisions involve more than providing an adequate income. The same was true of the program evaluations and the data analyses used by proponents and opponents of the legislation. Most focused on work placement rates, sanctioning of recipients for refusing to enroll in job search or work programs, shifts in benefit levels and costs, and the like. Other studies focused on factors explaining welfare dynamics—time spent on and off welfare rolls (Bane and Ellwood 1994; Ellwood 1988).

As central as economic decisions are, parenting is more complicated than earning enough to support one's children. It involves decisions about safeguarding children's health and physical security, nurturing their emotional and intellectual development, strengthening their bonds to their families, and making choices about their well-being. Policymakers' neglect of these dimensions of parenting would matter less if economic policies did not also affect choices about nurturing. But decisions about work and welfare receipt are influenced not only by a parent's employment history, education, job market conditions, and welfare requirements, but also by decisions about children's medical needs, by neighborhood quality and schooling decisions, and by assessments—mistaken or not—of what will provide the best life for the family.

This does not imply that economic support must be traded off against emotional support; the research in this book shows that in many cases, paid employment can help parents accomplish other parenting tasks. But the failure to examine how decisions about work or welfare receipt are, for parents, decisions about other factors as well means that policy based strictly on measurable economic calculations will confront unexpected obstacles.

While not prepared specifically as commentary on PRWORA, the chapters in this book illuminate some of the pitfalls that it may face. The mothers profiled in the chapter by Ariel Kalil, Heidi Schweingruber, Marijata Daniel-Echols, and Ashli Breen, for instance, not only share PRWORA's concern with responsible parenting, but also agree that paid employment might improve their parenting. Their appreciation of the "extras" that wages can provide for their children, and the break from their children that employment provides and that allows them to return to parenting with more patience, does not contradict the assumptions behind PRWORA. But the analysis provided by Kalil et al. explains that responsibility and good parenting sometimes point away from employment. When mothers left welfare, obtaining medical care for children was much more problematic. The fear of poor-quality child care, especially given financial constraints, kept other mothers from working. The long hours required for mothers to support their children on a low-wage job meant less time with children, and thus less emotional nurturance and less control over their children's behavior.

Kalil et al.'s chapter, of course, is not the only research that has emphasized the barriers that the lack of medical insurance, child care, or sufficient wages pose to employment for single mothers. But their discussions with young mothers show that these problems are seen as parenting problems, not employment problems. The difference in perspective is more than semantic. If the standard of comparison were simply whether work raised family income, a combination of work supports and sanctions could convince most women to choose work. But if mothers instead apply a calculus that emphasizes parenting, the benefits and costs of working will be modified by the extent to which they affect her parenting tasks. For instance, mothers might reject a night shift job with good fringe benefits and subsidies for child care, in favor of a day job with lower wages and health and child-care benefits, if they believed that quality child care was only available during the day. A mother might also leave a "good job" because a child gets involved with the wrong crowd after school, or refuse to cooperate on child support because it might disrupt her relationship with in-laws who baby-sit for her. Such decisions seem irrational from a purely financial standpoint, but make sense in her parental role.

The importance of considering these parenting dimensions is also evident in Waldo E. Johnson Jr.'s chapter on nonresident fathers. Like the mothers interviewed by Kalil et al., the fathers interviewed by Johnson agree that responsible fatherhood requires them to assume financial responsibility for their children. This belief can backfire, however, when fathers who are unable to provide their share of child support feel unable to parent in noneconomic ways—participating in their children's physical care, teaching them, or spending time with them. Their and their partners' sense that they are failed providers leads them to avoid their children out of embarrassment, and their partners to deny access in response. In some cases, the fathers admit, losing access to their children can prod them to work harder to provide support. But when fathers cannot find work or earn enough to provide support, their children end up with neither financial nor emotional nurturing from their fathers.

PRWORA made no attempt to address the structural and individual reasons behind fathers' inability to pay support. By simply reinforcing the obligation to pay without instituting any policies to increase the ability to pay, it reinforces the absent father problem, at least for this segment of the population. It will discourage some men who cannot pay support from being close to their children, lest they be discovered and sanctioned for the failure to pay. In addition, by enhancing the belief that parental responsibility is economic, it unwittingly downgrades the other dimensions of responsible parenting.

Johnson also points out that fathers and mothers are not exclusively parents: they are the children of their own parents and may be adolescents themselves. These multiple roles affect the ways these fathers parent. Just as many mothers in both the Kalil et al. and the Johnson study must live with their parents or depend on them for baby-sitting or other services, many of the fathers continue to share housing with their families of origin, and/or rely on them in between jobs, even though their families are usually poor as well. In return, they assume a continuing responsibility to contribute to the family income when they can. Failure to pay child support, in other words, may be a response to other, equally pressing family responsibilities. Johnson also points out that because many of these fathers are young themselves, their inability to live up to their own and the community's expectations of them as providers becomes a developmentally significant experience of failure. To the extent that this affects their employment prospects and parenting in the future, the effects of child support enforcement reverberate beyond the immediate well-being of the child, the mother, and the nonresident father.

The context of policy thus extends beyond those individuals directly targeted by a policy's provisions. It encompasses their support systems and their neighborhoods. Not only does a mother's poverty determine which child-care alternatives are affordable, her neighborhood determines which alternatives are within reach: poor neighborhoods rarely have the customer base to support quality child-care centers. Yet, the knowledge that available day-care alternatives are inadequate leads some mothers to believe that responsible parenting means *not* leaving children in the care of strangers. A father's sense of the need to contribute to his own mother's budget will vary depending on whether he lives in her home, whether she is in financial need, and whether she contributes to the support of his children. Thus, not only his own, but his mother's poverty, and not only his, but his mother's sense of family responsibility, affects his ability to pay child support and to parent his children.

Understanding these contexts enlarges the set of reasons for potential policy failure: not merely irresponsibility or economic irrationality, but also different conceptions of responsibility and contending responsibilities. It expands the range of places to look for policy effects: not only at benefit rolls, wages, or child support collection, but also at children's relationships with both parents, and at family strategies for managing economic pressure. And it increases the lessons that can be learned from policy success: not only how to encourage mothers to work or fathers to pay, but also how a successful policy helps mothers and fathers to manage competing responsibilities, or to change their definitions of responsible parenting.

Assessing Scope and Generalizability in Interpretive Research

As this chapter suggests and the following chapters document, interpretive research can improve our understanding of policy problems and make policy solutions more accessible and acceptable to the people they target. This understanding, however, comes at a price. In its use of small samples whose members are interviewed and observed at length, and respondent-directed interviews with formats that are not easily standardized, interpretive work often sacrifices breadth for depth. This means that the scope of a problem is harder to determine: the incidence of a particular problem in an interpretivist's sample is not representative of the incidence of that problem in the population. The sample the researcher has chosen may not be representative of most, let alone all, with similar problems; the unemployed women studied by a particular researcher, for instance, may not be typical of unemployed women generally. Thus, policy suggestions derived from an interpretivist study may be correct for women resembling those the researcher studied, but of limited relevance because few women actually fall into that group.

Understanding the nature of the problem, however, also leads to solutions for confronting it. The most obvious is to employ comparisons, both within the research itself and across research studies. For instance, some researchers combine different study groups in one project, to work out the ways in which similar contexts resemble each other, or are distinctive (Edin and Lein 1997; Newman 1988, 1999; Sullivan 1989). Others employ a more descriptive form of qualitative work to add depth to work that otherwise tests hypotheses using quantitative data. In these combinations, the qualitative work often deals less with interpretations of behavior, and more with information about behavior or attitudes that is not collected in standard socioeconomic surveys[2] (Rank 1994; Wilson 1996).

A third approach is to consider different, but related, qualitative studies, bringing out similar findings and critiquing divergent ones. This is the approach this book takes. Many details discussed in one study are echoed by others. For instance, families draw economic sustenance from an extended kinship and friendship network in the chapters by Hicks-Bartlett, Pattillo-McCoy, and Kalil et al. Reeves's portrait of young men who, even when working, still need to live with their mothers to support themselves is confirmed by the young men in Young's and Johnson's chapters. The role that neighbors and friends play in transmitting information about jobs and education and in monitoring children's behavior is the subject of O'Connor's chapter but is also evident in the memories of Barclay-McLaughlin's respondents and in Pattillo-McCoy's chapter. Similarly, Reeves's respondents cite their need for social support on the job, which is consistent with findings about the value of this kind of support for securing the job in the first place.

Of course, cross-study verification does not reveal the proportion of all low-income individuals who might believe or behave in a particular way. For instance, even several studies that have a small number of participants, combined, cannot tell whether "most" or "a significant minority" of the population in question is enmeshed in family support networks. But finding family support networks across several studies does establish that they exist in different venues and operate consistently across them. This should encourage policymakers to reexamine assumptions that individuals or nuclear families are modal economic units, to think about how policies might be altered to better satisfy the needs of a variety of family forms, and to further investigate the extent of the phenomenon and the situations associated with it.

A separate research issue is the process of interpretation itself. The advantage of emphasizing respondents' interpretations, as opposed to surveys that emphasize behavior, is the addition of a context with which to understand behavior. The researcher does not assume that interpretations of behavior are widely shared, or that the meaning and value of behavior is self-evident. The methodological problem that remains is that respondents, in creating explanations for their actions, always tell a partial story. They explain what they see as important, as different, as a choice, but they miss decisions that are so everyday or commonplace to them so as to be taken for granted. If the researcher is lucky, he will realize that the respondent is making assumptions that are not widely shared, and question them. But if those assumptions are as invisible to her as they are to her respondents, the researcher may miss an important piece of the puzzle.

A similar problem arises when a researcher assumes that the information respondents give him is accurate. Cynics sometimes raise this as the problem of deception or "lying" and suggest that interpretivists are often naive. Of course, respondents in interpretive research can lie, just as respondents to surveys can lie about their preferences or behavior. The same type of safeguards apply for both types of research. A more difficult problem than deliberate deception, though, is that of skewed perceptions. This can occur when respondents, unacquainted with academic notions of causation, identify "causes" that are neither necessary or sufficient, or when the respondents upon whom the researcher relies are the most interesting, most articulate, or most colorful personalities, who may not be representative of the group. Skewed perceptions also result because what the researcher observes is always influenced, to some extent, by the researcher's presence, by the interview process, and by what the researcher thinks is salient.

Here, again, cross-researcher compilations of similar studies can help. Because so much of the work of interpretation depends on the interaction between researcher and participant, seeing how similar research participants respond to different researchers can remind the reader to factor rapport, emphasis, and tone into the analysis. For instance, the young mothers who talked to the relatively young research team of Kalil et al. were more able to express a desire for independence than the similar mothers, who, talking to Hicks-Bartlett, accepted and valued their obligations to and their support from kin.

This difference in perspective does not show that one group or the other is lying, or that one researcher or the other is deceived. Instead it illustrates the strength of interpersonal obligations. Were those obligations easily dismissed, mothers would not need to express frustration. Were they less crucial to their well-being, mothers would not need to justify the sacrifices they make.

Similarly, the comparison between the Reaves and Young chapters shows that different features of a situation can be salient in different contexts. The unemployed and underemployed men that Young interviews do not focus on racism, while the successfully employed men that Reaves interviews do. This raises interesting questions: Is racism less salient to Young's respondents because they have so little contact with the work world? Are accusations of racism too threatening to these unemployed men because the existence of racism suggests that personal attitude and willpower may not be enough to find them jobs? Or is the experience of racism simply so much a part of their everyday existence that it is, paradoxically, not salient as a topic of discussion? Conversely, Young's chapter raises questions for Reaves's analysis: Could the overvaluation of their own skills, so evident in Young's respondents, be one of the reasons why Reaves's successfully employed respondents feel underappreciated? Might the lack of contact between Reaves's respondents and their white co-workers blind them to non-race-related reasons for their lack of promotions, just as the men in Young's chapter were too isolated to realize how the work world worked? Looking across the studies to see how common features of the environment might be recognized as salient by one researcher while being taken for granted by another thus adds to the explanatory power of both.

As this implies, variability across interpretivist researchers does not signal inherent flaws in the work or the method. The touchstone of interpretive work is not replication: two researchers in the same neighborhood, talking to the same people, will not get identical answers. Instead, the touchstone of interpretive work is connection and consistency across studies: those two researchers should find that their conclusions illuminate, deepen, and fit into the world mapped out by the other's research. Interpretive work is no less subject to verification than surveys or evaluations, where replication is a goal, if not a commonly employed technique. But that verification is of a different kind.

Conclusion

It is currently fashionable to talk of the importance of hearing the "voices" of the ignored or dispossessed. Used without care, this can mean as little as throwing a colorful quote into an article or book to prove a predetermined point. At the other extreme, it can herald a romantic belief that because people know their own situations best, only they can solve their own problems, and only if they are given as many resources and as much power as they request.

Both of these alternatives are dangerous because they discredit the important contribution made by interpretive work, which seeks to explain the "voices" of people affected by a particular situation, problem, or policy. Those who dismiss the effort to bring the perspectives of the poor to poverty policy as biased forget that without such efforts, the bias is that of the researcher, who substitutes her own view of human nature or human motivation, her models of incentives and behavior, in place of an understanding of the situation at hand. That bias is often overlooked because, by definition, its assumptions sound plausible to the research and policy community. Its cost shows up only later, as policies face unanticipated obstacles, people refuse to respond to carefully designed incentives, or the consequences of well-meaning policies are more negative than positive.

This does not mean that interpretive work can stand alone. Just as traditional surveys and evaluations need an interpretive context, interpretive work needs some understanding of generalizability for good policy to be made. That requires a knowledge of the extent of the problems that interpretive work identifies, a multifaceted picture of the situation that is often possible only through comparisons, and an assessment of how researcher-respondent interactions might influence the analysis. Interpretive work benefits both from complementary work in hypothesis testing and a rigorous assessment of its validity.

Given these, however, the acceptance of interpretive work as relevant for policy-making is long overdue. By showcasing a generation of poverty scholars who base their interpretive work on a thorough knowledge of the most up-to-date quantitative research on poverty, collections such as this one are a start. They exemplify the type of collaborative work, within and across research traditions, that can make policy for the poor, and particularly for African-American poor, more sensitive and more appropriate to those that policy serves.

NOTES

1. One of the goals of "community-based research," for instance, is to give research participants an active role in shaping research that they also have access to afterward.

2. In other work I have argued that the difference is one between "positivist" and "interpretivist" qualitative work; see Lin (1998).

References

Anderson, Elijah. 1990. *Streetwise: Race, Class, and Change in an Urban Community.* Chicago: University of Chicago Press.

Auletta, Ken. 1982. *The Underclass.* New York: Random House.

Bane, Mary Jo, and David Ellwood. 1994. *Welfare Realities: From Rhetoric to Reform.* Cambridge: Harvard University Press.

Bourgois, Philippe. 1995. *In Search of Respect: Selling Crack in El Barrio.* New York: Cambridge University Press.

Brooks-Gunn, Jeanne, Gregory Duncan, and Lawrence Aber, eds. 1997. *Neighborhood Poverty: Context and Consequences for Children, Vol. 1.* New York: Russell Sage Foundation.

Conger, Rand, and Glen Elder Jr. 1994. *Families in Troubled Times.* New York: Walter de Gruyter.

Corcoran, Mary. 1995. "Rags to Rags: Poverty and Mobility in the United States." *Annual Review of Sociology* 21:237–67.

Dash, Leon. 1996. *Rosa Lee: A Mother and Her Family in Urban America.* New York: Basic Books.

DiIulio, John. 1996. "Saving the Children: Crime and Social Policy." In *Social Policies for Children,* ed. Irwin Garfinkel, Jennifer L. Hochschild, and Sara S. McLanahan, 202–56. Washington, DC: The Brookings Institution.

Edin, Kathryn, and Laura Lein. 1997. *Making Ends Meet: How Single Mothers Survive Welfare and Low-Wage Work.* New York: Russell Sage Foundation.

Ellwood, David. 1988. *Poor Support.* New York: Basic Books.

Hannerz, Ulf. 1969. *Soulside: Inquiries into Ghetto Culture and Community.* New York: Columbia University Press.

Jargowsky, Paul. 1997. *Poverty and Place: Ghettos, Barrios, and the American City.* New York: Russell Sage Foundation.

Kotlowitz, Alex. 1991. *There Are No Children Here.* New York: Doubleday.

Liebow, Elliot. 1967. *Tally's Corner: A Study of Negro Streetcorner Men.* Boston: Little, Brown.

Lin, Ann Chih. 1998. "Bridging Positivist and Interpretivist Approaches to Qualitative Methods." *Policy Studies Journal* 26 (1): 162–80.

Massey, Douglas S., and Nancy Denton. 1993. *American Apartheid: Segregation and the Making of the Underclass.* Cambridge: Harvard University Press.

Maynard, Rebecca, ed. 1997. *Kids Having Kids: Economic Costs and Social Consequences of Teen Pregnancy.* Washington, DC: Urban Institute Press.

McLoyd, Vonnie. 1998. "Socio-economic Disadvantage and Child Development." *American Psychologist* 53 (2): 185–204.

Newman, Katherine. 1988. *Falling from Grace: The Experience of Downward Mobility in the American Middle Class.* New York: Free Press.

———. 1999. *No Shame in My Game: The Working Poor in the Inner City.* New York: Knopf and the Russell Sage Foundation.

Personal Responsibility and Work Opportunity Reconciliation Act. 1996. Public Law 104–193.

Rank, Mark. 1994. *Living on the Edge: The Realities of Welfare in America.* New York: Columbia University Press.

Stack, Carol. 1974. *All Our Kin: Strategies for Survival in a Black Community.* New York: Harper and Row.

Sullivan, Mercer. 1989. *"Getting Paid": Youth Crime and Work in the Inner City.* Ithaca, NY: Cornell University Press.

Wilson, William Julius. 1987. *The Truly Disadvantaged: The Inner City, the Underclass, and Public Policy.* Chicago: University of Chicago Press.

———. 1996. *When Work Disappears: The World of the New Urban Poor.* New York: Knopf.

PART 1
Neighborhood: Family and Community as Supports

CHAPTER 2

Between a Rock and a Hard Place: The Labyrinth of Working and Parenting in a Poor Community

Sharon Hicks-Bartlett

It was a quiet summer night in Meadow View. The crisp air and blue-black sky were tranquil. Suddenly the night's stillness was pierced by screams and yells of chilling distress. Shots rang out. No one could recall how many. At times like this, people move away from windows. Someone surely summoned the police. Although the station is only two minutes from any point in the community, the police take their time showing up. Events inside Lillie's apartment stunned the occupants and made it difficult later to remember exactly what transpired that terrible night. Things happened quickly. Everyone agreed, however, that men with guns broke into the apartment, yelling, cussing, and looking for Lillie's teenage son. When the boy refused to step forward, the gunmen threatened to kill everyone. Lillie's son finally identified himself. At this point, things spun out of control.

All the gunmen wanted was Lillie's only son. But this was more than Lillie was willing to give. A slight woman, barely five feet, three inches, Lillie leapt in front of him, shielding him, flailing her arms, screaming and pleading for them not to hurt her child. They didn't. In split-second pandemonium, they killed Lillie instead. Dead at the age of forty-two, leaving five children and one grandchild.

Few people were able to maintain their equanimity during Lillie's funeral. Many wept openly as versions of what transpired that night circulated through the large, crowded church. A self-described, longtime family friend sang a mournful rendition of Lillie's "favorite" song, *"It's So Hard to Say Goodbye to Yesterday."* The minister railed at the unsaved souls, insisting that only those who had not accepted the Lord should experience difficulty saying good-bye. His words were less a eulogy than a stern lecture to those who were "living by the sword." As sounds of sobbing filled the church, the minister bellowed at those who refused to identify Lillie's killers. The woman with whom I attended the funeral pointed out Lillie's ex-husband, who evidently had come up north to pay his respects and to retrieve his son. The community denounced the father for his son's refusal to cooperate with police. But silence, the father believed, was the only way to save his son's life. Following the funeral, father and son would be heading south to live.

At the funeral people whispered about the shame of it all, how things here had gone from bad to worse, how people couldn't even be safe at home, and how they feared for the future. They talked about the possible fallout from the killing. Might there be a retaliation murder like the one that occurred years before, when one young man shot another, only to be killed later by the brother of the man he had murdered days before? Back then, the community's lone undertaker prepared the bodies of both men. For the community's viewing convenience, the bodies were placed in adjacent parlors at the same time. Even then, many years before Lillie's murder, people were horrified by what was happening to Meadow View. Today, people continue to shake their heads in dismay, declaring that "people have simply gone mad."

In Meadow View families struggle to survive. Few do so unscathed. Even for those a step or two above the poorest, living in Meadow View is a merciless challenge. As residents often remark, "stuff is always happening here." The strain of rebounding from one crisis before the next occurs depletes the body and mind. Lillie's story captures the violence that can transpire here.

In discussing how we experience place, Tony Hiss explains that whether we realize it or not, we all react "consciously and unconsciously" to where we reside and work. "[P]laces have an impact on our sense of self, our sense of safety, the kind of work we get done, the ways we interact with other people, even our ability to function as citizens in a democracy . . . the places where we spend our time affect the people we are and can become" (Hiss 1990, xi). Meadow View is one of the nation's poorest suburbs; it is isolated from jobs, quality schools, and adequate community resources. In Meadow View, for the greatest numbers of family members to survive, space must be strategically and carefully managed, which requires a level of vigilance that burdens families and reinforces their interdependency. But despite the gloomy state of affairs here, residents are tied to this terrain and to each other in real and symbolic ways. Despite all its problems, people call this place home. The stigma attached to coming from this place engenders in many a defensive bond that strengthens intergroup relations at the same time that it threatens to rip them apart. Affective bonds are always at risk because material, social, and financial need is unremitting. Already vulnerable families struggle to fulfill each other's needs, and this very exertion reinforces a "collective ethos" that binds people together (Jones 1986, 229).

Here, people manage working and parenting by relying on loose, family-based networks that minimize risk and center on meeting immediate needs. These networks provide the only security available to families in the face of recurrent threats to their physical well-being, isolation from jobs both within and outside their neighborhoods, and meager finances. Personal sacrifices, made for the good of the family unit, strain already limited family resources. Not surprisingly, the help of relatives who are themselves poor is never enough to change one's life situation. But when "self-sufficiency" is promoted as a policy objective without attention to the central role that family members play for one another, it is easy to overlook the fact that family and community sufficiency is required for the problems of the poor to be fully addressed.

Meadow View is a small black suburb outside a major midwestern city. This chapter is based on more than nine years of fieldwork in Meadow View. The daily lives of ten women were explored with an emphasis on family, community, and work. Four of the ten women were first interviewed during an earlier project; the others were added during research for this project, which took place during an eighteen-month period beginning in the summer of 1995 and ending in December 1996. The women, all of whom are mothers, were engaged in conversations of both a general and specific nature. Most of the interviews were tape-recorded and transcribed verbatim. Formal interviews ranged from two to more than five per person. In addition, my impromptu visits to homes produced many opportunities to talk, woman to woman, about a variety of topics.

These mothers were located through old contacts in the community, a worker at a community center, and one or two key informants. I explained to all the participants that I was interested in learning about family and community life. Consent forms that proffered more information about the study were disseminated to everyone. Participation was unanimous. Initially, no mention of money was made. Upon completion of the first interview, ten dollars was given to each informant. No mention of money was made or offered thereafter.

Interviews transpired in one of two places, with the vast majority occurring in private homes. A small number of first interviews were conducted in a vacant office at the community center. Subsequent interviews took place in the mothers' homes at their convenience. In addition, I often dropped by for informal "interviews."

All of the mothers are African-American. They represent a cross section of the women I have interviewed over my many years of involvement in the community. Each mother has had work experience, which tends to be part-time and low wage. Welfare use has ranged from a few months to more than ten years. All the women acquired their first job as teens in a federally funded summer youth employment program. Two of the women later secured either part-time or full-time work as adults in the same program. The other women typically hold jobs in service, retail, or manufacturing. With the exception of Sissy, the mother with the most education and work experience in the group, the mothers often talk of desiring jobs in the caregiving fields.

A Suburb in Name Only

Although Meadow View is a suburb situated near a once-booming industrial region, it looks like the rural south, with its unpaved roads, two outhouses, and a creek set deep in the woods. Most of its nearly forty-five hundred residents, whether employed or not, are low income and black. By 1990, 49.2 percent of the population was below poverty level. Per capita income is just over $4,500. A large stamping plant sits outside the community, but few Meadow View residents hold these skilled and semiskilled jobs. By any measure, unemployment and underemployment are pervasive, creating a community dependent on government assistance. For those sixteen and over, Meadow View's unemployment rate is 26 percent. Local officials set the "real" unemployment rate higher than 50 percent. One glance around the community on any summer day gives credence to a community perception that "almost everybody is out of work."

Meadow View has always been a poor community. But not until it became poor *and* black did it develop such intractable problems. In the shift from a poor white community to a poor black community, Meadow View became a choice locale for low-income public housing projects. Now, 65 percent of housing is government projects. Their construction in this particular suburb, as opposed to other nearby middle-class suburbs, is a prime example of the collusion among local, state, and federal agencies to perpetuate racial and class segregation within Meadow View. This small community was particularly attractive to those who preferred suburban living but could only afford it where rock-bottom housing prices and regional housing discrimination allowed them to live.

Rajah, who is married and the mother of seven boys and an infant daughter, voices her trepidation about Meadow View; she routinely checks for opportunities to move to other suburbs.

> I've been looking and looking for a house for my kids. Looking forever! I got to get away from here before I go crazy or something happens to my boys. I'm sick of the water, I'm sick of the drugs, I'm sick

of living here. This is insane! Too much stuff is happening all the time, something is always going on.

Theoretically, Rajah's income and housing subsidy would permit her to leave Meadow View. But if she succeeds, she will most likely relocate to another overwhelmingly poor, black suburb. Her subsidy was once a ticket into a safer, more economically viable suburb in the area. Now, those who want to leave often find themselves blocked as a result of a political battle between county and local housing authorities that restricts the mobility of the Section 8 certificates in this region (Hicks-Bartlett forthcoming). Leaving the community is even more difficult for those with little income and no housing subsidy.

Economic stability, adequate community resources, healthy infrastructure, strong institutions, a robust tax base, fiscal viability, and effective local government are some indicators of community well-being. Meadow View falls short on every single one. Like other old black suburbs, Meadow View's local government strains to keep afloat financially (Logan 1983/1988). Ironically, although Meadow View provides fewer services to its residents than its nearby suburban neighbors, its per capita expenditures are higher than theirs. This is because the local government's weak property tax base is insufficient to provide adequate services or maintain its deteriorating infrastructure. Delaying needed repairs to save money often costs more in the long run. Several times, the local government has teetered on the brink of bankruptcy. On more than one occasion both the police and fire department have gone on strike, imperiling the safety of residents. Except for church, few institutional supports are available to supplement and reinforce parental efforts. Community-sanctioned outlets for youth do not exist. Local services are so inadequate (e.g., years ago the local library had to be closed due to its unsafe structure and lack of operating funds) that people must go outside the community for most things.

In the summer of 1996, more than one hundred fifty people were arrested in a series of drug busts conducted by undercover sting operations. Previous raids had done little to clean up the community's drug trade. The latest round of sweeps came on the heels of the arrest of the police chief for allegedly permitting the drug trade to flourish with impunity, which had been rumored for years. More than a decade of police "passes" have brought down not only the police chief but also six current and former police officers, all of whom now face serious charges and lengthy prison sentences. Such corruption and graft lead many parents to believe that the job of protecting children from the fallout of this destitute place is their responsibility alone.

Surviving a summer requires considerable vigilance and management of one's space. Hot homes drive people outdoors to enjoy the camaraderie on the street. At the same time, an unremitting flow of out-of-state cars scouting for drug dealers stir feelings of besiegement and spark endless discussions of safety, drugs, and violence. Drugs control certain streets, making them difficult to maneuver. Late-model, expensive automobiles, with white people at the wheel, block traffic along some streets. These outsiders are the topic of considerable community discussion, distrust, suspicion, and anger. The mother of two young children summed up her feelings regarding these invasions:

> We can't even drive through their neighborhoods. But they can come here and do whatever they want. They don't care about nothing but getting drugs, but we the one's suppose to be so bad. We the ones *they* don't want to live by.

Often communities like this become a market for all sorts of spillover vice. Women and young girls are propositioned by strangers hunting for drugs and sexual thrills. Although men of all types scout the community for willing females, white males, perhaps because of their high visibility, evoke the greatest ire.

The fear of getting caught in the crossfire of a drug shoot-out and the concern that one's child will either use, deal drugs, or be caught up in spillover crime as a victim or participant preoccupy parents. Parents assert that "you've got to watch out for your own." Meadow View has become a place where children must learn the community's alarm call: "hit the deck" or simply, "get down." Watching children here is endless, exacting work. As one mother comments:

> We ain't been doing nothing but staying inside. They been shooting the last two nights. Girl, I'm scared to look out the window. My nerves is already bad, now they really messed up. Seems like every time I try to fall asleep, racing cars or shooting wakes me up. You gotta keep yours inside—if you want 'em safe.

During interviews, mothers habitually peek out the window. This seemingly small gesture is repeated in households throughout the community. Parents survey the landscape, tirelessly scanning the environment, monitoring slow-moving cars, scrutinizing suspicious gatherings—behavior all rooted in indisputable facts of daily life. Before venturing out, people caution each other to "be careful." Some avoid going out at night altogether for fear of getting "caught" out after dark.

Young boys risk being seduced into illegal work. A fieldnote entry describes the challenges a parent can face. Mabel, mother of eight, expressed considerable angst about her sons. Her daughters worried her less because she had more success keeping them at home. One son, a particularly quiet youth of fifteen named Mark, was approached to work as a "lookout" for a local drug dealer. Fearing his mother's wrath, the boy rebuffed the offers. Later, a rather persistent drug dealer invited himself to Mabel's house to ask permission for the youth to work for him. Mabel listened patiently to the dealer's request. When he finished, she said, "Leave my son alone. . . . He can't work for you. Just leave him alone!" She was dead serious and hoped her steely glare transmitted that spirit.

Fearing that Mark would eventually turn to drug work, Mabel first thought of sending him south to live with his father's family. When this proved not to be a viable option, she tried to get him into a special program where he would leave the community to work on an out-of-state farm, safe from Meadow View streets. "For three years I wouldn't have to worry about him getting killed or something," she sighed. The program seemed a perfect solution. One problem remained, however. Because her son had never been in serious trouble, he was not eligible to enter the program through normal channels. Only if she abdicated her parental rights, formally declaring herself unfit, could he be admitted. The logic that required her son to be in trouble before he could receive help seemed inane to Mabel. She weighed her options and declared that if giving up her rights was the only way to save her son, so be it. As she explains it:

> I don't care too much about giving up my rights, if it can help him. He knows I'm his momma and I know I'm his momma. No piece of paper can change that. When he gets out, I'm quite sure he'll look me up and quite naturally he'll be grown and can understand what I had to do.

Mabel escaped having to surrender her parental rights. Her son managed to avoid drug work on his own. To Mabel, what happened seemed worse in some ways. A young cousin, while showing Mark his gun, accidentally shot and seriously wounded Mark in the head. Now, for the rest of his life, he will ingest medicines to control his seizures.

To separate working and parenting from this situational context is to fail to appreciate how bound the two are. Parents in nonpoor areas expect certain community qualities and services that support parenting. There is a vast difference, however, between the communities in which the poor and nonpoor reside, particularly those in which poor minority and poor non-minority live (Wilson 1987, 1996). While protecting children is a universal parental behavior, in Meadow View it can require extreme measures; it is labor-intensive, emotionally draining work. The need to protect children and the vigilance this requires create major barriers to working and parenting, especially when the two are attempted simultaneously. The mother of four young boys reveals what transpired one day.

> Girl, a boy got shot the other day. Right out here in front of my apartment. He couldn't have been no more than fifteen. They killed him right out in broad day light. I was so glad my kids wasn't outside 'cause usually they would be right out there playing. But I had just made them come in a few minutes before. It took the ambulance a long time to get here. I was so scared . . . Blood, all in the street—it's still there. I just think about my kids. Girl what if they were out there. They coulda' got kill, too.

Frightened by her experience, she immediately requested, to no avail, that the project housing authority relocate her family to a safer area. Mothers like this woman cannot but think that if they were not at home to make their children come in, their children might be the next victims. Meadow View lacks before- and afterschool programs that could engage children in constructive activities while parents work. Ironically, the luxury of such programs belongs to parents who live in neighborhoods where tax dollars can support such services or to parents who can purchase whatever care they desire for their children. But in Meadow View, where the need for such programs is so much greater, parents have neither the income nor the institutional supports to establish them.

Adults and children feel the effects of this stressful environment. Meadow View mothers often complain of "nerve problems." Some children become fearful and edgy. Others obsess about danger or being shot. Like Meadow View adults, children become extremely preoccupied with the environment and its inherent dangers. "Hypervigilance" is striking, seen in the ". . . scan[ning] [of] their surroundings for danger and over-interpret[ing] the actions of others . . ." (Brownlee 1996, 72). Nightmares about being chased, hurt, or killed are common. In one family, the stress on a mother and her two children, ages six and ten, is palpable. In discussing her children's fears, the mother laments:

> I can't get them out of my bed. You know, they are too big to be sleeping with me. But they too scared to be in the room by themselves. They got good beds to sleep in, but I can't get them in them for nothing. They sleep in here real good, but now I don't get any sleep. And my back stay hurt with one on each side kicking me, and I can't get comfortable. I really don't sleep at night. I catnap in the day, when they in school.

This sleep-deprived mother frequently complains of physical ailments. The only time she rests is when her children are at school. The many implications this would have on working outside the home are obvious.

The constancy of trauma and fear in their environment causes other problems in children. One report found that children who experience early trauma (e.g., witnessing or fearing violence) show measurable physiological and chemical changes in the body and brain (Brownlee 1996, 72). When frightened, they react in a "fight-or-flight" response. The body attempts to compensate by releasing certain stress hormones. In affected children, normal physiological and chemical reactions jump track, producing abnormal levels and imbalances in the body. The impact on learning for children in these environments has been well documented (Garbarino et al. 1992; Prothrow-Stith and Weissman 1993). Affected children have a shorter attention span; language and critical thinking suffers. High levels of these harmful chemical changes create children who are ripe for a host of learning difficulties. Children in these environments may also misconstrue normal play as aggressive and get into physical altercations.

All of these challenges influence parental decisions about work and family. This does not mean that those who face such barriers should be exempt from paid labor. When faced with objective situations that require hypervigilance (e.g., children who require extraordinary nurturing, fear management, patience, and care of chronic health problems), most mothers concentrate on performing their maternal role above all else. Those lucky enough to find others they trust to care for their children are able to work—at least on and off—because of it. Without such support, employed work is difficult and sometimes impossible to sustain. Yet money for survival is as necessary as care for children and families. The support networks that spring up to meet these challenges address this dilemma, but in ways that lessen the significance of individual achievement and self-sufficiency.

Kin Matters

Meadow View families depend heavily on each other. Individuals and families expect to share with others. In addition to financial support, families provide an array of essential services, without which most would not be able to work, attend school, or enroll in training programs. All of the families discussed here are involved in extensive helping networks that can buckle under the weight of a widening circle of needy members. Just how critical to survival these networks are is exemplified by one mother's family.

Wanda once lived in a two-bedroom project apartment with her two children. It also provided temporary quarters for her two brothers and two cousins, whom her parents raised after their mother died. Although she now works as a teacher's aide, Wanda received welfare for more than ten years. Throughout much of this time, she cared for her invalid mother. On occasion, Wanda received money from her parents but this was neither regular nor expected. To avoid placing the mother in a nursing home, Wanda's father, who worked full-time at a factory in a neighboring state, sought his children's help in caring for their mother. Since Wanda had a small child to care for, she was the designated sibling to help her mother and her employed siblings who might need occasional help. Two sisters, one employed in clerical work, the other in factory work, sometimes called on Wanda for child care. Providing care to those who need it is highly valued, particularly over low-wage work that may only slightly improve the individual's life while potentially burdening and making matters worse for the extended kin network.

Known for being able to stretch her welfare check, Wanda was often called on for a loan or a meal or a place to stay for a few days. She earned extra income by operating an in-house "store," a table set up in her kitchen from which she sold soda, potato chips, and candy to neighborhood youth; at best, her efforts rarely generated more than $30 a month. Although Wanda had her own share of money worries, she rarely refused anyone in need. For unexpected emergencies, she kept twenty dollars stashed away. Wanda's only complaint was that she did not have anyone as generous on whom *she* could rely. Although she felt she gave more than she ever received, Wanda did benefit from some invaluable help from this arrangement.

During her second pregnancy, Wanda moved from her parents' home into a subsidized apartment. Soon afterward, an assortment of relatives moved in and out. Until they found jobs, they were neither asked nor expected to help financially. When two relatives acquired jobs at a rehabilitation center, through another relative, they began giving Wanda money, helping with groceries and continuing to baby-sit. Whether working or not, they baby-sat whenever needed. Not only did this allow Wanda respite from her children, it also relieved the ennui of being housebound. Wanda benefited, too, from the protection and security of having men present.

> I don't mind having them here, they are good company. Plus, I know that no one is going to come in here on me when they know that a man lives here. . . . They help out just by being here. Plus it's good for my kids to be around their uncles and cousins.

Years later, while living alone with her two children, Wanda suffered a near fatal brain aneurysm. Her family sprang into action. During her nearly six-month rehabilitation, the extended family focused on Wanda's health. At the time, Wanda's brother Donnie had been planning to go to Mississippi for a long-awaited job. Unemployed for years, he looked forward to finally getting work—even though it required a major relocation. Because the other siblings were engaged in full- or part-time work, they were less available to attend to Wanda's needs. Together, the family decided that Donnie should move into Wanda's apartment and assume primary care of her children and her personal affairs. Other relatives helped out on weekends. When asked how he felt about having to give up his job, Donnie remarked, "You can always get another job, but you can't get another sister" (see also Stack 1990).

Wanda and her family viewed her miraculous recovery as a sign from God that she should improve her life. With the help of her caseworker, she enrolled in a community college and eventually became a teacher's aide. During Wanda's course work, Donnie, still unemployed, continued to live with her and help out, without pressure from his family to get a job. Caring for Wanda was a job that everyone in the family valued. Donnie never mentioned going South again. Until she finished school and found a job, Donnie selflessly contributed his unpaid labor to the family and Wanda's dreams. Now and then, Wanda gave him money, but he did not receive regular pay. Without his help, her recovery would have been difficult; her schooling would have been impossible. His child care and household work allowed Wanda to recover fully, reach a goal sparked by her illness, and obtain a job.

Most families will respond supportively to each other in times of crisis. In this sense, Wanda and her family are not unique. What is truly notable in Meadow View families is the degree to which individuals are summoned to meet the needs of others and to suppress personal goals to do so (see also Rank 1994). A great deal of working and schooling is made possible only because of the willingness of others to set aside self-interest. Many who manage to hold jobs have kin willing to defer individual pursuits for the sake of others. Because poor families cannot purchase the care their families need, they must supply it to each other.

Exploring the complicated arrangements mothers must make to work and parent simultaneously reveals how tenuous these arrangements are and how even a slight error can trigger a full-blown, snowballing crisis in families. Children's illness is a universal barrier to working that all parents face, particularly parents of young children. According to Heymann, Earle, and Egleston (1996), fully one-fourth of all parents reported that they had no sick leave available to take care of sick relatives, including their children. But children's ailments often require them to miss school. An estimated ten million children have some sort of chronic disorder. Not surprisingly, poor children have poorer health. They have a higher incidence of chronic ailments, while their working parents have the least amount of sick leave to tend to them. Sissy, a young mother who worked in retail, tells how she finally had to quit her job because of her infant's chronic respiratory condition.

> My sister was watching him but he just kept a cold. He'd have one a couple of weeks. Then he'd be okay a couple of weeks. Then he'd get sick again. I had to keep taking off to take him back and forth to the doctor. He wasn't eating right at all. My baby was so sick! They wanted to put tubes in his ears. When he couldn't breathe, my sister would call me at work and I had to rush home to take him to the hospital. She couldn't take him because she had to watch her own baby. So I had to quit because I was taking off a lot. I wasn't making no money. They were going to fire me because I had so many problems with the baby. I don't know if they believed me. My mother said I need to think about my baby and stay at home to take care of him myself. So I quit.

A preference for family/friend child care over other types of care derives from the conviction that only family can be depended on to deal flexibly with frequent emergencies.

In Meadow View the importance of caregiving can compete with a work ethic that values paid labor over nonpaid caring work. Anyone trying to combine simultaneous working and parenting can identify with Darla, an unemployed mother. Darla has four sons who attend school with her sister's three daughters. Her sister, a pregnant, single mother, works as a file clerk. By 7:30 A.M. the girls arrive at Darla's apartment. When it is time, they walk to school with Darla's two school-aged sons. After school, the five children return to Darla's, where the girls remain until their mother arrives. When the mother is late, the girls stay over or are retrieved by another family member. Before and after school, Darla is in charge of seven children under the age of eleven. She prepares snacks and sometimes entire meals for the children.

During the time we were meeting, Darla was battling cervical cancer. While often in severe physical discomfort and under medication that made her somnolent and temperamental, she took care of these children. She received little money from her sister but often was rewarded with free weekends while her boys slept at their cousin's house, a respite Darla enjoyed. Occasionally, the boys received gifts of clothing or other small items. On payday, Darla's sister brought over groceries for the children. The arrangement helped both women. As Darla explained:

> I help out my sister, she's got her hands full with the girls. And she's pregnant, too! Since I got to be here anyway, I might as well take care of hers, too. You can't just leave your kids with anybody. She knows

I'll do right by my nieces—I wanted girls, she was the one wanted boys. She's not going to leave her kids with just anybody.

When Darla recovered from the cancer, she found a job at a department store. Immediately, her job altered her sister's child-care arrangements and created new child-care needs for Darla. Now her nieces spend their before-school time in the care of another aunt, who just happened to quit her job because of doctor-ordered bed rest due to pregnancy complications. The girls continue to go to Darla's after school; until she arrives home from work, the children are now in the care of Darla's new boyfriend.[1]

The strain that such child-care arrangements can place on families is also evident from Vicki's story. Vicki, mother of two teenage daughters, once worked nights at a local bar, in part so that she could take care of her young nephew during the day. Her child-care work began soon after she got home from work in the early mornings, forcing her to get by on little sleep. Although she did receive pay for caring for Tony, whose mother, Kelly, worked on a cleanup crew at a local animal shelter,[2] the pay was sporadic due to Kelly's variable work hours. But as Vicki explained, this far-from-ideal situation was still the best option that the family, as a whole, had.

> I took care of Tony 'cause Kelly really didn't have anyone to watch him. She was going to get him in Head Start but someone had to get him there and go get him later. I didn't want to have to walk there and back [twice]. It was just easier to bring him over here in the morning. That way he'd be in one place all day. . . . That's why I wasn't really looking for a full-time day job then. She'd really have a hard time finding someone if I worked full-time, days.

When Vicki was unable to keep Tony because of foot surgery, another sister reluctantly used a week of her vacation time to fill in. This help was offered more out of duty to the larger family than respect for her sister. As she tells it:

> You know my sister and I don't get along at all! But that don't have nothing to do with Tony. I sure don't want to spend my vacation watching him. But somebody's got to watch him 'til Vicki gets back on her feet. My mother don't need to be bothered with this boy, she's too old. So I just took off to take care of him.

In a community without child-care programs for young and school-age children, someone willing and able to provide such care is highly valued. Child care, essential to all working parents with dependent children, is especially critical here. Mothers all want their children to receive the best care, to develop preschool skills, and to be involved in constructive activities with other children. Middle-class parents can purchase this care with greater assurance that it will be reliable and responsive to their needs.[3] Being able to purchase child care allows parents to exercise some control over the quality of that care. Quality is desired by poor mothers also. But few are fortunate enough to be able to take advantage of a program like Head Start because it fails to serve all those who want it or need it. Moreover, such programs are typically structured around a clock that conflicts with the working schedules of full-time mothers. Thus, poor mothers take what they can get. It is important to keep this point in mind when trying to understand why significant numbers of poor families' children are cared for by relatives.

Relatives can be intrinsically good caretakers and many are. But the preference for relatives must also be understood as part of an economic reality: mothers can trust and negotiate with family and friends in ways they could not with institutions. Given a choice, it is not clear that Kelly would have chosen one sleep-deprived sister and another disapproving one to care for her son. The help they offered was better than nothing. Even if her sisters were ideal caretakers, Kelly might simply wish to avoid reliance on custodial care done out of obligation. But it is unlikely that Kelly could have found a quality child-care provider who would have allowed her to pay erratically, or one who would take her son even when doing so violated the provider's self-interest. As another mother makes clear:

> . . . Beggars can't be too choosy. I'm grateful I got family that will help out. It's better than nothing. I don't particularly like them over there, but right now I can't do no better. And for what I'm paying, I can't be telling people how to run their house. I'm just grateful I have someone that can help me. It's better than nothing.

While limited options make one grateful for what one gets, they can place children at risk. Custodial care performed by caregivers with limited skills, poor health, little knowledge of normal child development, and unsafe homes creates anxiety for working mothers.[4] But out of a desperate need for care, mothers may pardon poor quality and disregard potentially hazardous situations. They make do, forever ready to establish new plans if absolutely necessary. High standards for the quality of child care one will accept is a luxury few Meadow View mothers can afford if they also want to work.

The symbiosis between working poor mothers and "nonworking" "welfare-taking" mothers makes it impossible to draw moral and ethical distinctions between the two. These mothers serve as lifelines to each other.

A work ethic that always defines workers as more deserving than non-workers misses this connection (Katz 1989). Given limited education, lack of job prospects, child-care needs, and inadequate transportation, these mothers recognize their dependence on others. They realize their ability to endure on low wages is possible, in large part, because of the misfortunes of other poor women whose labor helps them with their child-care needs. Those "lucky" enough to get a job realize that keeping it most often is directly related to someone else's current unemployment. And one frequently hears, "There but for the grace of God go I."

Reliance on the family can actually intensify after a job is obtained. One suddenly needs to find regular child care, to borrow money "til payday," to scrounge clothes to wear to work, to borrow bus fare or endlessly pursue other transportation means; these needs can ultimately weigh on everyone. Mabel, a mother who recently secured factory work, depends exclusively on her family's services. Just as the children are leaving for school, the mother is arriving home from work. When they return home, Mabel is often sleeping before departing for her graveyard shift. An older daughter who is a student at a local community college prepares the children for school in the morning and arranges her schedule to be home when the children return from school.[5] Without this help Mabel would not be able to keep her job. A parent working nights must maintain a schedule that is not conducive to rearing young children. Things are difficult, leading Mabel to wonder at times if she really is better off working. She comments on her ongoing struggles:

> You know, if it wasn't for [my family] I wouldn't make it. I'd be in the hole a lot. When I finish paying my bills, ain't much left. I like my job, especially getting paid every Friday, but it's hard to make it. I try to give a little to [her daughter] for helping with the kids. [Referring to the used car she recently purchased to get to her job]; I'm deep in the hole now 'cause of that piece of car. Seems like soon as I got it, it needed some of everything done to it and that ate up my little money. And the car still ain't right. It's bad when you work and still can't do no better. Girl, sometimes my brother has to get up out of his sleep and take me to work.

Life can be as tough for employed poor mothers as it is for welfare-receiving mothers who work within the home. Having a job may *feel* worse in some ways for employed poor mothers who see that working has made their lives more complicated and unmanageable than before. One mother comments on her attempts to make it:

I don't expect nothing on welfare so I make do with nothing. But when I was working, I expected to make it and seem like I was worse. I couldn't really stay up on it. I needed things to wear more, I needed money to pay for getting back and forth to work, the kids needed snacks when they went over to [a relative's house] and I had to send enough for her kids too, I wasn't really paid much. . . . And I could never get regular hours and that made it hard if I had to be there before they went to school. When [youngest child] is in school full-time, I can probably work more.

Alluding to the help she requires, another "self-sufficient" working mother states:

I'm squeezing by. This has been a good month . . . knock on wood! I'm just gonna keep my fingers crossed—that's all I can do. You know, as soon as you think you doing all right, something happens to remind you, you not. I ain't had to ask my family for nothing this month, and I hope it stays that way. I know my family gets tired of me begging, 'cause I get tired of me begging, too.

Rarely does this mother get through a month without the help of relatives and close friends. Her mother "keeps a freezer full of meat," allowing her to borrow food when money is tight. Such borrowing, in turn, exacts a cost from those who may have a little more than their poorest relatives but are also living close to the financial edge themselves. In fact, a tension exists between the pursuit of individual goals and the needs of the family. One woman explains the pressures she felt at college:

You know I knew my family needed me. I knew they were depending on my stipend. I'd call, and they would be having problems. I felt bad being here, having all this and they were having a hard time. I decided to come home after my first year and get a job to help out my family. I can always go to college at home.

This woman never finished her four-year business degree. She did, however, manage to complete two years of junior college. Until she was twenty-seven, she lived with her mother and siblings in a crowded project apartment. When she left home, she moved to an apartment a few blocks away.

Even young women with the opportunity to make a better life for themselves relinquish it to meet pressing family obligations. The assumption that working makes one better off is not always true. For whom are things better off? In this context, it is questionable that children are better off. Without reliable, affordable, quality child care for multi-aged children, it is doubtful that these mothers, who worry incessantly about the safety of their children, feel that they are better off. It makes sense to value their children's health and safety above low-wage work. When low-wage work wins out, it is in part because these mothers want to work badly and have managed to secure the support they need from others in hopes of making work pay. Many learn that work does not always pay, and that when it does, it does so primarily because of the current non-labor-force participation of others.

Some of the problems mothers face would be more easily resolved if Meadow View residents were able to work in their neighborhood. But Meadow View suffers from a lack of jobs and little transportation to where the jobs are. Family-based networks often refer workers to jobs and provide transportation alternatives. But when nearly everyone in one's network is poor, isolated from good opportunities, or dependent upon unreliable transportation, the network can provide only minimal assistance.

Finding Work, Reaching Work

One of the ironies of employment in Meadow View is that when poor mothers exchange their informal, family caretaking roles for paid, outside employment, the employment they find often involves caring for other people. In this region the demand for home health-care work is high, corresponding with a Department of Labor prediction that home health care will have the largest job growth of any industry between 1994 and 2005 (Eisler 1997). But while people everywhere must rely increasingly on purchased care, caregiving work is low paying and receives little credit for being important and necessary work (Abel and Nelson 1990; DeVault 1991; Stack 1974; Tronto 1994). These positions tend to be low wage, labor intensive, and little more than a "ghetto" for women, minorities and illegal immigrants (Eisler 1997; Statham, Miller, and Mauksch 1988). But the "soft" skills these mothers possess from years of traditional female work are usually enough to secure a job in these female-dominated fields. At least five of the ten mothers in my study have worked in nursing homes or in home health care. When asked what type of work they felt qualified for, all but one felt they could get a job in caregiving because as one mother put it, "that's mostly what I've been doing all along."

Home health care has advantages that other low-wage work does not; it allows for some flexibility in work schedules, which is especially important for single mothers (Schein 1995). Because of high demand for these workers, mothers can enter and exit the field at will, depending on the availability of help at home. Home health care also allows for more autonomy than other types of service work. Working in private homes, women can be their own bosses. Workers also develop strong relationships with their charges and often develop a sense of loyalty to the patient. They feel positive about providing a much-needed service to those less fortunate.

Even these advantages, however, are often insufficient to compensate for the job stress and low pay. Full-time pay at some agencies is $7 per hour, a pittance for a breadwinner. Home health care remains a poorly regulated industry, whose profits depend on unskilled, poorly trained, and uncertified workers. Currently the supply of workers is high, giving agencies little incentive to invest in better training for better-qualified workers, or to share with workers the industry's considerable profits. Without better training and industry regulations, the psychological stress and backbreaking physical demands of the job ultimately take their toll. Vicki, who has worked more than once in home health care, explains:

> I stayed with old man Jones for three years. Broke my heart when he died. I told them I didn't wanna work for no one for a while. I just couldn't take it. I needed a break. I had to leave.

Maggie is married, in her fifties, and mother of two adult children. She has worked as a nurse's aide and as a home health-care worker. When asked what she does for a living, she responds, "I'm a nurse." Due to health problems, she is currently on disability. She appears clinically depressed about not being able to work and is worried about her health. She is trying to will herself back to health because she "can't afford to be sick" much longer. She comments:

> I worked in a home for years before I quit. I left 'cause it was too hard and you get so attached to those old people. I remember coming in the room and this lady I'd taken care of had died. They'd already stripped her bed and cleaned the room. Nobody told me nothing. I just didn't want to be around all that death—took me a long time to get over that. . . . No, I will not work in the old folks homes again.

Many women suffer from the physical demands of the work:

> After awhile, moving people gets hard. That's dead weight you're trying to move, 'cause a lot of them can't move by themselves. You change diapers on grown people, clean up after them, bathe them, dress them. After awhile you just can't do it. You go home sore and hurting when you get through. I like the people and helping, but I was killing myself.

Like people everywhere, many people in Meadow View get jobs through family and friend networks. Those seeking work regularly interrogate others about job leads. But workers who sponsor relatives run the risk of damaging their own reputation if the relatives do not succeed. For instance, Wanda's brother, John, who held a respected position at a residential rehabilitation center, sponsored two cousins, a brother, and a sister for jobs. On his recommendation, all were hired, and eventually everyone quit. One resigned because he feared being fired. Because he worked a different shift than his relatives, he had to "bum" rides to and from work. Without reliable transportation, he was habitually late. The sister, who worked in the laundry, hated the drudgery of the work and claimed her supervisor was unfair and mistreated her. She left and eventually found other employment. A third quit after a disagreement with another co-worker. Of the four who terminated, one remained unemployed for more than a year. John, embarrassed, vowed never to sponsor anyone again. His sister explains why she believes things did not work out:

> They didn't really like the work. See, John has a good job there, he don't get messed over. But the rest of them . . . they caught it coming and going. And the whites kept on John about his relatives, what they did and didn't do.

On the other hand, if an employee works out well, an employer may come to view the sponsor as a reliable source for bringing responsible workers into the workplace. In Mabel's family, job sponsoring has worked out for two siblings in their early twenties.

> Both of them work at Brown's Chicken now. Ron got the job first and when his boss asked him if he knew some good workers, he told him about Juanda. Now they both are there. They're doing good, they like it. They get called in to do extra work all the time when somebody doesn't show up.

Many of the mothers I interviewed have acquired jobs through similar networks; they recognize their personal and skill limitations. They know that "good" jobs (i.e., full-time jobs that pay above minimum wage, with benefits) are not the jobs they will secure. For the most part they find jobs that are temporary, part-time, devoid of benefits, and always low paying.

The unavailability of good jobs is not the only obstacle that these mothers in Meadow View confront when they try to obtain employment. Simply getting to one's place of employment is difficult. It is widely accepted that urban communities are usually removed from suburban jobs, housing, quality schools, and other amenities. But the same isolation plagues old black suburbs. The significance of race is an indisputable fact in suburban development (Logan 1983/1988; see also Farley 1976). Decisions regarding transportation, suburban zoning codes, restrictive racial covenants in real estate investment and lending practices, redlining, and other discriminatory practices have historically been racially influenced (Massey and Denton 1993). Meadow View is not only a community that lacks industry, it is also situated in a region that is geographically isolated. Workers need to travel well beyond its borders to find work. Even though hordes of suburban workers access a highly developed transportation system that brings them to city jobs each day, traveling between suburbs in this region is much more difficult. And when Meadow View workers find jobs in the city that can be reached by public transportation, they may not be able to afford the commute. A round trip from Meadow View to the city costs almost ten dollars. To take advantage of travel discounts offered to frequent riders, one must purchase a monthly ticket, requiring a considerable outlay of money up front.

Amy, the mother of four young boys, is in her late twenties. At the age of nineteen she won custody of her five siblings after her mother died and her father abandoned them. Until recently and for ten years, she received welfare. She then got a job in a suburb not far from Meadow View and hoped that she would be able to walk the two miles from the bus to her job. The only problem she anticipated was inclement weather. When asked about arranging a daily taxi pickup from the bus, she reminded me that such luxuries were beyond her means and that the region does not have a dependable taxi service. Instead, Amy created an elaborate strategy for getting herself and her current boyfriend to and from work, which involved a carefully managed arrangement with a former boyfriend. This man, who was considerably older than Amy, considered her four children his responsibility—although he was the biological father of only the third child. Initially he agreed to drive Amy and her new boyfriend to work; if he was in a generous mood and did not have to work himself, he would even loan his car to her. But this arrangement was inherently unstable. When friends and other intimates are repeatedly called on for transportation, there is a good chance that personal mood and disposition will eventually get in the way. Amy tells of her experience calling on her former boyfriend:

> We were paying my ex-boyfriend to take Curtis (her new boyfriend) to work. No problems. Then he started getting an attitude and saying he couldn't take him. Now he knew there was no other way for him to get there. But because he was mad at me, he wanted to pull out.

Her new boyfriend worked part-time at a fast-food establishment. No bus routes went near his job and a cab was out of the question. Finally, the couple agreed to pay the ex-boyfriend more money until they could find another means of transportation. Because her plan was highly unreliable and filled with tension, Amy experienced considerable anxiety each day about getting to work.

Meadow View mothers unanimously desire work. They attempt it whenever they can. But they fail often, and not because they lack motivation or a work ethic. They fall short because the demands of simultaneous parenting and working eventually spin out of control, even with family support. They fail because the jobs for which they qualify turn out to be awful in the long run and eventually clash with family demands. They fail also because they work in job markets that discriminate against female breadwinners. In response, mothers quit. They hope to return at a more opportune time. Settings like Meadow View place considerable burdens on families, making it difficult, and often impossible, to parent and work successfully.

Summary

Barriers of space and place are not unique to Meadow View. Poverty and racial segregation, conjoined with spatial isolation and disconnection from the city that it lies near, prevent this suburb from receiving many basic services. The inability to afford a quality police and fire department, for example, exacerbate many problems here. Crime and fear of random violence force parents to become hypervigilant about their children, especially because the suburb has no institutional supports—afterschool programs, daycare providers—to help parents keep their children safely occupied. Parents must rely on family networks, but such networks are often strained by the demands placed on them. For people here, options are extremely limited.

Keeping children safe consumes parents and influences decisions about looking for work outside the home. Mothers, who assume much of the parenting, easily become overwhelmed by the unrelenting demands of this environment. The community is devoid of adequate resources such as a public library, youth services, and recreation programs. Poor pay tempts some police officers and firefighters to partner with the drug economy, leaving residents unprotected and vulnerable to random violence. Consequently, considerable effort is devoted to watching and protecting children. One must be forever vigilant about keeping children near and troublemakers far, a task that is not easy.

In Meadow View, the family is key to survival. Families provide transportation, housing, food, job leads, and emotional succor. Child care, a service that every working mother with dependent children requires, is provided by relatives and friends who are outside the labor force. Because of this, mothers' work is inextricably linked to the nonwork or misfortunes of other women who may or may not be employed. Since few can afford to actually purchase the care they need, child care provided by industry chains is out of reach for these families, both financially and geographically. Although mothers appreciate the custodial care the family provides, they have limited alternatives. Head Start fails to reach all those who need it, and those who use it must make elaborate plans to retrieve children, whose school schedules do not correspond with a regular, full-time workday. Child care here is prone to disruptions and is unreliable. Unexpected illnesses interrupt work, making mothers more likely to be tardy, absent, and distracted on the job.

These family networks are not without tensions. As more and more families experience hardships, the networks become increasingly stressed. It is difficult to meet everyone's needs. In some families, substance abuse has created a need to provide shelter for children and the substance abuser. Eventually the core group of givers becomes overwhelmed, forced to make tragic choices as to who can and who cannot be salvaged.

The emphasis from both the political right and left focuses on reducing welfare dependency rather than on eliminating poverty (Schram 1995). The right, with its emphasis on the individual as the key to achievement, sees the problem as a lack of good character, behavior, and sound morals. The liberal left, with its stress on developing one's human capital (Gans 1995; Handler 1995) argues that with the proper schooling, job preparation, and skills, the poor can assimilate into the world of work and perform like other Americans. But neither understands the multiple effects of poverty on poor mothers (single or married) who live in a community context that manufactures major barriers to simultaneous working and parenting. Work does not exist in isolation from family and community (see McKnight 1995). What is missing from both camps is an understanding of the daily demands on families trapped in an economically depressed and racially segregated community that is also geographically isolated and lacks the most basic resources.

Over time, such conditions create deep and multiple needs in both people and institutions. Parenting in an impoverished, unsafe community forces parents to make decisions about employment and self-sufficiency based on how they can best protect their children and hold on to the coping strategies that have worked in the past. Being thrust into low-wage work, without substitute supports and services or a method for maintaining what has already been carved out, puts already vulnerable families and children at great risk. Parents need the security of knowing that the most vulnerable among them, their children and the elderly, will be safe, cared for, and protected.

Successful work programs will need to go beyond teaching job skills to consider community issues that program participants confront regularly. At the very least, work programs should address issues of community space, family obligation, local institutional support, and how these forces, alone and together, affect parents' ability to be productive workers and effective parents. For poor people to be simultaneously good workers and good parents, they need access to the same supports and resources that other working citizens have. Policymakers must develop a perspective that incorporates the full array of forces that go into work and parenting decisions (Dickerson 1995; McKnight 1995). Lacking this, policymakers will create policies and programs that have little relevance to the real, day-to-day world in which the poor struggle to survive.

NOTES

1. Although few talked about leaving children with boyfriends for this chapter, previous fieldwork suggests that this is often done out of desperation and rarely considered an ideal situation. The risk to children left with unskilled and unwilling caregivers needs to be examined from a child safety perspective.

2. This animal shelter worker has held several nursing home jobs but found them emotionally stressful, unpleasant, and difficult to manage without a car.

3. As more middle-class families experience problems with abusive child-care workers and poorly managed child-care chains, this is less true.

4. Living conditions in Meadow View are often unsafe. Over 34 percent of Meadow View's housing is considered "substandard."

5. The daughter's need to adjust her college schedule to accommodate the child-care needs of her family could be a barrier for completing her education. The potential exists that she will leave school due to unexpressed pressures to help her family, that family needs supersede her own. An afterschool program could ease this type of child-care issue. For now, the daughter's school schedule is secondary to her family's needs.

REFERENCES

Abel, E. K., and M. K. Nelson, eds. 1990. *Circles of Care: Work and Identity in Women's Lives.* Albany: State University of New York Press.

Brownlee, S. 1996. "The Biology of Soul Murder." *U.S. News & World Report,* 11 November, 121:71–73.

DeVault, M. L. 1991. *Feeding the Family: The Social Organization of Caring as Gendered Work.* Chicago: University of Chicago Press.

Dickerson, B. J., ed. 1995. *African American Single Mothers: Understanding Their Lives and Families.* Thousand Oaks, CA: Sage.

Eisler, P. 1997. "Home Health Care: 'All the Components for Disaster.'" *USA Today,* Special Home Health Care Report 4D:Life, 18 March.

Farley, R. 1976. "Components of Suburban Population Growth." In *The Changing Face of the Suburbs,* ed. B. Schwartz. Chicago: University of Chicago Press.

Gans, H. J. 1995. *The War Against the Poor: The Underclass and Antipoverty Policy.* New York: Basic Books.

Garbarino, J., N. Dubrow, K. Kostelny, and C. Pardo, eds. 1992. *Children in Danger: Coping with The Consequences of Community Violence.* San Francisco: Jossey-Bass.

Handler, J. F. 1995. *The Poverty of Welfare Reform.* New Haven: Yale University Press.

Heymann, S. J., A. Earle, and B. Egleston. 1996. "Parental Availability for the Care of Sick Children." *Pediatrics: The Journal of the American Academy of Pediatrics* 98:226–230.

Hicks-Bartlett, S. T. Forthcoming. *Kin of Mine: Community and Family Life in a Low Income Suburb.*

Hiss, T. 1990. *The Experience of Place.* New York, Vintage Books.

Jones, J. 1986. *Labor of Love, Labor of Sorrow: Black Women, Work and the Family, From Slavery to the Present.* New York: Basic Books.

Katz, M. B. 1989. *The Undeserving Poor: From the War on Poverty to the War on Welfare.* New York: Pantheon Books.

Logan, J. R. 1983/1988. "Realities of Black Suburbanization." In *New Perspectives on the American Community,* compiled by Roland L. Warren and Larry Lyon, 231–40. Homewood, IL: Dorsey Press.

Massey, D. S., and N. A. Denton. 1993. *American Apartheid: Segregation and the Making of the Underclass.* Cambridge: Harvard University Press.

McKnight, J. 1995. *The Careless Society: Community and Its Counterfeits.* New York: Basic Books.

Prothrow-Stith, D., and M. Weissman. 1993. *Deadly Consequences.* New York: HarperCollins.

Rank, M. R. 1994. *Living on the Edge: The Realities of Welfare in America.* New York: Columbia University Press.

Schein, V. E. 1995. *Working from the Margins: Voices of Mothers in Poverty.* Ithaca and London: ILR Press.

Schram, S. F. 1995. *Words of Welfare: The Poverty of Social Science and the Social Science of Poverty.* Minneapolis: University of Minnesota Press.

Stack, C. B. 1974. *All Our Kin: Strategies for Survival in a Black Community.* New York: Harper & Row.

Stack, C. B. 1990. "Different Voices, Different Visions: Gender, Culture and Moral Reasoning." In *Uncertain Terms: Negotiating Gender in American Culture,* eds. F. Ginsburg and A. L. Tsing, 19–27. Boston: Beacon Press.

Statham, A., E. M. Miller, and H. O. Mauksch, eds. 1988. *The Worth of Women's Work: A Qualitative Synthesis.* New York: State University of New York Press.

Tronto, J. C. 1994. *Moral Boundaries: A Political Argument for an Ethic of Care.* New York: Routledge.

Wilson, W. J. 1987. *The Truly Disadvantaged: The Inner City, the Underclass, and Public Policy.* Chicago: University of Chicago Press.

———. 1996. *When Work Disappears: The World of the New Urban Poor.* New York: Knopf.

CHAPTER 3

Communal Isolation: Narrowing the Pathways to Goal Attainment and Work

Gina Barclay-McLaughlin

> When we first moved into the projects it was so different. I
> have great memories of my past, growing up. We loved our
> neighbors. They cared about us, we cared about them. Neigh-
> bors looked out for each other, especially for the children, in
> those days. Man, it's so different now. You better stay out of
> folks' way. That's what it has become.
>
> [Skylan resident]

William Julius Wilson's pathbreaking 1987 work, *The Truly Disadvantaged,*
introduced the concept of "social isolation" to describe the situation of the
inner-city African-American poor. These communities, he wrote, suffered
from social isolation—"the lack of contact or of sustained interaction with
individuals and institutions that represent mainstream society" (Wilson
1987, 60). The absence of middle-class families, of stores and churches, of
high-achieving schools, and of workers with steady jobs in these areas of
concentrated poverty meant that the inner-city poor had limited access to
job networks and to behavior patterns associated with full-time work. Ending this isolation, he argued, was crucial if concentrated, multigenerational
poverty was to be ended. Thus, he argued that tight labor market policies
combined with universal family allowance and child provision programs
were necessary to connect the socially isolated poor to the job market and
to maintain them as workers (Wilson 1987, 163). As the poor gained more
economic resources, they would be able to "follow the path worn by many
other former ghetto residents and move to safer and more desirable neighborhoods" (Wilson 1987, 158).

Wilson's concept of social isolation has had a powerful influence on
the study of poverty, reviving an entire body of research on neighborhood
effects (Brooks-Gunn et al. 1993; Brooks-Gunn, Duncan, and Aber 1997;
Huston, McLoyd, and Garcia-Coll 1994; Jencks and Mayer 1990; McLoyd
1990). This work supplements earlier research by providing an important
focus on context. But little of this work has captured the voices of the poor,

their perceptions of daily life in poor communities, and the extent to which they feel supported or hindered in their aspirations and pursuit of goals. Few scholars have contributed to our understanding of the perspective of the poor, especially concerning the impact of neighborhood.

The voices of the poor continue to be excluded from the debate about their future. Current policy debate fluctuates between those who argue that the poor could find work if they wished (Mead 1986; Murray 1984); those who argue that enterprise zones and other business ventures will revitalize communities through the restoration of buildings and structures, infrastructure rebuilding, youth development and services, and entrepreneurship (Grant and Johnson 1995; Green 1991; Halpern 1995; Hollowell 1996; Kasinitz and Rosenberg 1993); and those, like Wilson, who expect that inner-city neighborhoods will eventually be abandoned as individual African-Americans become more economically able to leave.

New conceptual models that embrace the perspectives of the poor are needed to address the complex and dynamic nature of poverty and the influence it has on processes for achieving successful employment and self-sufficiency (Burge 1991; Coulton and Pandey 1992; Dilworth-Anderson, Burton, and Boulin-Johnson 1993; Hicks-Bartlett, this volume). Individuals are not affected by their contexts in the same manner, nor do they perceive or utilize resources and supports in similar ways (Burton and Jarrett 1991; Burton, Obeidallah, and Allison 1996; MacLeod 1995; Monroe 1989; Stevenson 1998).

Wilson (1996) acknowledges that some residents living in poor inner-city environments are more able to describe the influence of declining opportunities, economic restructuring, and the exodus of social and human resources than are social scientists who investigate them. Yet there is a paucity of literature that allows us to gain a sense of how the poor identify and assess their own problems and needs. Still less is available on the ways they envision or value supports or strategies for successful goal attainment. Clearly, work and workers are needed in inner-city neighborhoods. But present policies linked to efforts to reform welfare have focused on job procurement without sufficient understanding of the context, mechanisms, and processes that produce and maintain successful outcomes. How might the perspective of the poor aid our understanding? How might they contribute to the development of more effective policies and models for reform? How might their assessment of problems, needs, barriers, and supports provide increased understanding and contribute to more positive outcomes? What are their views on processes and mechanisms that have contributed to the decline in their opportunities? What resources and supports have contributed in the past to the resilience and success of neighborhood residents by supporting their dreams and aspirations?

Communal Isolation

One of the rapidly declining resources is the community interdependence that was once such a positive force in many poor neighborhoods. A communal system of support is valued in poor neighborhoods as a resource for sustaining a healthy existence (Hicks-Bartlett, this volume; Stack and Burton 1993). The deterioration of this interdependence is certainly linked to the lack of legitimate economic opportunities and the subsequent growth of crime and gang activities.

I call the consequence of this loss *communal isolation*. Other forms of isolation, poor from rich, black from white, are more widely recognized and studied by scholars. Neighborhoods experience communal isolation when people are denied access to a communal system of support. Neighborhood residents who share so much in common withdraw from each other and from opportunities to provide traditional support, guidance, direction, and a range of more tangible resources. Young people may be left alone to face challenging periods and situations, and to form and pursue their goals without guidance. All who value the cultural traditions of community feel the loss. In the community I study, Skylan, this loss is a hardship for residents who value community not only as a resource in transforming dreams into attainable goals but also as an anchor and shield in a society they perceive to be unfair and unjust.

Skylan is the largest of six public housing projects located near the center of Hopeville, a community in a major midwestern American city. Its twenty-eight towering high-rise structures pierce the sky in a two-mile stretch across the southwest section of Hopeville. It is a stark and even overwhelming landscape. Until increasing patterns of out-migration emerged recently, Skylan housed as many as twenty thousand residents, and unofficial counts suggest there was an even larger population.

Some residents triumphed over the poverty that has always been well known in this housing project. In large part, they attribute their achievement to the community support and resources once available to them in Skylan. Their stories show how families in Skylan once created a viable community of neighbors who socialized together, parented one another's children, and provided the role models, resources, and support for one another's aspirations. But their stories also show how that community support has deteriorated and how it cannot even be replaced by the opportunity to move elsewhere.

An accumulation of disturbing factors contributes to the demise of community in Skylan, chief among them poor educational opportunities and performance, a high rate of unemployment, the scourge of drugs, a surge in crime, and neighborhoods tyrannized by gangs. Fear of crime and violence causes people to withdraw, to seek safety and stay out of other people's business. If it is dangerous to be out and about in the neighborhood, opportunities for social exchange and the development of networks vanish. As one resident put it, "In the old days people cared about the neighborhood and did their share to help take care of it. Today it seems like nobody cares anymore, and they don't make an effort to do their share."

Understanding the importance of community interdependence in the past, and learning how communal isolation has replaced it, is crucial to the study of poverty. Policies that support the aspirations and opportunities of the inner-city poor must combat the growth of communal isolation. The first step in this effort must be to pay attention to the perspectives of the poor themselves.

Methods

Current conceptual work on poverty fails to reflect an in-depth understanding of its complex and dynamic nature. As Skylan residents demonstrate, individuals are not affected in the same manner, and we cannot be assured of a predictable response or outcome. How do we describe and understand the dynamic nature and interrelationship of the effects of poverty? What implications do these effects have for discussions of reform?

Most inquiries into poverty are conducted by outsiders possessing comparatively little, if any, affiliation with the group under investigation (Evered and Louis 1981; Newman 1994). As Newman (1994) asserts, most scholars have few direct experiences of poverty. Generally, they have achieved their knowledge of poverty by "remote control." Cooperrider and Srivastva's (1990) work on appreciative inquiry implies that their distance from poverty explains why it is often difficult for scholars to fully grasp and appreciate the daily life experiences of the poor and the meanings they attach to these experiences.

Evered and Louis's (1981) insider/outsider mode of inquiry is an attempt to capture features of the physical and psychological distance researchers have from the setting or phenomenon under study. The authors posit that meanings achieved by measurement and logic give little, if any, consideration to context. Although Schein (1984) contends that outsiders can ask critical questions that delve into unconscious assumptions often made by insiders, he asserts that knowledge gained from the inside is extraordinarily valuable.

Qualitative studies seek understanding from the inside to gain a sense of the reality for the individuals studied, to explore and understand meanings from their perspective, and to learn how these meanings influence and shape behaviors and outcomes (Anderson 1992; Hicks-Bartlett, this volume; Newman 1994; Stack 1996). Although external perspectives inform our thinking, their limited purview is inadequate for understanding the inherent complexities of the insiders' view (Louis and Bartunek 1992). Substantive reform requires an understanding of the complex and multifaceted nature of the processes (individual, family, and community) that shape and influence human behaviors and mediate their effects (Huston, McLoyd, and Garcia-Coll 1994; Masten 1999; McLoyd 1990).

The growing body of literature denigrating the morality and values of the poor has done little, if anything, to shed light on how to help them, nor have structural explanations of poverty provided viable policies for effective change. What is missing from the picture is a clear understanding of the processes that link structural factors to the behaviors of the poor. Currently, major gaps in our understanding of welfare present formidable challenges to the field (Corcoran 1995). For example, Corcoran argues that available theories on neighborhood effects and the data and methods used to examine them are inadequate for understanding complex relationships and influences. Although Wilson's (1987) notion of social isolation emphasizes structural constraints and how these constraints impinge on people's lives, he does not adequately explore their relationship to the day-to-day realities of poverty.

Communities vary and change over time (Jargowsky 1994, 1997). As is the case with Skylan, some communities are geographically isolated and have limited access to resources, services, and opportunities. Other poor communities are situated in close proximity to a range of resources and can access opportunities and needed services. Communities with only 10 percent of residents living in poverty function differently than communities in which the overwhelming majority of the residents live below the poverty level and must compete for limited opportunities and resources (Jargowsky 1994).

In this analysis, I have identified themes from a series of long interviews conducted January through December 1996. In sharing this information, I make no claims that the residents of Skylan are representative of poor people throughout the country. My informants' interpretations of their experiences are not linear, as are the findings from bivariate and multivariate analyses. Sometimes, making connections can be difficult and cumbersome. Yet it is my hope that my informants' experiences will shed new light and lead to greater understanding.

Data for this qualitative study were primarily collected in the homes of past and present residents of the community through a series of face-to-face interviews. A few interviews were conducted at an alternate site, at the request of the informant. For the most part, respondents were interviewed at least twice. Informants were recruited with the assistance of a community-based intervention program serving the Skylan community. However, over time the informal network within the community generated far more respondents than the twenty to twenty-five originally planned for study; more than twice that number wanted to participate and share their stories. Twenty-five informants were interviewed; they were the first to schedule the series of required interviews. All were either participants in the community-based intervention program or community staff in either the intervention program or with one of the Hopeville community social service agencies.

The study was designed to capture residents' general perceptions about daily living and functioning in the Skylan community as individuals and as parents. Although studies have been conducted here for generations, entering Skylan is no easy undertaking for a researcher. As a result of my experiences, I am aware that establishing trust is the ultimate challenge. Developing rapport, understanding meaning, using language appropriately are all important tools to facilitate open communication. My experiences in this community have increased my understanding of the value of using an assortment of tools, instruments, and styles and reinforced my sense of the importance of familiarity, respect, and sensitivity. It requires "doing time," a process for developing competence and understanding meaning from the participant's perspective (Barclay-McLaughlin 1997). Doing time allows for the development of close intimate relationships between the interviewer and the research informant. The relationship that emerges from the process encourages participants to "drop their guard," share experiences, and reveal information usually unavailable to those outside the individual's inner circle. Ultimately, doing time conveys to participating informants that the relationship with the interviewer is respected and valued and what is shared will be handled in that spirit (Barclay-McLaughlin 1997).

I used the long interview format with a set of guiding questions. My first questions were designed to capture accounts of respondents' earliest dreams and aspirations about their future and early memories of life in Skylan. These initial questions generally evoked a smile or even laughter. Respondents often closed their eyes or leaned back in their seats as though they were attempting to drift back in time. Clearly there once were good times to remember; it was not always the place it is today.

Hopeville and Skylan: The Early Days

Early settlers of Hopeville included Americans born of English, Scotch, and Irish heritage. By the turn of the century, as this population migrated out, German Jewish families moved southward into Hopeville. Although a few African-Americans lived in Hopeville as early as 1890, a significant shift in its racial composition occurred after 1920 as African-Americans migrated into the area in greater numbers (Philpott 1991; Spear 1967). During the Great Migration more than fifty years ago, Hopeville was the symbol of upward mobility for thousands of African-Americans exiting the South in search of new opportunities and an escape from the demoralizing effects of racism and discrimination (Drake 1993; Grossman 1989; Lemann 1992). The growing demand for industrial workers following World War I contributed to this influx. Also, for a brief period during this era, economic benefits made it possible for a few African-Americans to buy homes in the neighborhood. As the African-American migration pattern into the area escalated, whites took flight further south to areas where black home ownership was prohibited. By 1940, 98 percent of Hopeville's population of one hundred thousand was African-American (Hirsch 1998).

Many African-Americans migrated north in search of the American dream—economic opportunities and a better quality of life—perceived to be beyond their grasp in the South. Stories and reports about opportunities in the North were sent back, generating excitement among family and friends. But while opportunities were clearly better in the North, the migrants soon found that they were not free of restrictions (Hirsch 1998; Spear 1967). The real estate codes of the time supported segregation policies and confined African-Americans to certain areas of the city. This limited opportunities for home ownership. Despite clear indications that the development of new housing was unable to keep pace with rapid increases in the population, discriminatory policies supported by local and national governments made it impossible for African-Americans to find adequate housing elsewhere. These policies, imposed on a community already challenged by inadequate resources and space, contributed to rapid and systematic neighborhood deterioration.

Toward the end of the 1950s, demolition activities in Hopeville, authorized by the city's Land Clearance Commission, resulted in a sharp decline of the neighborhood population. By the beginning of the 1960s, the population had dropped from one hundred fourteen thousand to eighty thousand. However, in 1960, the city invested in the development of 4,289 new units (in contrast to the 1,636 developed during the 1950s), developing the community of Skylan in the southwest corner of Hopeville.

The new structures attracted many people. Most saw them as an interim step; few thought Skylan ideal for living or raising a family. Continuing segregation policies and a lack of adequate income, however, kept most residents there. Some informants wanted it to be known that segregation is not their notion of the American dream, nor the context they envisioned for raising a family. The move into Skylan was only meant to be a transition—one step closer to the dream, offering time to plan and save. Seventy-five percent of the informants, however, have lived in the neighborhood for fifteen years or more. Although not ideal, Skylan did become a community for them and for their children.

As they describe the Skylan of their youth and adolescence, residents explain what a neighborhood of communal interdependence consists of: neighbors who interact with each other, creating visible bonds of trust and enforcing norms of behavior; parents and secondary parents who nurture children and support aspirations; and extended family, teachers, and friends who provide role models and links to the world outside of the community.

Long-term residents, among the first cohort of occupants, vividly recall the excitement of brand new buildings surrounded by attractive grassy areas, plants and flowers, all well groomed by housing staff, many of whom were hired from the community. Buildings were systematically maintained, including services to hallways, stairways, elevators, incinerators, and other areas. Play areas for children were maintained in a manner that gave parents a degree of comfort about the safety of their children. In contrast to their previous living conditions, many early residents viewed the apartments as decent, affordable housing, a relief from deplorable "slum" dwellings, and a transitional step toward the American dream. One longtime Skylan resident said:

> Oh God, . . . I was proud of where I came from and I knew that it was the projects. That's when we had grass around Skylan. Yes, beautiful surroundings. I was in awe as I grew up. I was, like, this must be the life right here. The grass is green.

Ms. Ray, who has lived in Skylan most of her life, recalled that for her parents, the move was an escape from the substandard apartment they were renting, closer to the city. Ms. Ray described pre-Skylan existence in this manner:

> Most of the time it was hard to function during the cold winter days. We never had enough heat. Even when it [the furnace] was supposed to be working, you could barely feel it [the heat]. As a matter of fact, for a long time we didn't even have hot water. My father used to put plastic over the windows to keep out the cold air that came from the strong wind.

Therefore, when Ms. Ray's mother learned from her sister about new low-income housing under construction in Hopeville, the sisters envisioned the move as a welcome relief and an interim step toward their ultimate dream—space, land, and home ownership. Ms. Ray's father grudgingly consented to move:

> My father didn't want to hear it. He said that's too many poor people piled up on top of each other. But my mother was convincing and when he saw those brand-new apartments with new kitchens, bathrooms, and appliances, and especially reliable heat and hot running water, he gave in. My mother was so excited. No rats and low rent. She said we could save enough and eventually own our house just like she and my father dreamed with enough space to raise their children decently and provide a good future for them.

Ms. Jones, who has lived in Skylan for more than twenty years, remembered her parents' decision to move there, in search of more affordable and suitable housing. Convinced that they were moving toward a better quality of life, they were among the first to move into Skylan.

> I don't think my parents ever believed they would live in Skylan forever, but they saw it as a good step for the future. When we first moved into Skylan, it was so different. I have great memories of my past growing up. We loved our neighbors. They [neighbors] cared about us, we cared about them. Neighbors looked out for each other, especially for the children in those days.

As Ms. Jones described the communal network of support that surrounded her when she was growing up, she emphasized the fact that it challenged myths about family structure and a lack of resources within the community.

> When jobs were there people worked, mothers and fathers . . . People who don't know us want to believe we didn't have fathers in here [Skylan]. Mrs. J was a waitress. Her husband was with the city transportation system. Mrs. K was an accountant, I forgot what [her husband] did. Ms. L was a housewife, but her husband was something in accounting. I think he did something with numbers, too. Ms. E, she worked and her husband worked. I think he was a laborer, too. It seemed as though everyone had a mom and dad. You noticed I named mother and father . . . nuclear families, right there in Skylan.

As a child, she didn't feel the stigma that now haunts residents of Skylan. Reflecting on her childhood, she describes it in this manner:

It was just like you could sit on the porch in Skylan. . . . Now, we're on a porch, in front of our house. We just looking at people downstairs. They're sitting on a little bench in the playground, just having a good time. We are sitting there eating pizza, and I remember so vividly having those conversations. Laughing. Just having a good time. How do these people in the project do that today? It was fun. Mama would fry chicken, and I would sneak in there and get me and Nita . . . a piece. And mama would say, I know I fried about eight. Four are gone! We were sitting up there, sucking on a bone. This is what I remember . . . that chicken and just sitting on that porch just talking. Just talking. That was fun for us. This is what I'll always remember, because I was not afraid being out. It was just good old fun. Fun that you wished would never go away. You almost hate to grow up, because those childhood memories are so precious. They are so precious.

Ms. Jones described the support from neighbors and the responsibility they demonstrated with children of the neighborhood. Children understood the standards and rules of the community, and neighbors were empowered to enforce them. Child rearing was not just the responsibility of the family; it had the support of the community. Children could interact safely, knowing they were under watchful eyes.

The neighbors were neighbors. They would hit you in a second. [Ms. Jones said smiling and beaming with approval] If you were doing something wrong, and your momma and daddy were at work, you got spanked. They were secondary parents. That really helped us out. I really believe. But now, you're afraid to touch anybody else's child. I really appreciated that when I look back on it. Ms. Jackson was there. She really got me. Ms. Jackson sure did tell on me.
   Ms. Jackson was our next-door neighbor. We lived in 604. She lived in 605, Ms. Nelson lived in 603. So I was surrounded. Ms. Wilson was at 601. Ms. Jones was at 602. You know, you knew all of your neighbors and they knew you. Okay. You weren't supposed to be outside until your parents got in and you know how you used to sneak out. They were always watching us and that was good.

Ms. Smith, another longtime Skylan resident, described the critical role neighbors played in her and her siblings' development:

We had our neighbors who were mom as well as our mom. They did have their nose all in our business especially if they seen us doing stuff that was wrong. You had to believe that we did get in trouble because my mom did find out.

When I was growing up everybody was together; we had a unity. It was unified, and everybody did trick [tattle]. They tricked, they told, and parents believed. They told. They saw stuff that went on, they told [your parents] and we got in trouble for it. It was still a lot of fun. We played broomball, rode bikes. We were able to ride our bikes all over the place. We didn't have to worry about the police harassing us. . . . It was a quiet place. Growing up in the projects, we didn't know that we were poor. Some people would say that you were poor. It was just a lot of fun, it was just like growing up in a house or should I say a condominium?

Ms. Jones, who lived a sheltered life, in a family that supported her educational aspirations, went on to college at the University of Wisconsin at Madison. As a young person growing up in Skylan, she didn't feel the stigma that now haunts neighborhood residents.

It seemed like the older I got, the more uncomfortable I became. Because when I went off to college, the University of Wisconsin is predominantly white. I would talk to the girls. So when I talked to them about my childhood, they'd say, "God, you had a great childhood."

About her early years in Skylan, Ms. Jones concludes:

And I will tell anybody about my childhood, because I was proud of it. It's not only because I came from Skylan. It was what I learned from being a part of a Skylan. It's almost like survival. You had to survive.

Although the benefits were not always articulated in great detail, it was clear from the messages informants conveyed that children were exposed to and learned to deal with different parenting styles and methods of adult interactions. Parents were able to exchange values, beliefs, and attitudes about child rearing, and these exchanges served to reinforce them on a neighborhood level. This greatly contributed to a sense of community cohesiveness.

Theories of development suggest that as children grow, they engage in exploration and experiments that contribute to their sense of awareness and knowledge of the world and the roles they can play within it (Baumrind 1989; J. Johnson and C. Johnson 1987; Wachs and Gruen 1982). All children need models and experiences for creating dreams and exploring possibilities. In a caring and nurturing environment, dreams can emerge and serve as building blocks toward the development of long-term goals and fulfillment. As their dreams develop, children must have access to human and social resources to support and nurture them. Healthy neighborhoods provide this. The guidance and support of resource people who serve as role models and mentors can assist in the development of realistic goals and strategies for goal attainment. In a healthy community, children can trust adults to support curious exploration, link them to available opportunities and services, offer guidance as they use them, provide encouragement when they are faced with frustration and disappointments, and praise and celebrate the successful achievement of milestones along the way. This is also true for adults seeking a second chance to pursue long-held dreams or new opportunities for success. In Skylan, there are few windows for dreaming.

The Loss of a Viable Community

In the early to mid-1980s, a series of physical and social changes in Skylan had far-reaching consequences. Housing policies and regulations generated a tremendous exodus of working-class families from Skylan. Economic decline and labor market shifts on a national level also had rippling effects. With a decline in public funding there was no safety net to sustain the physical and social infrastructure of the neighborhood. Working-class families were no longer encouraged to remain as tenants, since they would be penalized for earnings beyond a certain income level. Moreover, growing rates of unemployment, due to the closing of factories and the resulting loss of other related jobs, significantly lowered the income status of families who qualified to remain. These factors added to the burdens of a community already saddled with poor architectural planning and design.

As businesses abandoned the area, it became increasingly difficult to obtain even basic services. The physical appearance of Skylan swiftly deteriorated: substantial numbers of neighborhood supermarkets, drugstores, laundromats, and other commercial services vanished. Loss of critical social services further contributed to Skylan's rapid decline. Cutbacks in federal funding, public mismanagement, and funding abuse help to explain the current state of affairs.

It is evident that little attention or effort has been given to the upkeep and maintenance of Skylan. After only twenty years, elevators in the buildings seldom functioned. On occasion, residents were trapped in them for hours. Often, incinerators burned uncontrollably with clouds of smoke pouring out along the entrance to apartments, seeping into homes, polluting and contributing to a range of respiratory illnesses. Parents described wetting old clothes and newspapers and lining the doorways and windowsills to block out the toxic pollutants. Residents say the burning of incinerators reduced garbage and waste not routinely picked up by the city. The outdated heating system made it difficult to regulate and control heating in an efficient and economical manner. Some apartments were overheated and residents were forced to open their windows to have any level of comfort. Other apartments were inadequately heated. Parents often tried to compensate, using flames from the burners of the cooking stove or unsafe space heaters, causing fires.

Poor service for broken plumbing was and continues to be a frequent complaint. Pipes often freeze during the winter and sometimes burst, spilling raw sewage. Stairways are dark, haunting pathways. Rats roam through the stairways and apartments; many complaints have been lodged about attacks and bites. Children have had to learn how to maneuver around rats trapped in the corridors. Adults joke that even cats run at the sight of a Skylan rat.

The many vacant apartments reinforce the impression of a community under siege. Most informants believe vacant apartments attract and support criminals and dangerous activities. They are often occupied illegally for gang and drug activities. Robbers can gain access to adjacent apartments. One informant described how entrance was gained to her apartment by removing the medicine cabinet from a shared wall while her family was away from home. Another described a similar break-in in which robbers entered during the night as the family slept.

For safety reasons, a decision was made to enclose the front of each floor with wire mesh to protect children from falling off patios or being hit by objects from above. From the second-floor landing to the top floor, across the entire façade, the building is encased in heavy wire. It looks like a prison. Residents suggest, with dark humor, that it offers basic training for future incarceration.

Throughout the 1980s, Skylaners increasingly perceived themselves as hostages within their own community, portrayed by the media as an "underclass out of control." They restricted their movements to the neighborhood and away from the avenues that connected them to the world beyond. Moving about the neighborhood, interacting with family and friends, and enjoying community traditions became more of a challenge with the escalation of violence, drugs, and dangerous criminal and gang-related incidents.

Parents found it unsafe to allow their children to play outside on the grounds, even within their view. Children and youth became increasingly homebound. There were fewer opportunities for children and youth to learn how to form and engage in important relationships with peers and to do so in a healthy and supportive context, the foundation for responsible adulthood.

Such changes have threatened the safety of residents and have reduced opportunities for neighborhood members to mingle and share. Moreover, they prevent the exchange and reinforcement of values and customs that had sustained the community over time. A major consequence has been a decline in adult-child interactions and adult exchanges, important elements of the communal system of support that served as a mechanism to ensure that cultural values and norms were shared, understood, and embraced. Formal and informal gatherings reinforced these values for daily living. Adults, especially those deemed as elders, understood their responsibility to look out for children, to provide guidance and serve as surrogate parents. The system was based on established and shared standards; children were disciplined whenever necessary, based on a standard that was culturally grounded and appropriate. Children not only understood family and community standards, but expected neighbors to enforce them in the same manner as their parents. The communal system, therefore, served as a system of checks and balances.

Skylan residents now interact far less frequently with neighbors or within formal or informal group settings. Informants report they make fewer visits to each other and consider it unsafe to gather outside in the neighborhood. Such occasions used to provide important ways to learn other perspectives on culture, parenting, expectations, and dreams. These interactions promoted community cohesiveness. Interactions were not only instructional, but cathartic. Families have now become isolated, confined to the small and inadequate living space of their apartments.

Informants report that this confinement can be stressful for both children and parents, and costly to the process of parent-child interactions. Children need space for healthy growth and development. One parent shared her assessment of the situation:

> We don't need a parenting class to know our children need space to grow and develop; that's just common sense if you got children. What we need is the space for them to do it where they can feel safe. We need more playgrounds with decent playground equipment; more recreation centers like the "Y," and places like that, safe. That's what we need, safe places for children and that can put their family at ease. I don't need somebody wasting my time telling me what I need that I already know. That's common sense. I ain't stupid. I need them to help me keep the neighborhood safe. Like a good police department that knows how to do its job. More policemen that do their jobs and protect children from gangs and drugs and stuff like that. That's what we need up in here. You know what I mean?

There is less consensus among parents, however, as to whether child rearing in Skylan is more challenging for families with young children or adolescents. There are consequences at each developmental stage. Generally, parents with toddlers and preschoolers seem to agree that healthy development requires safety and space to explore and experiment. In the typical, tiny standard rooms of Skylan apartments, frequently cluttered, lacking storage space, and often serving as a refuge for relatives and friends who are homeless, there is little freedom for childhood exploration and play. Additionally, special efforts to control rodents and other pests (a serious problem in all of the buildings) further restrict play areas for children and contribute to parents' urge to be overprotective, a practical choice given the context. One resident described the level of fear:

> [In the summer, the neighborhood kids] have two months out [of school.] During those two months, if someone did a count on the kids that made it through the summer vacation, the ones that were caught up in drive-by shootings, rapes, murders—those numbers are so alarming that sometimes I hate when summer comes, because you know some kids that graduate are not going to make it to college. They're not going to make it to the army. That's what bothers me. I almost hate for it to come. It's scary. I don't have children, but I know so many other children are out there in front of their door, playing, playing rope and somebody drives by and shoots them. They are not involved in drugs and they're playing right in front of their house and shot.

Concerns, constraints, and stress generated by these and other factors create tension and conflict in parent-child interactions. Without clear understanding of the context and its contribution to these adaptive behavioral forms of parenting, styles of parenting in Skylan can be easily misunderstood as norms of parenting among the African-American population.

Parents of adolescent children interviewed argue that challenges to parenting are greatest at this developmental stage. Many parents of adolescents are overwhelmed by fear and anxiety about drug activities, gang involvement, and other forms of negative or criminal behaviors. These developmental insults threaten, seduce, and rob their children of a normal life, obstructing short- and long-term opportunities and creating roadblocks to fulfillment of dreams and goals. Parental anxieties often shape and influence parent-youth interactions and force parents to be unusually protective in their attempt to form a barrier against negative competition from the environment. Parents are aware that young people need safe environments and positive social support and opportunities for exploration and healthy development. Many agree that overprotectiveness and other forms of adaptive parenting behaviors employed to avert environmental insults may threaten desired outcomes, especially long-term goals. Adaptive parenting styles (often identified in the literature as restrictive parenting) are not fully understood by adolescents who characteristically at this stage feel invincible. As one resident described it:

> You know the scary part is that some of these kids are not afraid today, because they have that attitude, Oh, that won't happen to me. I won't get shot. Or, they're not gonna mug me, they know me around here. That's that mentality. Talk to any of the youth in the area, they say I'm not afraid. Afraid of what? If I'm going to die, I'm going to die.

Adolescence is a developmental stage that typically resists adult guidance and authority. In communities like Skylan, where children and youth may be especially vulnerable, heightened parental control, perceived by parents as protective, more often generates youth rebellion. Young people interpret such control as a lack of trust. Long-term goals and the foundation children need for achievement and attainment are sacrificed and replaced by more immediate survival strategies.

Although some parents desperately seek alternative environments for their children, trying to engage them in constructive activities outside the neighborhood during every available moment, managing this alternative is costly to the parent and child. Today, it is not uncommon for parents to see gang identification or minimal affiliation as a measure of protection and safety for their kids. Parents know that youth who are unable to declare some connection to a given gang may suffer deadly consequences.

Violence, drugs, and crime are not the only things that restrict vision, limit access, and minimize the utilization of opportunities and resources, but they are the ones that force their victims to shift priorities and to center their energies on survival. With depleted personal and psychological resources, residents' visions and goals for a successful life slip to the background. These negative patterns within Skylan are often sensationalized and exploited by popular media, stigmatizing Skylan residents and contributing to various forms of isolation and misunderstanding. Outsiders become fearful of entering the community, even when they are eager and willing to share resources. Residents often appear reluctant to interact with outsiders and hesitant to engage with their neighbors. Thus, they are restricted from knowing about or accessing resources within their reach.

As Skylan residents internalize these negative media images of themselves and their neighborhood, they also develop psychological barriers to cultivating internal and external support. Embarrassment and feelings of low self-esteem undermine their confidence and desire to generate or connect to networks of support, especially those needed for career attainment and employment options. This closing down of options, the retreat from the wider world, also has a profound impact on the children of Skylan and those in other communities like it around the country.

One resident expressed it vividly:

> Today, if you try to tell people what's going on about their kids, you're nosy; they're ready to fight and it's a whole bunch of other stuff. Like the little saying, "It takes a village to raise one child," but the village—if you don't have that togetherness—you can't even raise your own. It's by force that you have to stay out of peoples' business now today, not by choice.

Residents of Skylan reflected on the factors that contributed to the demise of community. Ms. Jones said, sadly:

> We didn't have that violence. It's so different today. I'm afraid. I work in this community. Some people know me. A lot of them don't. But I can't walk through the community saying what I did when I was a child, because a lot has changed since then.

Ms. Ray, who grew up in Skylan and still resides there, reminisced about the past, attempting to put it into perspective:

> Some things weren't as clear to me as they are today. I didn't have the insight and understanding I have today as an adult; but I still have vivid memories of some of the things that happened to our family as we grew up in this neighborhood. As a child I watched my parents' dream wither and the effect it had on us growing up. My father lost his job when the stockyard closed down. He started drinking heavily and staying away from home more and more. My parents started arguing and fighting a lot. We weren't the only family with this kind of experience. It was happening all around us. Lots of men in the community lost their jobs, and it changed the quality of their family life. I thought a lot about it after I took this urban studies class.

Like many informants, Mr. Brown, a young man who grew up in Skylan, believes that drugs were the main contributor to the breakdown of a sense of community:

> Yeah, they tried to recruit me. I had to fight every day. It was a gang called. . . . They would wait for us every day. If we ran to Wabash, we

were safe. Then you'd have to go back. It was a no-win situation. You just got tired of running. Then you said, if you don't whoop me, I'm going to whoop you.

Mr. Brown believes that part of the problem in Skylan is that young people lack adequate role models and appropriate activities:

> But there are no role models over there. There's nothing for them to do over there. There are no activities. That's why kids get caught up in gangs now and drugs. They have nobody to lead them on living the right way. [It used to be] somebody else's parent would see you doing something, they would whoop your butt and when you got home you'd get more.
>
> But now, nine out of ten—most of those parents now are on drugs. Fathers aren't there or using drugs himself. When the kid comes home, the mother's so drugged out. . . . That's where the gangs come in at. The kids don't have nobody to love them.

Escalating violence and gang and drug activities have forced many to flee the neighborhood in search of a safer environment. Residents describe the area as extremely dangerous and believe that only those with absolutely no alternative remain. Most informants interviewed who remain in Skylan said they would take advantage of any opportunity to move out. Only a few expressed reluctance, based on anxiety about the unknown. A sense of community no longer binds them, nor do they seem to think that they will find it elsewhere; they believe the problems in Skylan exist throughout the city and are impossible to escape.

The Lessons of Skylan

There is little disagreement that public housing has failed, especially for many urban locations. It has become evident that the policies that created Skylan and similar communities contributed to the density and intensity of neighborhood poverty. These policies, or the lack of them, failed to support and enhance quality life for low-income residents, particularly the communities of high-rise buildings with dense concentrations of poverty. Officials now acknowledge that an alternative housing plan is essential. Skylan residents feel they have been and continue to be left out of decisions that influence their lives and the future of their community. Many community leaders and residents believe that the Skylan public housing development and other vertical housing for the rapidly growing African-American population were designed to restrict horizontal housing expansion. Some say that despite heated debates among city politicians and intensive protest from African-American community leaders and concerned individuals, little consideration has been given to the long-term impact of such developments on children and families, and the values residents hold for nurturing and maintaining a sense of community.

The lack of concern about community views further undermines community trust and is especially significant given the history of Skylan itself. Although community advocacy groups have tried to organize meetings to address some of these concerns, residents feel they have been deliberately excluded from discussions that would give them an opportunity to participate in decisions that affect their future and fulfillment of their dreams. Many blame the political system and believe they are powerless to challenge it. One person attending a community meeting expressed it in this manner, "[It's] a done deal, and you know how powerful City Hall is."

We have learned through the voices of Skylan residents that unsafe environments inhibit healthy family and community functioning. Such environments breed violence and distrust and destroy the fabric of the community, essential for supporting communal interdependence. The outcome, as we see today in Skylan and other poor neighborhoods across the nation, is communal isolation—withdrawal, mistrust, intense loneliness, feelings of despair and hopelessness. Similar to the pattern in many cities across the country, the decision to address this looming problem has resulted in the demolition of a series of high-rise public housing projects. Many residents believe, however, this decision did not evolve out of concern for the residents. Alternatively, they believe decisions were made because communities like Skylan were built on real estate that is rapidly increasing in value and ideally situated for profitable development ventures.

I attended a community meeting where decisions for the redevelopment of Skylan and other public housing sites in Hopeville were announced. The residents responded with mixed reviews. Some questioned the intent of the decisions; for others, the announcement confirmed lingering mistrust. "Everybody knows they want this area back. This is prime land. We aren't stupid. They want this piece of land." Some residents see community conflict as a conspiracy, a deliberate attempt to divide and conquer for a takeover. "We don't have to let it happen. We have a choice. We can let them divide us or we can wake up and smell the coffee."

As families are forced to relocate, due to demolition of the buildings, some of the displaced residents from Skylan are finally gaining access to programs such as Section 8. The Section 8 program does not address concerns associated with building strong and supportive communities; it does allow families who qualify to obtain affordable housing through the aid of government subsidies. Qualified applicants are sometimes able to negotiate and select rentals beyond the geographical boundaries normally designated for public housing. More than 1.4 million households in the United States have received vouchers and certificates, giving them the option to select from privately owned rental housing.

Several residents reported years of waiting to qualify for Section 8 rental assistance. After they submitted preliminary applications, their names were placed on a waiting list. Ms. Bennett waited more than five years to become eligible for assistance. She reported being shocked by the arrival of the notice of approval:

> I was so surprised; I couldn't believe my eyes when I got the notice about my Section 8. I hugged my daughter and we screamed and danced around the room together. I just remember being so happy about moving out of this place . . . especially happy for my daughter because she was having a lot of problems. Most of her classmates live in nice neighborhoods, and she was getting angrier by the day about living in Skylan. Every day she was more and more ashamed to let her friends know that she lived in the projects. I wanted her to go to this school so bad, but seeing her so unhappy and mad with me; it was just a problem.

Although the family remained in Hopeville in a high-rise building nearly one mile east of Skylan, the substantial difference in settings gave Ms. Bennett a new level of hope. She and her daughter shared their feelings about their new setting. They expressed appreciation for everything from gardens and grass, to working elevators, to the sense of safety and security as they moved in and out of the building to engage in normal routine activities of family life. Ms. Bennett described her feelings about the change in this way, "It was like a mountain had rolled off my back." Her daughter added, "I don't ever want to go back, not even to spend the night with my cousins."

It struck me that Ms. Bennett and her daughter's description of their new residence echoed the narratives shared by older Skylan residents as they reflected on an earlier, more hopeful era in Skylan. In their new home setting they no longer seemed as preoccupied with surviving the immediate threats to health and safety that they had grown accustomed to in Skylan. Instead, Ms. Bennett said she had more energy to think about other priorities and plan for achieving goals and aspirations for herself and her daughter. Ms. Bennett was also pleased to discover that residents of the new community valued the communal tradition familiar to her during an earlier period in Skylan. The welcome she and her daughter received from neighbors and the subsequent relationships and exchanges that evolved between them were supportive. Through Section 8 she was not only able to relocate to a safer environment; it was also a neighborhood where she felt welcomed and experienced support anchored in the values and traditions she considered important to the goals and aspirations she had for herself and her daughter.

For Ms. Bennett, Section 8 was an opportunity for a new environment, one with a comfortable fit. But such programs are no panacea. Although they may aid families to relocate to new and safer settings, these families may still suffer from communal isolation—a lack of culturally valued support and interactions within their neighborhood context. For example, Ms. Smith expressed ambivalence about her relocation through Section 8. Admittedly, her new residence is an attractive newly renovated three-level townhouse located nearly fifteen miles from Skylan in a middle- and working-class community in the northwest section of the city. The well-groomed gated backyard allows her children to play free of imminent danger. Although she was disappointed to learn that her children did not rank as well academically as they did in Skylan, Ms. Smith was pleased to discover the new public school offered far more resources to support the dreams she has for her children. Yet Ms. Smith's comments seem to suggest that something important was still missing: "If I could only pick it all up and put it in Skylan."

Further elaboration revealed that the community support Ms. Smith remembered and valued from earlier days in Skylan was missing in her new location. She didn't receive a warm welcome from her new neighbors upon entering her new context, nor did she experience the support, reminiscent of earlier life in Skylan, that she sought. For example, Ms. Smith's oldest son often suffered from asthma. Whenever he was ill, both children were absent from school. As Ms. Smith explained, this would have been an uncommon occurrence during earlier days in Skylan: "Someone would see to it that my other son got to school." With little, if any, interaction with her neighbors, whom she scarcely knew, Ms. Smith expressed reluctance about entrusting her child to a neighbor. She said she is often very lonely and returns to Skylan as often as possible seeking the community support that Skylan had lost in recent years and that she had anticipated finding in her new setting. She wondered whether her new environment would eventually support her in achieving the goals she has for herself and her children. Despite her criticism of the decline of Skylan, Ms. Smith believes some resources she needs to support her as an individual and parent still remain in Skylan: "Sometimes I think it is better to drag my children back across town, back to Skylan."

Over the years, as I have observed children and families of Skylan and elsewhere in low-income communities, I have become intrigued by the early development of dreams and the pathways taken toward attainment. Similar to any community across the country, Skylan children and their families dream. Some share well-formulated goals; others are able to articulate a plan. Yet it is obvious that not all communities have access to the same level of opportunities, to appropriate resources, and to the support needed, especially technical guidance and mentorship, for dreams to be nurtured and hope to emerge and be realized. Too often, the dreams of early residents of Skylan vanished; individuals lacked the guidance or emotional support needed for progress and achievement. Other individuals experienced frustration and disappointments as they wandered aimlessly in search of avenues to achieve success. For too many, these frustrations and disappointments contribute to a sense of hopelessness and despair. Some give up; still too many wander off along paths that are destructive to themselves and others. This sense of hopelessness and despair is a loss of human potential; it is also a cost for the individual and often to their families. For the society at large, this is a burden and cost that often leads to resentment and alienation.

Reflections from Skylan residents offer many lessons: Effective policies must ensure that neighborhoods and communities are safe contexts where dreams can develop and flourish with a sense of hope and fulfillment. Communities must have appropriate resources, support, and opportunities to generate and sustain the hopes and dreams of individuals and families. In a healthy functioning community, residents can trust, share, and gain additional resources unavailable within their own context. It is the collective contributions and exchanges that create a sense of communal interdependence to sustain the vitality of the community, even during periods of hardship.

REFERENCES

Barclay-McLaughlin, G. 1997. "Research Program Insights: New Perspectives and Challenges When Including Families of Color." Paper presented at Rush University Summer Research Facilitation Workshop, Chicago, IL (July).

Baumrind, D. 1989. "Rearing Competent Children." In *Child Development Today and Tomorrow,* ed. W. Damon, 349–78. San Francisco: Jossey-Bass.

Brooks-Gunn, J., G. J. Duncan, and L. Aber, eds. 1997. *Neighborhood Poverty: Context and Consequences for Children.* New York: Russell Sage Foundation.

Brooks-Gunn, J., G. J. Duncan, P. K. Klebanov, and N. Sealand. 1993. "Do Neighborhoods Influence Child and Adolescent Development?" *American Journal of Sociology* 99 (2): 353–95.

Burge, P. L. 1991. "Single Parents' Work and Family Demands." In *Work and Family: Educational Implications,* ed. B. Felstehausen and J. B. Schultz, 186–99. Peoria, IL: Macmillan/McGraw-Hill.

Burton, L. M., and R. L. Jarrett. 1991. "Studying African-American Family Structure and Process in Underclass Neighborhoods: Conceptual Considerations." Paper presented at the American Sociological Association Conference, Cincinnati, Ohio.

Burton, L. M., D. A. Obeidallah, and K. Allison. 1996. "Ethnographic Insights on Social Context and Adolescent Development among Inner-City African-American Teens." In *Ethnography and Human Development: Context and Meaning in Social Inquiry,* ed. R. Jesser, A. Colby, and R. A. Shwder, 395–418. Chicago: University of Chicago Press.

Coulton, C., and S. Pandey. 1992. "Geographic Concentration of Poverty and Risk to Children in Urban Neighborhoods." *American Behavioral Scientist* 35 (Jan./Feb.): 238–57.

Cooperrider, D. L, and S. Srivastva. 1990. "Appreciative Inquiry in Organizational Life." *Research in Organizational Change and Development* 1:129–69.

Corcoran, M. 1995. "Rags to Rags: Poverty and Mobility in the United States." *Annual Review of Sociology* 21:237–67.

Dilworth-Anderson, P., L. M. Burton, and L. Boulin-Johnson. 1993. "Reframing Theories for Understanding Race, Ethnicity, and Families." In *Sourcebook of Family Theories and Methods: A Contextual Approach,* ed. P. G. Boss, W. J. Doherty, R. LaRossa, W. R. Schumm, and S. K. Steinmetz, 627–49. New York: Plenum Press.

Drake, S. C. 1993. *Black Metropolis: A Study of Negro Life in a Northern City.* Chicago: University of Chicago Press.

Evered, R., and M. R. Louis. 1981. "Alternative Perspectives in the Organizational Sciences: 'Inquiry from the Inside' and 'Inquiry from the Outside.'" *Academy of Management Review* 6:385–95.

Grant, D. M., and J. H. Johnson. 1995. "Conservative Policymaking and Growing Urban Inequality in the 1980s." In *The Politics of Wealth and Inequality,* ed. R. E. Ratcliff, M. L. Oliver, and T. M. Shapiro, vol. 5 of Research in Politics and Society, ed. G. Moore and J. A. White, 127–59. Greenwich, CT: JAI Press.

Grossman, J. R. 1989. *Land of Hope: Chicago, Black Southerners, and the Great Migration.* Chicago: University of Chicago Press.

Halpern, R. 1995. *Rebuilding the Inner City: A History of Neighborhood Initiatives to Address Poverty in the United States.* New York: Columbia University Press.

Hirsch, A. 1998. *Making the Second Ghetto.* Chicago: University of Chicago Press.

Hollowell, M. J. 1996. *Empowerment Zones, Enterprise Zones, and Renaissance Zones: The New Vocabulary of Urban Development.* Troy, MI: Homeward Bound Seminars.

Hunter, A. G., and M. E. Ensminger. 1992. "Diversity and Fluidity in Children's Living Arrangements: Family Transitions in an Urban Afro-American Community." *Journal of Marriage and the Family* 54:418–26.

Huston, A., V. McLoyd, and C. Garcia-Coll. 1994. "Children and Poverty: Issues in Contemporary Research." *Child Development* 65 (April): 275–82.

Jargowsky, P. A. 1994. "Ghetto Poverty Among Blacks in the 1980's." *Journal of Policy Analysis and Management* 13 (2): 288–310.

———. 1997. *Poverty and Place: Ghettos, Barrios, and the American City.* New York: Russell Sage Foundation.

Jencks, C., and S. E. Mayer. 1990. "The Social Consequences of Growing Up in a Poor Neighborhood." In *Inner-city Poverty in the United States,* ed. L. E. Lynn and M. G. McGeary, 111–86. Washington, DC: National Academy Press.

Johnson, J., and C. Johnson. 1987. *Play and Early Childhood Development.* New York: HarperCollins.

Julion, W., D. Gross, and G. Barclay-McLaughlin. In press. "Recruiting Families of Color from the Inner City: Insights from the Recruiters." *Nursing Outlook.*

Lemann, Nicholas. 1992. *The Promised Land: The Great Black Migration and How It Changed America.* New York: Vintage Books.

Louis, M., and J. Bartunek. 1992. "Insider/Outsider Research Teams: Collaboration Across Diverse Perspectives." *Journal of Management Inquiry* 1 (2): 101–10.

MacLeod, J. 1995. *Ain't No Makin' It: Aspirations and Attainment in a Low-Income Neighborhood.* Boulder, CO: Westview Press.

Masten, A. 1999. *Cultural Processes in Child Development (Minnesota Symposium on Child Psychology, vol. 29).* Hillsdale, NJ: Erlbaum.

McLoyd, V. (1990). "The Impact of Economic Hardships on Black Families and Children: Psychological Distress, Parenting, and Socioemotional Development." Special Issue: Minority Children. *Child Development* 61 (2): 311–46.

Mead, M. L. (1986). *Beyond Entitlement: The Social Obligations of Citizenship.* New York: The Free Press.

Monroe, S. 1989. *Brothers, Black and Poor: A True Story of Courage and Survival.* New York: Ballantine.

Murray, C. 1984. *Losing Ground: American Social Policy 1950–1980.* New York: Basic Books.

Newman, K. 1994. *Working Poor: Low Wage Employment in the Lives of Harlem Youth.* Interview with the author on the unpublished manuscript.

Philpott, T. L. 1978. *The Slum and the Ghetto: Neighborhood Deterioration and Middle-Class Reform, Chicago, 1880–1930.* New York: Oxford University Press.

Schein, E. H. 1984. "Coming to a New Awareness of Organizational Culture." *Sloan Management Review* 25:3–16.

Spear, A. 1967. *Black Chicago: The Making of a Negro Ghetto.* Chicago: University of Chicago Press.

Stack, C. B., and L. M. Burton. 1993. "Kinscripts." *Journal of Comparative Family Studies* 24 (2): 150–70.

Stevenson, H. 1998. "Raising Safe Villages: Cultural Ecological Factors That Influence the Emotional Adjustment of Adolescents." *Journal of Black Psychology* 24 (1): 44–59.

Wachs, T. D., and G. E. Gruen. 1982. *Early Experience and Human Development.* New York: Plenum.

Wilson, W. J. 1987. *The Truly Disadvantaged: The Inner City, the Underclass and Public Policy.* Chicago: University of Chicago Press.

———. 1996. *When Work Disappears: The World of the New Urban Poor.* New York: Knopf.

CHAPTER 4

Negotiating Adolescence in a Black Middle-Class Neighborhood

Mary Pattillo-McCoy

The branches of the Gibbs family tree extend far and wide in Groveland, a black middle-class neighborhood on Chicago's South Side.[1] Mr. and Mrs. Gibbs, the trunk of the family tree, moved into Groveland in 1961 and raised six daughters there. Three of them, including Anna Gibbs Morris, are now raising their own families in the neighborhood. Last year, Anna Morris's nineteen-year-old daughter, Neisha, had the family's first great-grandson, Tim Jr. The Gibbs family has spent more than thirty-five years in the neighborhood, with four generations living in one square block.

Much has changed since the Gibbs family moved into Groveland. One significant change has been the increase in gang activity. Little Tim's father, Tim Ward Sr., is in a gang, as were many of Neisha Morris's boyfriends before Tim. Drug dealing often goes hand in hand with being in gangs. Neisha's mother is both angry and sad as she watches Neisha's boyfriends fall prey to the fast life. "Neisha and [her cousin] Kima done lost too many friends to all that shit," Anna Morris began telling me one evening. She continued:

> You know, Neisha just can't take it no more. She lost two boyfriends. And she really took this last one hard. I just hate to see her go through alla that. The first one was like her first boyfriend. You know, he was a nice boy; I liked him. But they just be out there doin' they thang. And they shot him. This last one, Sugar, we just buried. And I really took this second one hard. They done lost ten friends already. Close friends, too. But still, they still choosin' these little boys who out there like that. I mean, they ain't bad people, but they get caught up in all that stuff sellin' drugs.

This short sketch of the Gibbs family reveals some of the challenges facing the cohort of adolescents and young adults to which Neisha belongs. I locate these particular stories within a discussion of how race and class structure neighborhood experiences. Racial segregation and disproportionate black poverty combine to concentrate disadvantage in a growing number of isolated urban neighborhoods (Jargowsky 1997; Massey and Denton 1993; Wilson 1996). Although the social problems in poor neighborhoods have been well documented, less attention has been paid to the effects of segregation and poverty on middle-class African-Americans, the focus of this chapter.

In the post–civil rights era, African-Americans have made significant progress in various occupations that were once closed to them, and a sizable black middle class has emerged as a result. However, the black middle class remains a vulnerable group that is clustered in lower-middle-class occupations and, because of its recent emergence, lacks any substantial wealth (Landry 1987; Oliver and Shapiro 1995). Most Groveland residents are not doctors, lawyers, or business executives; they are more likely to be government bureaucrats, social workers, and office administrators. In 1993, only 18 percent of black families nationally—compared with 38 percent of white families—earned more than $50,000 (Smith and Horton 1997). Thus, the label "middle class" among African-Americans refers to a lower-paid group of white-collar workers than it connotes among whites.

Black middle-class families tend to live in racially segregated neighborhoods. The black middle class is distinct because of its spatial proximity to poor neighborhoods and cross-class kin and social ties. Middle-class status for black youth like Neisha is only a partial buffer from the problems associated with concentrated poverty. Middle-class black families and the teenagers in them face threats to their development from which their white counterparts are often spared, because of the different neighborhood contexts in which the two groups reside.

High poverty rates in black communities beget greater lifestyle diversity within them. Middle-class black youth grow up with friends from a variety of social backgrounds; middle-class parents have less control over the experiences to which their children are exposed, less control than they would in a more homogeneously middle-class setting. While parents do try to control their children's social interactions, they face tough competition. This is Anna Morris's dilemma with her daughter Neisha, who continues to be attracted to neighborhood boys who are headed for trouble. Black middle-class youth have a number of resources that enable successful outcomes, but they also face substantial roadblocks. It is especially important to make this point because many believe that the more comfortable socioeconomic status of middle-class black youth should make them more like whites. One might assume that the black middle class is in a good position to equal whites on a variety of measures. However, we find that for both youth and adults, and on indicators as diverse as out-of-wedlock childbearing and participation in crime, middle-class blacks and whites still do not look the same.

One of the areas in which middle-class blacks differ from whites with similar incomes is in educational performance. Using the most extensive controls for family income and wealth does not eradicate the significant test-score gap between blacks and whites. Middle-class blacks perform worse than middle-class whites on a variety of aptitude and achievement tests (Jencks and Phillips 1998). Although this chapter does not focus exclusively on schooling, the stories of Groveland youth direct attention to the unique neighborhood contexts in which black middle-class youth are educated and socialized as one way to begin to understand this gap in performance. For example, Douglas Massey and his colleagues (1987) show that as neighborhoods become more segregated and poverty becomes more concentrated in black neighborhoods, the quality of the schools declines. In majority white census tracts where blacks are just beginning to move in, 19 percent of students in the local schools test below the fifteenth percentile. But in tracts under rapid racial transition, the percentage of students testing below the fifteenth percentile rises to 32 percent. In established black tracts, this rises to 40 percent. Middle-income African-American students who attend these schools suffer from their overall poor performance and are profoundly affected by low teacher expectations and a slower pace of instruction.

This scenario plays out in Groveland. The likelihood of graduating from the area high school is only about a fifty-fifty proposition. Middle-income students must resist this trend. To beat the odds, a number of families pay for Catholic high schools where graduation rates are much higher and a large proportion of the graduates go on to college. But for those families who cannot afford private school (or choose not to make the financial sacrifice), or whose children are not chosen from the long waiting lists for magnet schools, the local public schools, with their lower graduation rates and less rigorous curricula, are their only option. It is necessary to understand the local context in which middle-class black youth operate to understand the choices they make, choices that can sometimes lead to negative outcomes.

Elijah Anderson (1994) describes the continuum of lifestyles in poor, inner-city neighborhoods; he defines the two extremes as "decent" and "street" lifestyles. Decent families are "loving," "committed to middle-class values," and "willing to sacrifice for their children," whereas the code of the streets revolves around the maintenance of respect, often through violent or otherwise oppositional means. At the heart of decision making for Groveland youth is the constant *negotiation and balancing* of decent and street lifestyles.[2] The Groveland case illustrates that no youth and no family (and, indeed, no neighborhood) is fully street or decent. Focusing on the negative, or street, behaviors of black youth in places such as Groveland obscures understanding of the complex range of values, including many decent ones, which these youth incorporate. In black middle-class neighborhoods there are substantial resources for nonstreet alternatives, but the streets have a definite allure for youth traversing the rebellious period of adolescence. Black middle-class youth participate in peer groups that embrace components of both street and decent lifestyles; I would contend that is also true of poor black youth, despite the prevalent negative stereotypes. This chapter explores the necessary negotiation of these two lifestyles through the examples of three Groveland youth—Neisha Morris, Charisse Baker, and Tyson Reed.

Research Setting

Considerable information is available on the life choices of poor youth in areas of concentrated poverty from many powerful ethnographic accounts, including the ones in this volume. Substantial quantitative research also investigates the effects of poor neighborhoods (Brooks-Gunn et al. 1993; Jencks and Mayer 1990). But there is little study of the majority of African-Americans who are working and middle class. The possibilities for downward mobility among middle-class black youth as a result of the heterogeneous lifestyles to which they are exposed must also be considered in formulating a policy agenda for improving the social well-being of African-Americans.

African-Americans of every socioeconomic status live in qualitatively different kinds of neighborhoods than their white counterparts. In a revealing exercise, Sampson and Wilson (1995) used census data to locate structurally similar black and white neighborhoods as defined by the percentage who are poor and the percentage in single-parent families. They found that "the 'worst' urban contexts in which whites reside are considerably better than the average context of black communities" (p. 42). Doing similar comparisons, Massey and Denton (1993) concluded that for blacks, "high incomes do not buy entree to residential circumstances that can serve as springboards for future socioeconomic mobility" (p. 153).

How do these contexts affect the processes of adolescent socialization in middle-class black neighborhoods? Groveland, a middle-class black neighborhood on the South Side of Chicago, provides an empirical context in which to investigate this question. The neighborhood has just under twelve thousand residents, over 95 percent of whom are African-American. The annual median family income in Groveland is nearly $40,000, while the comparable figure for the entire city of Chicago is just over $30,000. Over

60 percent of Groveland's employed residents work in white-collar jobs, although the majority of these workers are in lower-middle-class occupations in the technical, sales, and administrative support categories.

The houses in Groveland are mostly single-family brick homes, and over 70 percent of the residents are owners. By income and occupational criteria, as well as the American value of home ownership, Groveland is a middle-class neighborhood, and residents refer to it as such. However, in 1990, nearly 12 percent of Grovelandites were unemployed, and the same percentage of Groveland families had incomes below the poverty line, reflecting the considerable diversity within this middle-class neighborhood. Among the six neighborhoods that border Groveland, all but one have lower median family incomes, and only two have an equivalent or lower poverty rate. Nearby Treelawn, where many Groveland youth go to high school, has a median family income of just under $18,000, not even half the median family income in Groveland. Its poverty rate of over 30 percent is almost triple that of Groveland.

The black middle class lives in closer proximity to areas of concentrated poverty and among more poor families than the white middle class (Darden 1987; Erbe 1975; Farley 1991; Villemez 1980). In addition, all of these contiguous neighborhoods are over 90 percent black, illustrating the hypersegregation of Chicago (Massey and Denton 1993). Such intense segregation shows the extent to which the white middle class has been able to distance itself from urban poverty.

Research Method

Research in Groveland was conducted as an ethnographic community study (e.g., Suttles 1968; Whyte 1943). Although this chapter focuses on youth in Groveland, the study from which the data are drawn was an investigation of broad neighborhood processes. For the first two and a half years, this research was part of the Comparative Neighborhood Study (CNS). The CNS studied four ethnically distinct Chicago neighborhoods, focusing on racial discourse, culture, and social organization. With these general topics in mind, the field staff was instructed to get involved in a wide range of formal organizations—such as churches, business associations, political groups, and social service institutions—and foster informal ties with local families. Key leaders as well as residents were interviewed, and field data were collected from an array of local meetings.

The CNS aimed to match fieldworkers and neighborhoods by race and to place a mixed-gender research team in each neighborhood. As a black female, I was paired with a black male to study Groveland. A number of methodological considerations arise from the practice of matching neighborhoods and researchers by race. "Insider" research (Brewer 1986; Merton 1972) can be especially fruitful because many of the initial obstacles to entry are minimized. From my first few encounters in the neighborhood, I understood that Groveland was similar to the black middle-class neighborhood where I was raised. There were often fewer than six degrees of separation between myself and the residents of Groveland; we knew many people in common. With the black Catholics I shared knowledge of black Catholic leaders in the Midwest. I had mutual acquaintances among the young adults who had gone to college on the East Coast. And the neighborhood's political boss was my uncle's best friend. My research partner, who had grown up in Chicago, had even more familiar connections.

These connections and the relative ease of association had important repercussions, especially at the interpretive end. Such closeness to the community made it difficult to see certain behavior with a critical eye or to question the logic behind people's statements. As a fellow African-American I was supposed to know the answers to many questions that ethnographers must ask to get beyond mere description. I was in constant danger of letting my own insider knowledge prevent me from sufficiently probing the residents of Groveland for their own interpretations. Overall, being African-American facilitated entry and the formation of informal ties, but it was also necessary that I consciously assume an outsider position.

When the CNS ended, I had many close ties with Groveland residents. I was the director of the church choir; I was involved in the church's community action group; I had stuffed envelopes for the alderman's reelection campaign; and I had coached cheerleading at the local park. I started to see my Groveland friends at the grocery store, driving on the freeway, and at movie theaters throughout Chicago. I decided to continue the research by moving into Groveland and conducting more interviews with residents. At this point, my interests became focused on the experiences of Groveland youths, but I remained committed to looking at them in their family and community contexts (see also Brooks-Gunn 1995).

I interviewed thirty-one Groveland residents to augment the participant observation data. The interview sample was chosen to represent various age groups (youth, young adult, and mature adult) and socioeconomic statuses (low, working to middle, and upper-middle income). Eleven of the thirty-one interviews were with youth (twenty-one years old and younger). This number, however, represents a very small proportion of the young people with whom I associated in the church youth groups and in recreational activities at Groveland Park. I chose the three youth featured in this chapter for both pragmatic and substantive reasons. In the cases of Neisha Morris and Charisse Baker, I had come to know them and their families quite well over my years in Groveland. I had substantial data from informal interactions with them, as well as the interviews themselves. In the case of Tyson Reed, I did not know him personally when he was referred to me by his best friend, whom I had also interviewed and knew informally. Nonetheless, Tyson's interview was the longest interview of the thirty-one I conducted, and he was especially forthcoming with personal information and stories.

In addition to the quality and quantity of the data I collected on these youth, the substance of their stories appropriately illustrates the street-decent balancing act that I observed among the majority of Groveland youth. All three occupied the intermediate position between street and decent orientations, yet there was important diversity among them. For example, Neisha and Charisse faced important choices about boyfriends and education. Joining gangs was not a salient issue for either of them. However, gang involvement and drug dealing were pervasive pressures and temptations for the young male, Tyson. Gender clearly shaped the nature and consequences of youthful rebellion. These three stories display a range of family situations, peer and school contexts, utilization of neighborhood resources, and individual personalities.

Groveland Youth Case Studies

Neisha Morris, Tyson Reed, and Charisse Baker are loosely connected through family and friendship ties. Neisha has a first cousin named Ray Gibbs who also grew up in Groveland; both are grandchildren in the four-generation Gibbs clan. Ray Gibbs and Tyson Reed are best friends, played football together at Groveland Park, and went to college together. Charisse Baker is more peripheral to this group and would probably not recognize the other two young people on a Groveland street, but she does have a weak tie: Neisha's current boyfriend, Tim Ward, grew up in his grandmother's house two blocks from Charisse's house. Tim also played basketball under Charisse's father at the local Catholic school gym. Charisse has a crush on Tim's younger brother who is in and out of jail. Charisse stays informed on the gossip of Tim's relationship with Neisha, although Charisse and Neisha have never met.

Neisha Morris

In addition to the Gibbs family on her mother's side, Neisha's father also grew up in Groveland and his family remains in the neighborhood. They are a close-knit and loving extended family. Neisha's mother, Anna Morris, is a dental assistant and her father is a park supervisor. She has a nine-year-old brother, Nate. Her parents were married for more than fifteen years, but because of Mr. Morris's drinking problem, they separated a year before I interviewed Neisha. His unpredictable and, according to Neisha, "crazy" behavior played an indirect role in Neisha's getting pregnant at eighteen. To avoid her father, she moved in with her nineteen-year-old boyfriend, Tim, at his grandmother's home.

> [My father] was too strict on me. That's when I met Tim, and I started spending the night with him every night. I got to the point where I felt like Tim took me away from my father, and havin' to come [home], and havin' to be bothered with that.

When Neisha got pregnant, she returned to her mother's house, bringing her boyfriend, Tim, along with her. By that time, Neisha's parents had separated.

The fragility of black middle-class households becomes manifest when there is a sudden shock, such as a separation. Mr. Morris earned a majority of the Morris's over $40,000 yearly income. As in most African-American families, wage income is the only means of support in the Morris household. White households have significantly more wealth in both physical and financial assets, which enables them to survive for longer periods of time when there is a crisis (Oliver and Shapiro 1995). With Mr. Morris gone, Neisha's mother looked for creative ways to keep the family comfortable. Tim's contributions, although illegally earned, helped to pay some bills.

Many of Neisha's first cousins also grew up in Groveland, and they span a wide range of life situations. One cousin is in jail in Iowa for assaulting someone who owed him money. Her cousin Ray, after being shot in the stomach, decided to change his life and joined Tyson Reed at Grambling State University, a historically black college in Louisiana. Another cousin graduated from college and is a graphic artist for a downtown design firm. Her closest cousin, Kima, has an informal beauty parlor in her grandmother's home to support herself and her three-year-old daughter.

This diversity of outcomes among Neisha's male and female cousins is not reflected by Neisha's closest girlfriends, however. All three are young single mothers like Neisha, searching for career direction. Neisha described them to me:

> My close friend, Libra, she's in college. She goes to Chicago State for nursing. Well, all my friends just had kids. So, Trenique's baby is one. Deshawn is one. And my friend Roxanne, her son's birthday is Thursday, so he makin' one. So, it's like Trenique didn't finish at Benton High

School 'cause she got pregnant. So she went to school and got her GED. So now she in school to do hair, Cosmetology School. And Roxanne, she not working either. She just trying to find out really what she wanna do with herself, you know.

Neisha and her girlfriends have much in common. In addition to being young mothers, the children's fathers are all in the drug business. Drug money fills the gaps between what their parents provide, what AFDC and food stamps provide, and what they need to support themselves and their children in the style to which they are accustomed. "I can't take care of me and my son off no aid check, not the way he can take care of us," Neisha commented about the discrepancy between public assistance and her standard of living. "It's like I won't have a lot of the stuff I want because my mother has to take care of her and my brother and this house." Yet Neisha knows she cannot fully rely on the unstable income of a drug dealer. "I got to do stuff for myself 'cause that [drug dealing] lifestyle, you could have it one day and the next day it could be gone."

For the Morris family, drug money is one of the safety nets that supports their once-middle-income family. Because of Tim's illegal income, Neisha has not needed to go on welfare, although she does receive food stamps. There is an interesting irony in the choice Neisha faces between turning to AFDC or turning to drug profits; neither are "decent," yet Neisha has decided there is more stigma in welfare than in drug money. From her perspective, at least the latter is gained through hard work. Mrs. Morris does not approve of Tim's business, but she also does not find it reprehensible. She is content that he does not store drugs in her house and does his business away from her family. Perhaps Mrs. Morris would not be as tolerant if the family had other means of support.

The integration and balancing of street and decent orientations is a constant in the Morris family. Mrs. Morris keeps her garden colorful and her lawn meticulously trimmed. The glass table in her living room never had a smudge on it. Her commitment to holding a job in the legal economy coexists with Tim's participation in the underground economy. Neisha is an unmarried, teen mother, but she chooses not to receive welfare. Mrs. Morris abhors the violence that accompanies the drug business. Yet she must improvise to keep the family afloat.

Neisha did not attend the local public elementary school. Instead, she was bused to a racially mixed magnet school. "I had some real high scores on my Iowa Tests," Neisha remembered. "And they told me to pick another school that I wanted to go to. And that's the school my mother picked, that offered an enrichment program there." Mrs. Morris was proactive in putting her daughter in a challenging academic environment, one clearly decent strategy to promote children's future success. However, young people do not always appreciate their parents' attempts to help them. Neisha could have continued on to the magnet high school that most of her classmates attended, but she was weary of the long commute and wanted to be with her neighborhood friends. She transferred to Benton High School.

Benton High School is in the Treelawn neighborhood, where over 30 percent of the residents are poor, and the median family income is quite low. Benton is not the closest school available to Groveland, but the closer two high schools have more serious gang problems, and one of those schools in particular is dominated by a rival gang. The Black Mobsters, the primary gang in Groveland, has little clout at the closest two high schools, but it predominates at Benton High School, which is why many Groveland teenagers choose it over the closer schools. While Benton is designated as a "preparatory academy," and nonneighborhood students like Neisha must achieve certain standardized test scores to get in, the overall graduation rate is only 59 percent. Neisha described the type of student at Benton:

> It's a lotta kids that's strictly into that school, strictly into going to school, all type of activities, honors, this and that. But a lotta people just be there to cut classes all day. Just to go to gym and lunch. And sometimes just come to school and don't even go in the building. And they bring down the school, the whole school. So basically it's half and half.

This is the type of school environment that differentiates the black and white middle class. Neisha can recognize the split in student motivation in her school, but she is less aware of how her school differs from predominately white schools in funding and resources. Although Neisha did graduate from Benton High, she was not part of the honors group, not because she wasn't smart, but because her attentions turned to friends and boys.

In summary, Neisha's family, schooling, and peers present various examples for Neisha to follow. Both of her parents work in stable jobs with good incomes. They remained married for fifteen years, until Mrs. Morris could no longer cope with Mr. Morris's drinking. They tended their home and yard. Neisha's mother chose a competitive magnet school, but also allowed Neisha to make her own choices about high school. Of Neisha's neighborhood friends, including her cousins, some went to college and have careers while others just made it out of high school and started a family. Many of the young men in Neisha's life are captivated by the fast-money drug business. Neisha's peers and family illustrate the mix of people who live in Groveland.

Tyson Reed

Tyson Reed was a member of the Black Mobsters in Groveland. The leader of the gang took a special interest in him and Neisha's cousin Ray Gibbs, because of their leadership skills. With the Black Mobsters, Tyson spent a few years selling drugs and guns. According to his friend Ray, many of their gang friends have "faded or disappeared." I asked Ray what he meant by this statement and he elaborated:

> It's probably three things. Well, I should say four things: either in jail, still out here doin' nothin' with theyself, some died, and then the other few like us probably trying to do something with theyselves like go to school, or get a job. Just get away.

Tyson and Ray have tried to get away from the gangs and drugs in Groveland by going to Grambling State University together.

Because of the schools Tyson Reed attended, his networks extend far beyond the boundaries of the neighborhood. "You gotta think about it," he instructed me:

> I grew up in Groveland, but [I was] always on the West Side. I went to Presley, and kids got bused in to go there, so I knew a lotta people. Then I went to Dayton, kids got bussed in to go there. Then I went down South and went to college, so I had a lotta friends there. Not to mention in between I played football—got a lotta friends—[and] wrestled.

Tyson went to elementary school at Presley Academy, a public magnet school outside of Groveland for which there is a long waiting list. A majority of Presley students perform above national norms on standardized tests. After Presley, Tyson attended Dayton Prep, a public high school in a racially mixed, middle-class neighborhood. Although Dayton Prep has changed over the years, and is neither as racially mixed nor as middle class as the neighborhood that surrounds it, it continues to send over 85 percent of its students to four-year colleges. It is one of the few Chicago public schools to which college admissions officers from elite universities make regular recruiting visits. That Tyson attended magnet schools was the result of his mother's insistence that he get a good education. Tyson's mother is a high-ranking official in the Chicago Public Schools. She had received her Ph.D. a few weeks before I interviewed Tyson and he proudly showed me her diploma. His mother's own continued schooling suggests that education is highly valued in the Reed family.

At twenty-two years old, Tyson does not have a close relationship with his mother, but he is beginning to realize the advantages of the kind of education his mother provided for him. He talked about this burgeoning appreciation:

> 'Cause you gotta learn how to appreciate stuff you got. I ain't never really appreciated what my mother used to do for me. Like sending me to Presley and Dayton. I ain't never appreciate that until, until I started to get fucked up a lot, and, you know, I really got on my own. I was like, "damn if it wasn't for that I'll be just as dumb as this mufucka over here." You know what I'm saying? Really, when you really think about it, you'on appreciate it 'til it's too late.

Once Tyson began to appreciate it, he started to use it to his advantage. He has just one course to complete to receive his B.A. in Criminal Justice. He plans to go to law school once he finishes college. In the meantime, he will work for the Board of Education, a job secured through his mother's connections.

Tyson does not know his father well, and he is intensely angry about his father's absence. "I know where he [is] at, but I don't wanna fuck with him," Tyson told me. Even though he does not want a relationship with his father, he recognizes the problems that arise because of absent parents:

> That's a real problem right there with the black community today with our kids and stuff. People just don't care. I mean, when the kids [are] young really it's the parents responsibility, well, duty, to be around 'em. You know, be around they friends, be around your family or whatever. Matter of fact, outta all my friends, I'll say 90 percent of them either live with their mother or live with their father. Only like 10 percent of my friends live with both of their parents.

From his own experiences, Tyson is convinced that he would not have gotten involved in gangs if his father had been around. Tyson's understanding of the connection between delinquency and a concentration of single-parent families is supported by empirical evidence. Single-parent families have fewer economic resources and lack the extra pair of eyes important for monitoring youths (McLanahan and Sandefur 1994; Sampson and Groves 1989; Steinberg 1987).

Charisse Baker

Charisse is the youngest of my three subjects, and much of her adolescent life is still unfolding. She is sixteen and lives with her mother and younger sister, Deanne, across the street from St. Mary's Catholic Church and School. Charisse's mother is a personnel assistant at a Chicago university and is taking classes there to get her bachelor's degree. Charisse's father is a Chicago firefighter. Although her father and mother are separated, she sees her father many times a week at the afterschool basketball hour he supervises at St. Mary's gym. Mr. and Ms. Baker remain friends, and Charisse has a very loving relationship with both parents. I first met Charisse at a St. Mary's boys' basketball game; the team is coached by Charisse's father. I was interviewing Mr. Baker when Charisse walked over to him and clung to him as only daughters can cling to their fathers. Later, Charisse's excited stories about her high school's father/daughter dance, and Mr. Baker's faithful attendance at graduations and performances, reinforced that positive first impression.

In addition to her biological parents, Charisse and her younger sister, Deanne, are being raised by the neighborhood family. "We [are] real close. Like all our neighbors know us because my dad grew up over here. Since the '60s." Many members of St. Mary's Church also play the role of surrogate parents. Charisse's late paternal grandmother was the school secretary. When Charisse was in elementary school at St. Mary's, she was always under the watchful eye of her grandmother and all of the staff who were her grandmother's friends. Also, Charisse's mother would bring her and her sister to choir practice when they were little girls, and there they acquired another ensemble of mothers and fathers.

After St. Mary's elementary school, Charisse went on to St. Agnes Catholic High School, her father's choice. St. Agnes is located in a south suburb of Chicago and is an integrated, all-girls Catholic school where 100 percent of the girls graduate, and over 95 percent of the girls go on to college. Many of the students come from lower-middle-class families like the Bakers. Charisse told a story about a recent St. Agnes graduate that illustrates the importance of education at St. Agnes, as well as the economic status of its students.

> I was hearin' about this one girl who went from St. Agnes. She got a full scholarship to Stanford. And she was, you know, she was a minority. She was talkin' about how e'rybody in Stanford drivin' to school with they little Rolls Royce and Corvettes. And she was on her little ten speed. She was like, "That's okay." She gettin' her education.

The possibility of a Stanford scholarship, as well as the graduation statistics at St. Agnes, are clearly among the reasons why Charisse's parents chose it over Benton High School, which is closer and free.

Most of Charisse's close friends went to St. Mary's and now go to St. Agnes with her, but her choice of boyfriends evidences signs of rebellion. For her father, the mere fact that she has boyfriends is rebellious. Yet Charisse has managed to have a very full social life when it comes to boys. Many of Charisse's male interests are older than she is and irregularly employed—although some are in and out of school. She meets many of them hanging out at the mall. One evening, members of the church's youth choir sat around talking about their relationships. Charisse cooed about her current boyfriend who had just graduated from high school but did not have a job and was uncertain about his future. Suddenly she started talking about another young man she had just met. "Charisse changes boyfriends like she changes her clothes," her sister joked, highlighting the impetuous nature of adolescent relationships.

Although these young men are not in gangs or selling drugs, many of them do not seem to share Charisse's strong career goals and commitment to attaining them. Some of them would not gain the approval of her parents. However, this full list of boyfriends has not clouded Charisse's focus. She told me, in her always bubbly, fast-talking manner:

> Okay, I would like to go the University of Illinois in Champaign-Urbana. I would like to major in marketing and I'm considering minoring in communications, because I talk a lot. And once I get a job, I get stable, then I can pursue a relationship. I'd like to get married and I want five kids. 'Cause I love children. I really do. I love children.

Charisse has a clear vision for her life—school, then marriage, then children. The content and order of these plans attest to mainstream values and aspirations. Her parents have made decisions about Charisse's schooling that will prepare her for college, that have instilled in her the Christian values in which they believe, and that have provided her a group of like-minded friends.

Yet Charisse's family, friends, and acquaintances are not all angels. "Any of my uncles might be in jail," Charisse responded when I asked if she knew anyone in jail. She continued, "I know one uncle I haven't talked to, he could be on parole. And I have a cousin who I know is on parole in Detroit, so he can't see nobody." About her neighbors, Charisse recalled, "I know Harris is in jail. He live around here. You know his brother Big Tim [Neisha's boyfriend]." These relationships show that Charisse is not completely isolated from delinquents, in either her neighborhood or her family. While Charisse's closest family and friends stress positive behaviors, her larger network could negatively affect her choices.

Negotiating Neighborhood Crossroads

Groveland is quite different from many of the other settings reported on in this volume, by virtue of its predominately (lower) middle-class composition. Many Groveland residents possess financial, social, and human capital that greatly facilitates parenting. Each of the three young people in this chapter have familial financial resources that have provided access to private schools, paid for sports equipment and dance classes, and generated some spending money for the movies, the prom, and an occasional trip or vacation. Charisse's parents have raised her in the Catholic Church and Catholic schools; Neisha has taken every dance class ever offered at Groveland Park and still wants to be a dance instructor with the full support and urging of both parents; and Tyson's mother used magnet schools to get her son a solid education and steer him toward college. At the neighborhood level, there are thriving local businesses; Groveland Park hosts a fully enrolled Summer Day Camp and other recreational activities; and many of the churches are well supported.

These families also have social connections to the work world. Even though Neisha dislikes her father, his job with the Chicago Park District helped her get a summer job. She admitted, "My daddy got a promotion to another park. He's a park supervisor, so I'll probably work at his park, you know, through the summer." Tyson also took advantage of his mother's connections and planned to work for the Chicago Board of Education. And Charisse's younger sister—who is not yet even sixteen years old—spends her summers filing and answering phones in her mother's office. Charisse works at the beauty salon owned by a family friend, who is also a member of St. Mary's Church.

Finally, Groveland residents have human capital skills that set examples for neighborhood youth. Tyson's mother's knowledge of the Chicago public education system surely influenced her decision to place her son in magnet schools. The fact that she had gone to college and graduate school no doubt facilitated Tyson's college application process, as well as nurtured his aspiration to go to law school. Similarly, because of their white-collar employment, both Neisha's and Charisse's mothers work with computers, fax machines, and other high-tech office equipment. Familiarity with such technology is now a prerequisite for future success. Groveland youth are in many ways privileged because of these resources. They enjoy opportunities that poor African-American youth do not.

Still, Groveland is not insulated from the social problems of poor neighborhoods. Groveland parents run up against the stubborn obstacles of underfunded and understaffed schools, crumbling housing nearby, poor city services, drugs, gangs, violence, and so on. As the geography and composition of Groveland illustrate, the neighborhood is part of a larger and poorer black community on Chicago's South Side. Groveland residents share many South Side institutions with other neighborhoods. The character of middle-class black neighborhoods and black communities generally

increases the choices that middle-class black youth can make during the rebellious adolescent period. Some of those choices can have very negative
outcomes. Many youth emerge from this unscathed, but others are left with
a variety of battle scars—gun shot wounds, criminal records, new babies,
subpar educations, or one less friend.

Most parents have strategies for raising their children that include steer-
ing them in positive directions. Middle-class resources provide certain safety
nets when self-sufficiency goals are frustrated. Although such resources may
be thin in any one family, as was the case for Neisha after her father left,
households are not disconnected from their extended family and community contexts. Together, impressive pooled resources provide extended alternatives and opportunities for Groveland youth. Even if a young person has
a child, she (usually she) is often provided with housing, child care and time
to continue her schooling, and sometimes even the social life she had before
she became a mother. For young people who have graduated from high
school, thinking about college or making plans to go to college is sufficient
activity to give them the freedom to work at odd jobs and live at home. This
principal support by parents, which is frequently motivated by their fears
of what awaits their children in dangerous neighborhood contexts, can continue well into a young person's late twenties and early thirties. While self-
sufficiency is the ultimate goal, families recognize that such success rests on
the sustained collaboration of family and community resources.

But parents cannot be with children at all times. Once parental strategies are chosen and enacted, and resources are expended, children inevitably
rebel against them. This rebellion, however, cannot go too far outside the
parameters of a young person's social and spatial milieu. As Furstenberg
(1993) points out, "the context in which parenting occurs influences both
the parents' style of management and their success in implementing their
goals" (p. 233). Neisha, Tyson, and Charisse all had particular areas of rebellion against their parents "management" and "goals," the consequences
(or outcomes) of which were affected by the neighborhood context. When
youths disagree with their parents about what their lives should be like, they
can draw from both street and decent activities available in the neighborhood as alternatives.

Tyson Reed

Tyson resisted some of his mother's positive parental strategies. He told me
about the kind of son his mother wanted him to be:

> Without all the gangbanging. Without knowing the people I know. She
> really ain't want me to play football. She wanted me to be on the swim

team. 'Cause I been swimming since I was like three months old. So I know how to swim real real good. And she would say, 'Well why'on you get on the swim team.' Yeah, awright, that's gay as hell. I mean, when you think about it, it ain't gay, but you thinkin', I'm a male, 17, 18, 19, 20 [years old]. In college, high school. How the hell I look competin', "Oh, I'ma beat you swimmin'," when I can run up and physically hit somebody. You know what I'm sayin'? Or even basketball, you can show your abilities or something. How I look, 'Oh, I'm gonna outswim you. Ah, I'm faster than you.' I mean, even with track, I think it's more manly than swimming.

Tyson rebelled against his mother's desire that he be a studious young man on the swim team. His resistance was tied to his adolescent concerns with masculinity, physicality, and image. His mother's suggestion of swimming as the sport of choice indicated to him that she must not understand the masculine pressures he faced as a young African-American male.

The absence of Tyson's father compounded his need to establish a masculine identity and further fueled his anger toward his mother. Searching for male role models and a fellowship of young men, Tyson got "plugged," Chicago slang for joining a gang. According to Tyson's friend, this was not difficult to do. His friend explained the process of becoming a Black Mobster:

It start off like two or three people'll join a gang, but you hang with them. So you too close to 'em to let somebody beat up on 'em. Somebody mess with them, you in it. So now they look at you as, you know what I'm saying, you with 'em. So now they want you, too. But pretty soon you start doing everything they doing. Everything they doing except being plugged. So you just plug. That's when it start.

This story once again illustrates that the shape of youthful rebellion can only go as far as the local options allow. Tyson did not have to search far to get involved in the Black Mobsters and their drug business; he simply had to be friends with people who were already members.

The absence of Tyson's father and the departure of his favorite uncle fostered his exploration of delinquent neighborhood networks. Tyson recalled how he got involved in selling drugs:

When I really needed somebody to teach me something, my uncle was there trying to help me. But after he went to college, and I was still in grammar school by myself, it wasn't nothing else to do but go across the street and do what I had to do. Awright, my mama might have a good job, but if my homey [friend] and me go up across the street and he get on and start sellin' drugs, now you honestly think I'ma sit there. That's a form of peer pressure, I know. But you gon' see him make all that money and ya'll together. You there anyway, fuck it. You might as well make you some money. That's how I felt about it, you know.

Tyson's "negotiations" are apparent in his words. He was a young man who felt somewhat directionless because of his father's and uncle's departure. He recognized that his mother's "good job" should count for something in his decision. Yet his friends were a strong force at this point in his life (the peer pressure he referred to), and fast money in this consumer age had an almost irresistible allure. Finally and most importantly for this focus on neighborhood context and options, Tyson just had to cross the street to carry out a decision to sell drugs.

In a neighborhood like Groveland, gangs and drug selling are attractive to these middle-class youth because of the fast money they are supposed to provide. Although Grovelandites frequently describe the neighborhood as "middle class," the black middle class is clustered at the lower-middle-class end of the distribution, which means that being black and middle class does not allow for much excess. To get the extra money to buy the newest sneakers or get the latest hairstyle, some Groveland youth turn to the Black Mobsters and their drug business. Yet Tyson's professional mother had a high income and an average-sized family on which to spend it. Tyson's explanation for selling drugs was that his mother was too miserly. "Your parents give you what you need and sometime they get you what you want," Tyson explained. "But when you sell drugs, you get you what you want." Tyson made a decision to sell drugs, despite his family's financial resources. The decision was affected by neighborhood composition and opportunity.[3]

The high poverty rates in neighborhoods inhabited by middle-class African-Americans mean that more young people in these neighborhoods will have fewer familial resources to connect them to positive activities like dance or swimming and buy for them the status symbols of contemporary youth consumer culture. For this economically disadvantaged portion of the population, commitment to mainstream behaviors may be attenuated (Sampson and Wilson 1995). These orientations can be transmitted to middle-class youth whose parents could provide some luxuries—as Tyson's mother could—but never enough to satisfy the wants of an American adolescent. Many black middle-class youth like Tyson are in search of a male peer group, are excited by the thrill of deviance, and desire the flashy material goods that an illegal income can buy. Finally, the opportunity for delinquent rebellion is readily available; kids don't have to travel far to get involved with the "wrong crowd."

Neisha Morris

Like Tyson, Neisha's family situation affects the nature of her rebellion, which is in turn circumscribed by the neighborhood milieu. Neisha's parents stayed together for most of her childhood years, provided for her financially, and enrolled her in positive activities. Her extended family continues to give her much love and encouragement. Yet her father's drinking problem often has negative consequences. He is very strict and does not want Neisha to talk on the phone with boys, or date them. Still, Neisha, like Charisse, finds a way to have a thriving social life, including boyfriends. Many of the young men Neisha chooses, however, have gone a similar route to Tyson's. Although Neisha's mother spoke somewhat negatively about her daughter's choice of boyfriends, they grew up in the neighborhood and Neisha's mother knows many of them to be generally good young men. These longtime neighborhood connections make it difficult to completely sever relationships with delinquent youth or criminal adults (Pattillo 1998).

For example, Kareem was one of Neisha's boyfriends before Tim. Kareem holds a leadership position in the Black Mobsters. Before his affiliation with the Black Mobsters, however, Neisha's mother, aunts, and grandmother all knew Kareem as just another neighborhood kid. Neisha described her early neighborhood memories of Kareem and how they eventually started dating:

> Kareem been likin' me for the longest. Even before he had money. I remember seein' him, he used to be sittin' on some crates over by the store with some ol' raggedy T-shirt on, and his fat just hanging. Well, this was before he had money. He would just keep on talking to me and kept on and kept on. Then, you know, he started makin' money. And I ain't think he even liked me any more. So, you know, I wasn't even thinkin' about it. But then, he just kept tryin' to get my number and shit. Finally, I just gave it to him. And that nigga called me about a hundred times that day. He just kept tryin' to talk to me. The first time we went out he gave me $300. I was like, "What's this for?" But, you know, I really started likin' him. He really real sweet and all.

Kareem is much more than a high-ranking gang member and drug dealer. He was the fat little boy who sat in front of the store, he is real sweet, and he has been persistent in his attentions to Neisha. Neisha could undoubtably find a boy in the neighborhood not affiliated with the Black Mobsters and not selling drugs, but money and power can be aphrodisiacs. The neighborhood cycle that fostered Tyson's entrance into the drug business also operates in Neisha's case in terms of shaping her choices of young men to date.

Charisse Baker

Because Charisse is younger than the other two, it is more difficult to thoroughly appraise her choices or gauge the impact of those choices. A number of factors in Charisse's upbringing converge to provide her parents with considerable control over the choices she can make. Although her parents are separated, her father continues to be a daily and positive presence in her life. Moreover, Charisse's intense involvement in the church leaves her little time for much else. When I asked Charisse how she spent her free time, she joked, "I got a lot of stuff that I have to do at the church. But I don't know if that's considered work or free time." She listed her involvements in St. Mary's, which included the parish pastoral council, youth group, youth council, gospel choir, and the hospitality committee. Also, the extra parenting that she is subject to by church members makes her all the more accountable for her actions.

Charisse's rebellion, like Neisha's, is through boys. And also like Neisha, her extended family (church and kin) knows many of the residents in Groveland—the good and the bad. Unlike Neisha, however, she and her sister's very good relationship with their father fortifies their consciences when choosing boyfriends and deciding what to do with them. Charisse's sister, Deanne, told me about her father's talk with her about boys:

> I think one good factor is the way my father approached me about boys. He told me when I was like only six or seven. He sat down and he was like, "Deanne, boys'll tell you anything to get you in the bed." [She laughs as she remembers her father's words]. I'm thinking that's not true. You know, I'm in, what, second grade? I ain't thinkin' along those lines. He specifically said all boys. He said they'd tell you anything. He was like, "They'll tell you they love you. They'll tell you anything to get you in the bed." He was like, "Don't do it!" He had that look on his face like if you do it, you in trouble. So, I didn't do it. Later on I found out that all boys aren't bad, but a lot of them are. So I kinda got the hint.

"What would happen if either of you got pregnant?" I asked both Charisse and Deanne. Charisse answered without hesitation:

> I would run away from home 'cause I think my parents would actually try to kill me. I think my daddy would kill me. I'm not being sarcastic at all. I would run away from home. I would call [my friend] Khadija and say Khadija, I gotta go. And I'd be up. And that's all seriousness. That's why I ain't doin' nothin' so I'on get nothin'.

Charisse's good relationship with her parents means that their words stick in her mind. While she tests the boundaries when it comes to boyfriends, she is not inclined to disregard her parents' advice and lessons.

However, the fact that Charisse's parents have been able to more closely supervise and influence her behavior does not mean that the neighborhood context is unimportant. On the contrary, the church is also a part of the neighborhood context, as is the Catholic school and many of the people who participate in these two institutions. Charisse's family's involvement in the church and school integrate positive family and neighborhood contexts for her. Almost all of Charisse's friends had parents who were paying a premium to send their children to Catholic school. And St. Mary's Church members include Groveland's state representative, an executive at the Coca-Cola Company, and an executive assistant at the Urban League, all of whom Charisse may interact with and learn from.

Charisse is by no means sheltered from the neighborhood trouble-makers. She knows the neighborhood gang members. She grew up with them just as Neisha did, which is how Charisse knows Neisha's boyfriend Tim, and his younger brother Harris. Many of the young men that play basketball at the church gym under Charisse's father's supervision are also gang members. Mr. Baker grew up in Groveland when the gangs were first forming. As a result, he knows many of the founding members as well as the younger cohort of gang members. Mr. Baker's familiarity with the neighborhood's roughnecks gives Charisse and her sister, Deanne, a certain feeling of security. Deanne commented, "I want people to know that that's my daddy 'cause I'on wanna be messed with or anything." Because of these associations, and her father's lessons, Charisse is, in Elijah Anderson's (1990) terms, streetwise.

Conclusion

Despite their rebellious forays, their street and decent balancing acts, and the fragility of the collective resources on which they depend, Neisha, Tyson, and Charisse may still be poised to duplicate their parents' middle-class status. Tyson will soon graduate from college, Charisse is determined to be a successful businesswoman, and Neisha still has aspirations to be a dance instructor and will have much help in raising little Tim. But they are not out of the woods. The need to reconcile street and decent lifestyles does not end at adolescence. Adults must also negotiate the neighborhood context, as well as their peer and family relationships. While people may, to some extent, choose their friends and neighbors, they cannot choose their relatives. Extended kinship bonds make it most difficult to limit association to people who are similar in class and lifestyle. If Neisha does well but her cousin Kima does not, for example, her close extended family will make it difficult to separate herself from Kima, assuming that she even desires to do so. Likewise, even though Tyson is planning to go to law school, he stays in touch with his neighborhood friends because he is determined not to lose his street edge. He is committed to making his own children (when he has them) well versed in the street, as he is. "Even if I do become a big-time lawyer, judge, or whatever, e'rybody ain't gon' be able to do that," Tyson reasoned. "So I can always know somebody in the ghetto. I'ma send my kids right over your uncle such-and-such and cousin such-and-such house to let you know how it feel if you didn't have this." Negotiating street and decent lifestyles is a continuous process for the black middle class.

Interview selection bias also qualifies an overly optimistic reading of these stories. The youth I interviewed and befriended were persevering. This is especially relevant for Tyson whose mere survival, as a black male, has been an accomplishment. I could not interview the friends who had just "faded or disappeared." I could not interview the women lost to drug addiction, whose children are being raised by grandparents (Burton 1992). Hence, these three young people in many ways represent those who are successful in maneuvering through their family, peer, school, and neighborhood environments. The road is perilous, and the stories of these three young people reveal the nuanced nature of family life and individual choices in black communities.

Other factors such as personal agency and family situation, of course, play a role in these young people's lives. Neisha scored high enough on standardized tests to attend a magnet high school, but instead wanted to be closer to her friends and so attended a less rigorous school. Tyson could have been his mother's angel by staying out of gangs and joining the swim team, but he chose otherwise. Charisse could still choose not to go to college. Family situations also have an impact; all three of these youth lived in single-mother homes at the time that I interviewed them. Children from single-parent homes are at high risk of dropping out of high school, having a teenage birth, and engaging in delinquent behaviors, no matter what their family, peer, school, or neighborhood contexts (Garfinkel and McLanahan 1986; McLanahan and Sandefur 1994). Areas with a preponderance of single-parent households are less able to monitor crime, especially because of the prevalence of unsupervised peer groups in such neighborhoods (Sampson and Groves 1989). Nearly 40 percent of Groveland households are headed by women. Yet even the children of two-parent households in Groveland exhibit the same balancing behaviors as Neisha, Tyson, and Charisse. Choices are made within the limits of what options are presented to these young people, and in this neighborhood context, many bad choices can be made with ease.

While being middle class provides substantial privileges, the precarious economic situation of the black middle class often renders stability and mobility an extended family, and sometimes even a community, effort. The Morris family pieced together financial resources from legal income, food stamps, and illegal drug sales, as well as nonpecuniary goods, such as child care given by Neisha's grandmother and the social support that Neisha's cousins and friends provided. The same was true in the Baker family, where the church provided positive activities (sometimes at a cost, but most times free) and created a network of adults to raise Charisse and her sister. The complexity of these arrangements and relationships underscores the importance of studying whole families in their ecological contexts, instead of focusing on the resources in one household, or limiting the discussion to the nuclear family. It is critical that policymakers understand the rippling effect that one person's situation can have on many others. Welfare reform, for example, not only affects women who are currently receiving assistance but also impacts the family and friends to whom they will turn for help as rules become more strict, or when the labor market is less hospitable.[4] Since African-American families have lower incomes and less wealth than whites, weakening the public safety net could lead to a particularly disastrous depletion of family resources among blacks.

The situation in Groveland sheds light on racial inequalities that persist. Black middle-class youth live in neighborhoods with more poverty, worse schools, and more crime than their white middle-class peers. This affects their educational performance, their choices about childbearing, and the nature of their adolescent rebellion. Just as neighborhood context is important for understanding poor youth in areas of concentrated poverty, it is equally important for understanding black middle-class youth who grow up in neighborhoods that are, in some ways, not even equivalent to those of poor whites. Socioeconomic status is complicated by the crosscutting reality of race, and the ways in which racial discrimination shapes neighborhood contexts.

Notes

1. All names of people and places are pseudonyms to ensure anonymity.
2. The use of Black English and slang provides a useful example. Massey and Denton (1993) call Black English a "language of segregation," but their discussion focuses on its use in poor black communities. As the field notes in this chapter reveal, however,

Black English is also widely used among the children of African-American professionals (and even among some of the professionals themselves), especially in casual settings. I frequently used Black English in conducting interviews to make them less formal and more comfortable for the interviewee. Speaking slang is one strategy for maintaining a connection to the streets. As one college-educated Groveland young adult remarked, "It's good to be educated, and it's good to have the street sense. But sometime you look like a damn fool when you try and mix 'em with the wrong crowd." Code-switching is part of the process of balancing street and decent orientations.

3. One important factor that I do not explore in this chapter is the role of the mass media in glamorizing deviance, especially gangs and drug dealing, and targeting urban youth as conspicuous consumers (see Nightingale 1993; Pattillo-McCoy 1999).

4. The research of Kathryn Edin and Laura Lein (1997) illustrates the same reliance on extended family networks and friends to make ends meet among poor women.

REFERENCES

Anderson, Elijah. 1994. "The Code of the Streets." *Atlantic Monthly* 273:80–94.
Anderson, Elijah. 1990. *Streetwise: Race, Class, and Change in an Urban Community.* Chicago: University of Chicago Press.
Brewer, Rose. 1986. "Research for Whom and by Whom: A Reconsideration of the Black Social Scientist as Insider." *The Wisconsin Sociologist* 23:19–28.
Brooks-Gunn, Jeanne. 1995. "Children in Families in Communities: Risk and Intervention in the Bronfenbrenner Tradition." In *Examining Lives in Context: Perspectives on the Ecology of Human Development,* ed. Phyllis Moen, Glen Elder Jr., and Kurt Löescher, 467–519. Washington, DC: American Psychological Association.
Brooks-Gunn, Jeanne, Greg Duncan, Pamela Kato Klebanov, and Naomi Sealand. 1993. "Do Neighborhoods Influence Child and Adolescent Development?" *American Journal of Sociology* 99:353–95.
Burton, Linda. 1992. "Black Grandparents Rearing Children of Drug Addicted Parents: Stressors, Outcomes, and Social Service Needs." *The Gerontologist* 32:744–51.
Darden, Joe T. 1987. "Socioeconomic Status and Racial Residential Segregation: Blacks and Hispanics in Chicago." *International Journal of Comparative Sociology* 28:1–13.
Edin, Kathryn, and Laura Lein. 1997. *Making Ends Meet: How Single Mothers Survive Welfare and Low-Wage Work.* New York: Russell Sage Foundation.
Erbe, Brigitte Mach. 1975. "Race and Socioeconomic Segregation." *American Sociological Review* 40:801–12.
Farley, Reynolds. 1991. "Residential Segregation of Social and Economic Groups among Blacks, 1970–80." In *The Urban Underclass,* ed. Christopher Jencks and Paul E. Peterson, 274–98. Washington, DC: The Brookings Institution.
Furstenberg, Frank Jr. 1993. "How Families Manage Risk and Opportunity in Dangerous Neighborhoods." In *Sociology and the Public Agenda,* ed. William Julius Wilson, 231–58. Newbury Park, CA: Sage.

Garfinkel, Irwin, and Sara S. McLanahan. 1986. *Single Mothers and Their Children: A New American Dilemma.* Washington, DC: Urban Institute Press.

Jargowsky, Paul. 1997. *Poverty and Place: Ghettos, Barrios, and the American City.* New York: Russell Sage Foundation.

Jencks, Christopher, and Susan Mayer. 1990. "The Social Consequences of Growing up in a Poor Neighborhood." In *Inner-City Poverty in the United States,* ed. Laurence Lynn and Michael McGeary, 187–222. Washington, DC: National Academy.

Jencks, Christopher, and Meredith Phillips, eds. 1998. *The Black-White Test Score Gap.* Washington, DC: The Brookings Institution.

Landry, Bart. 1987. *The New Black Middle Class.* Berkeley: University of California Press.

Massey, Douglas, Gretchen A. Condran, and Nancy A. Denton. 1987. "The Effect of Residential Segregation on Black Social and Economic Well-Being." *Social Forces* 66:29–57.

Massey, Douglas, and Nancy Denton. 1993. *American Apartheid: Segregation and the Making of the Underclass.* Cambridge: Harvard University Press.

McLanahan, Sara, and Gary Sandefur. 1994. *Growing Up with a Single Parent: What Hurts, What Helps.* Cambridge: Harvard University Press.

Merton, Robert K. 1972. "Insiders and Outsiders: A Chapter in the Sociology of Knowledge." *American Journal of Sociology* 78:9–47.

Nightingale, Carl Husemoller. 1993. *On the Edge: A History of Poor Black Children and Their American Dream.* New York: Basic Books.

Oliver, Melvin L., and Thomas M. Shapiro. 1995. *Black Wealth/White Wealth: A New Perspective on Racial Inequality.* New York: Routledge.

Pattillo, Mary E. 1998. "Sweet Mothers and Gangbangers: Managing Crime in a Black Middle Class Neighborhood." *Social Forces* 76:747–74.

Pattillo-McCoy, Mary. 1999. *Black Picket Fences: Privilege and Peril among the Black Middle Class.* Chicago: University of Chicago Press.

Sampson, Robert J., and W. Byron Groves. 1989. "Community Structure and Crime: Testing Social-Disorganization Theory." *American Journal of Sociology* 94:774–802.

Sampson, Robert J., and William Julius Wilson. 1995. "Toward a Theory of Race, Crime and Urban Inequality." In *Crime and Inequality,* ed. John Hagan and Ruth D. Peterson, 37–54. Stanford: Stanford University Press.

Smith, Jessie Carney, and Carrell Horton, eds. 1997. *Statistical Record of Black America,* 4th ed. Detroit, MI: Gale Research Press.

Suttles, Gerald. 1968. *The Social Order of the Slum: Ethnicity and Territory in the Inner City.* Chicago: University of Chicago Press.

Steinberg, Laurence. 1987. "Single Parents, Stepparents, and Susceptibility of Adolescents to Antisocial Peer Pressure." *Child Development* 58:269–75.

Villemez, Wayne. 1980. "Race, Class, and Neighborhood: Differences in the Residential Return on Individual Resources." *Social Forces* 59:414–30.

Whyte, William Foote. 1943. *Street Corner Society. The Social Structure of an Italian Slum.* Chicago: University of Chicago Press.

Wilson, William Julius. 1996. *When Work Disappears: The World of the New Urban Poor.* New York: Knopf.

PART 2
Employment:
From Removing Barriers
to Coping with Obstacles

CHAPTER 5

Dreamkeeping in the Inner City: Diminishing the Divide Between Aspirations and Expectations

Carla O'Connor

Bring me all of your dreams,
You dreamers,
Bring me all of your Heart melodies
That I may wrap them
In a blue cloud-cloth
Away from the too-rough fingers
Of the world.
                    "The Dream Keeper"
                    by Langston Hughes

This chapter visits six African-American high school girls who imagined a "better life" while growing up in poverty in inner-city Chicago: Cher (age = 15), Sabrina (age = 15), Tina (age = 15), Benita (age = 15), Janine (age = 17), and Collette (age = 16). They resided in neighborhoods where few were employed and many had not completed high school; gang violence was intense and social services were insufficient. Their families relied on AFDC and they lived in public housing.[1] All the girls but Collette had been born to a teenage mother, and Collette's mother was the only caretaker who had a job, packing boxes in a local factory. The caretakers of all the other young women were unemployed. None of the girls' parents or guardians had received a high school diploma, though the mothers of Cher and Collette had attained their GEDs. Benita lived with both of her maternal grandparents, and all of the other young women resided in homes headed by their single mothers. Janine was already the mother of two sons, ages seventeen months and six months.

Despite such savage realities, these girls imagined futures that stood in stark contrast to their current circumstances. The girls explained that they were "sick of living up in the projects." They "wanted nice car[s]" and spoke of living in "big house[s]." They wanted to be in neighborhoods where there was "quietness—ain't nobody shooting—ain't too much gangbanging either." Consequently, they talked about having a life in the "suburbs" or in more residential areas of Chicago like "out south . . . like in the 72s." And they also emphasized their desire to be "independent." They "[didn't] want to be on welfare" and "[live] off of the government."

In some cases, the young women also hoped to escape a past that was marred by drug addiction. Benita's mother had died of a drug overdose in 1984. Sabrina's mother had started doing drugs four years ago and had not worked since. Cher's mother had been in recovery for the last three months, but before then had been on drugs for as long as Cher could remember.

The girls believed that if they realized their educational and occupational ambitions, they could achieve the independence, material trappings, and social prestige they associated with the middle class. They could reside in communities different from those in which they had grown up. In essence, they dreamed the American dream, hoping to do better than their parents and guardians on all measures of social achievement. Only Cher and Sabrina, however, anticipated the realization of their aspirations. Somehow their dreams had been protected from the "too-rough fingers of the world." When I asked Sabrina, who wanted to become a computer scientist, what were the chances that her dreams would come true, she responded, "Oh, very high." Cher explained, "I see myself graduating from college, getting a good job as a business administrator—middle class. I could have what I want. It's mine. Just got to keep working hard."

In contrast, Collette, Janine, and Benita were pessimistic about their chances of "making it." They presumed that they, like their parents, would not go on to college, would experience unemployment, would rely on welfare, and would fail to acquire the material trappings that they desired. Collette explained:

> Well if I had a choice I'd be a teacher. I'd go to college . . . I would have a house out south . . . like in the 72s . . . [but my life] probably be messed up. I won't have the things I want. I'd feel sad cause I ain't have no house. Cause I ain't have a job. I probably be on welfare. Ain't going to be nothing that I want.

The remaining student, Tina was situated between these first two groups of young women. She was quasi-optimistic about her life chances. Unlike optimistic Cher and Sabrina, she did not anticipate attaining the status to which she aspired. She explained, "Where I would like to see myself is finishing up college and starting to teach—even if it's substituting. But I can't say if I'll really get to go to college." However, in contrast to pessimistic Collette, Janine, and Benita, Tina expected that she would at least surpass the educational, occupational, and social statuses of her mom. In her voice:

I have more education [than my mother]—so already my life will be better. I will have more money because I will have more education—my life will be better.

While Tina's limited expectations and Collette, Janine, and Benita's pessimism could have been predicted from their social backgrounds, Cher and Sabrina's optimism could not. Low socioeconomic status, having parents with low levels of education, being female, and living in areas of concentrated poverty have been shown to suppress educational and occupational aspirations (Allen 1980; Crowley and Shapiro 1982; Dawkins 1981; Marini 1984; Marini and Greenberger 1978; McLelland 1990; Sewell, Haller, and Portes 1969; Willis 1977). And when aspirations are high despite such background characteristics, the aspirants are less likely to expect the realization of their goals (Berman 1975; Crowley and Shapiro 1982; Marini 1978; Marini and Greenberger 1978).

Aspirations are idealistic orientations toward the future and reflect the hopes, wishes, and dreams of the individual. They represent life preferences "unsullied by anticipated constraints" (MacLeod 1987, 60). Expectations, however, take constraints squarely into account and represent realistic mobility orientations. Mickelson (1990, 46) refers to these realistic mobility orientations as concrete attitudes about social upgrading that are grounded in the different material realities that can limit social mobility. Thus, when marginalized individuals express high hopes for the future, they are less apt than higher-status persons to presume that they will achieve their desires, because they are more likely to recognize a host of situational factors (e.g., inadequate finances, an inequitable opportunity structure, and a differential reward system) that threaten to constrain their social mobility (Allen 1980; Berman 1975; Han 1969; Kerckhoff 1976; MacLeod 1987; Mickelson 1990; Ogbu 1974, 1987).

There is growing evidence that expectations, and not aspirations, are the more robust predictor of academic achievement and educational and occupational attainment (Hanson 1994; McLelland 1990; Mickelson 1990). Moreover, young women who express only limited mobility expectations are more likely to become teenage mothers, drop out of school, and find themselves relegated to low-skilled, low-wage work if any employment is to be found (Eckstrom et al. 1986; Fine and Zane 1989; Passmore 1987; Rosegrant 1985). If we are to better understand the process of upward mobility, productive participation in the labor force, and independence from governmental assistance, we must identify those factors that facilitate high expectations for the future, despite disadvantage. In other words, we must be able to explain how individuals like Cher and Sabrina develop optimistic expectations in the midst of circumstances that have been shown to limit the individual's assessment of her life chances.

Evidence abounds that structural constraints and institutionalized inequalities both within and outside of schools (e.g., differential teacher expectations, prejudicial ability grouping and tracking, inequitable school funding and financing of higher education, deindustrialization, job and housing discrimination) overwhelmingly account for why marginalized individuals are less likely to know success and mobility in the American context (e.g., American Association of University Women 1992; Bernstein 1977; Bourdieu and Passeron 1977; Bowles and Gintis 1976; Chunn 1989; Delpit 1995; Dusek and Joseph 1985; Fine 1991; Oakes 1985). Nevertheless, a pessimistic disposition toward the future can exacerbate oppressive conditions by making it less likely that one will take advantage of the opportunities, however limited, that one is afforded and thus will inadvertently intensify the income and employment problems one must confront (Fine and Rosenberg 1983).

In other words, it is not expectations in and of themselves that determine attainment, but how this social-psychological variable affects the probability that individuals will take actions that facilitate social upgrading and self-sufficiency. Sociologists, anthropologists, and psychologists have provided evidence that individuals' assessments of their prospects for success define the likelihood of their pursuing outcomes (e.g., higher levels of education, vocational training) and expressing behaviors (e.g., effort, hard work, perseverance, adherence to institutional norms and expectations) that are consistent with their goals and thus affect the likelihood that they will achieve their goals (e.g., Bandura 1982a, 1982b, 1986; Bourdieu 1977a, 1977b; Ford 1992; Ogbu 1974, 1987, 1994). Hochschild (1995) in particular has shown that although many poor African-Americans believe in the American dream—that personal aspirations may be achieved via hard work and effort—they are unlikely to translate that belief into action if (1) "they do not know how to start climbing the ladder of success" (p. 175); (2) they have a limited sense of confidence or self-efficacy; and (3) they recognize external factors that constrain their upward climb. In other words, unless low-income individuals have some sense that they can achieve their goals, they are unlikely to pursue them.[2]

By comparing the life stories of Cher and Sabrina with the other four girls who had similar aspirations for the future but were more pessimistic about their life chances, this chapter explores factors that determine how individuals who experience comparable degrees of disadvantage develop very different expectations for the future. I provide evidence that the social interactions of Cher and Sabrina gave them an advantage over their more pessimistic peers. Individual family members and teachers (sometimes referred to as significant others) provided them the social support necessary for enhancing their sense of efficacy. By persuading the girls of their capabilities, these significant others fostered the young women's confidence that they could achieve their ambitions. They also provided the scholastic assistance necessary for the girls to achieve academically, thereby enhancing the young women's chances for upward mobility. And, finally, they transmitted information about mobility strategies and pathways that enabled the young women to imagine realistic paths toward their goals. By contrast, the less optimistic girls received (1) ambiguous or contradictory messages about their potential for achieving their dreams, (2) inadequate or belated academic assistance, and (3) insufficient information about how they could climb the ladder of success in spite of external constraints. In short, while the future expectations and mobility of Cher and Sabrina were being nurtured by a number of individuals, Tina, Collette, Janine, and Benita failed to receive the same degree or quality of support.

The salience of individual sponsorship and support is troubling. It has been well documented that the neighborhood contexts in which these young women live are socially isolated, making it difficult for them to develop ties with individuals who have extensive knowledge of work- or education-related resources, information, strategies, and support that are likely to develop a strong sense of personal efficacy and facilitate upward mobility (Wilson 1987, 1996). Few will be lucky enough to meet people with the requisite knowledge to sponsor them effectively. Institutional sponsorship is therefore required. Formal institutions must adopt systems to provide the poor with work- or education-related resources, information, or strategies that generate the confidence and ability necessary for them to pursue social upgrading.

A secondary analysis, however, suggests that the young women in this study could not rely on their high school, the most significant formal institution in their lives, for such systematic support. I specifically consider how the dispositions of the teachers, the structure of teachers' work, and the organization of the counseling program did not support the girls' ambitions. By examining the culture and organization of the girls' high school, we can discover how the young women's expectations for the future and potential for self-sufficiency may have been circumscribed by an institution that is presumably designed to facilitate upward mobility.

Research Methods and Objectives

The life stories of the six girls featured in this chapter derive from a study of forty-six low-income[3] African-American students who attended two nonselective public high schools in Chicago (O'Connor 1996).[4] The data for this project were collected during the spring and fall of 1993, and the respondents were all sophomores during the 1992–1993 academic year.[5] The respondents were almost equally divided between males and females with each gender subsample equally represented by high and low achievers.[6]

Relying on the structured open-ended interview as the primary method of data collection, the project examined how the students conceived of the American opportunity structure and how they interpreted their own chances of achieving their aspirations. In light of these research emphases, the interview explored how students located race, class, and gender (if at all) in relation to hard work, individual effort, and education in explaining the process of status attainment. Interviews captured students' aspirations and expectations for the future and focused on how their biographies influenced their interpretations of opportunity, both at the level of the self and as a social phenomenon. Students discussed their experiences in the home, school, workforce, and neighborhood and recounted the status and functioning of significant others within these contexts. Since the respondents were both high and low achievers, the data garnered from the interviews also provided a means for examining how achievement varied with students' autobiographical accounts and perceptions of social and personal opportunity for mobility.

Selecting the Subsample for Study

Females were selected for this study because, as previously indicated, they are less likely than males to expect that they will achieve high levels of educational attainment and enter competitive, nontraditional occupations.[7] Women are also more likely to experience poverty and government dependency in their adult lives, and both of these social outcomes have been associated with low expectations of mobility.

The respondents were next selected because they had exaggerated risk profiles. Their social backgrounds included a greater number of factors that place individuals at risk for developing low expectations for the future, dropping out of high school, and being unemployed or marginally employed in the future. While the life of the average female respondent did not have more than four of the following eleven risk factors,[8] these six girls were in a subcategory of ten women who had seven or more of these factors:

1. Born to a teenage mother
2. Household headed by a single adult female
3. Caregiver addicted to drugs or alcohol

4. Head of household received less than a high school education
5. Head of household unemployed or working low-skilled, low-wage job
6. Parent or guardian involved in criminal activity
7. Family receiving AFDC or food stamps
8. Residing in public housing
9. Residing in an area of concentrated poverty
10. Participated in violent, criminal, or gang activity
11. Has a child or is pregnant

Of these ten girls only one had modest aspirations for the future (i.e., hoping only to graduate from high school and get "some kind of office work"). The remaining nine expressed interest in attending college. Six of these nine attended Burnside. Therefore, these six girls provided a "natural" opportunity to explore the role schools might play in reference to the students' future expectations and chances for self-sufficiency.

The life narratives of the six girls reveal how young women who attend the same public high school, share comparable background characteristics, and express similar aspirations for the future develop distinct interpretations of what their futures will bring. The two optimistic youth, Cher and Sabrina, are at the center of the discussion; their stories emphasize that significant others served as "keepers of their dreams" and increased their potential for self-sufficiency. The life stories of the more pessimistic youth (i.e., Tina, Benita, Janine, and Collette) confirm that the absence of support from significant others can affect expectations for the future and influence life chances. The discussion shows that the girls' expectations for the future were a function of (1) how others had defined their potential for mobility, (2) whether they had a basis for believing they could perform the tasks necessary to fulfill their ambitions, and (3) the extent to which they had insight into how they could navigate the pathways to their life dreams.

The Significance of Individual Sponsorship

Defining the Potential for Mobility

I begin by discussing how the optimistic girls recollect the expectations that had been established for them. Although Cher and Sabrina's mothers had been drug abusers and had not gone far in school, they were adamant that their girls have a better life. Sabrina explained:

[My mother] told me she don't want neither one of [her daughters] to be like her. She want me to be better. She said nobody in the family ever got as high as college. She want me to get further than college—do the best I can.

When Cher was asked whether anyone talked or acted in a way that made her feel that they believed school or education was important, she responded:

All of them did [i.e., her grandparents, Aunt Nee, and three first cousins]. My mother did too, even though she ain't go, you know. Parents always going to want you to do better than them. My mom she wants me to go to college and make something out of my life. That's what she's always saying she wants for me.

The extended kin of these young women reinforced the expectations of their mothers. Sabrina recalled how her Uncle Niles and his girlfriend, who had helped to raise her, were making plans for her future:

Every day my uncle and my aunty tell me I can't wait till my baby graduate from college. You going to do this for your graduation. We going to have this made. I'm going to have your dress made like this. What color you want your dress. I mean just actually making plans.

In accordance with Merton's (1968) theory of anticipatory socialization, these significant others not only may have enhanced Sabrina's positive orientation toward a social group (i.e., college graduates) to which she sought membership but also may have facilitated her ability to interpret this status shift as a given. Cher similarly indicated that her kinfolk expected great things of her. She reported that her Aunt Nee, who was "like a mother" to her, and two of her first cousins, Eileen and Deirdre, were "always harping on [her] about going to college."

If we presume that it is through the communication of expectations that individuals articulate what they believe others are capable of achieving (Haller and Portes 1973), such verbal messages may have persuaded Cher and Sabrina that their aspirations were realistic (Bandura 1982a, 1986). In comparison, the messages received by quasi-optimistic Tina and two of the pessimistic youth did not. Tina explained that both her uncle and her mother had expectations for her mobility. However, while her uncle unambiguously stated that he wanted Tina to be the "first girl" in the family to "finish high school and go on to college," her mother was more tentative in establishing college expectations for her. Tina explained that her mother told her to get enough education but if you can't go to college you just go to work with that [i.e., a high school diploma]. Cause if you can't go—you can't go. But if you can—just don't turn away from it—go.

Due to this expressed doubt about her chances of attending college, Tina may have been less convinced than Sabrina and Cher that college was a realistic option for her. She, nevertheless, had reason to have greater faith in her potential for mobility than either Collette or Janine.

While Tina's mother assumed that her daughter would receive at least a high school diploma and held out the possibility that she might attend college, the mothers of Collette and Janine had only expressed the desire that their daughters complete high school. Janine explained:

Because [my mother] ain't finish high school. Well she want all of her kids to finish high school. . . . So we can at least get some kind of job—some kind of legit job. See I ain't never—I never ain't really heard my mama say I want to see a high school diploma and then want to see a college diploma. She ain't really never say nothing like that. She said just as long as you have a high school diploma.

And unlike Tina, Janine and Collette did not indicate that anyone else they knew had established expectations for their mobility. These two pessimistic youth had received little verbal assurance that they had the potential for realizing their life goals. But while verbal assurance might facilitate a positive disposition toward the future, Benita's experience indicates that it is not necessarily sufficient.

Benita was still pessimistic about her life chances, though her grandfather consistently communicated his expectation that she would go to college:

My grandaddy he want me to hit the sky. He want me to go to school for college, the university—everything. He want me to do everything.

Benita, however, added, "But what he wants for me just don't feel real to me." When asked why his expectations didn't "feel real," she replied, "I don't know." Later in the interview, however, she stated that she did not believe that she was "smart enough" to go to college.[9] She explained that though her grandfather was "always tell[ing] [her that she was] smart and all of this" she did not feel comfortable with this definition of her ability because she had never done well in school. In her own words:

I felt funny [when he said that] because I wasn't used to hearing it. I ain't used to hear it from school or all my teachers.

Like the other pessimistic youth, Benita had not received the social support necessary for her to develop hard evidence that she was capable of meeting the tasks and demands associated with the roles to which she aspired.

Unlike Benita, Cher, Sabrina, and, to some extent, Tina had significant others who defined their potential for mobility as high, supporting their belief that they were capable of achieving their ambitions.

Status attainment research shows that the educational expectations of significant others is positively correlated with the target individual's mobility expectations (Porter 1974; Portes and Wilson 1976; Sewell, Haller and Ohlendorf 1970; Sewell, Haller, and Portes 1969). However, an individual's potential is inevitably confirmed or disavowed by the individual's experience with success and failure (Bandura 1982a, 1986; Ford 1992). Cher, Sabrina, and, to some extent, Tina facilitated their expectations with academic success. These girls had already learned that they could perform well in school.

Developing Capability Beliefs

Though their GPAs did not define them as high achievers in absolute terms, Cher, Sabrina, and Tina were clearly among the academic elite at Burnside High School. With GPAs of 3.2 (Tina), 2.8 (Cher), and 2.7 (Sabrina), they ranked second, tenth, and thirteenth in their sophomore class of 335 students. And though Burnside did not offer Advanced Placement classes, all three girls participated in varying degrees in the school's honors program. During their sophomore year, Cher was enrolled in two, and Sabrina in three, honors classes. Tina, however, was enrolled in only one honors class during that time. While Cher and Sabrina recall that with few exceptions they had been A-B students throughout grammar school,[10] Tina had been a C student until the seventh grade. As the following discussion will show, Tina's less rigorous academic schedule and relatively late academic blooming might be attributed to the fact that she had not received the same degree or quality of sponsorship as either Cher or Sabrina.

Unlike Tina, Cher and Sabrina recalled how their family members had prepped them for school success. Cher explained that when she "was real young like three and stuff" her cousins "would teach [her] address and stuff" and then would "brag" about the fact that "oh she know this she know that." She believed that this "attention made [her] want to do better." But this attention also ensured that she started school with numeracy and literacy skills that likely facilitated her academic achievement. Sabrina similarly received a "head start" from her Uncle Niles, who "played word games with [her]" and taught her "how to count" when she was "real little."

As the girls got older, family members continued to provide academic assistance. Cher stated that her Uncle James "helped [her] out education-wise." According to her:

> When he came over he used to try and bribe me to do math problems and stuff. And I would get upset if I didn't understand a problem—get mad—but he used to help me with my math and stuff.

And despite the drug addiction that plagued Sabrina's mother, she was often there to help Sabrina academically. Sabrina stated, "my mama didn't like math but she good in it and she would help me all the time when I was having trouble."

Both girls were in familial networks where individuals had the academic know-how and the wherewithal to jump-start and sustain academic achievement. But the optimistic students additionally identified a number of teachers who had "cared." They explained that these individuals "weren't just there to get the paycheck" or "to dress." They "took the time" to work with their students, and they also let the girls know when they were good at something. For example, Cher reported on Mr. Regis, her seventh-grade teacher:

> . . . by him being in a black school—a white man anyway he was kind of nervous—but he was always there for the students—tried to talk to them and help them and plus he would always tell me, you know, you write good and stuff.

Sabrina spoke of Ms. Davidson, her seventh- and eighth-grade teacher who was "just like a second mother" to her:

> I would get a 80 on a test. She would make me take it over for 100. I be like but ain't that good. Ain't that—that's a B. So what she want me to get a 100—a A.

Cher stated that her fourth-grade teacher "pushed [her] to do [her] best and be the best." And though both girls reported that it was easier to find grammar school teachers who "steady push, push, push, push you to do your best where[as] high school teachers push, push, that's all," they both had secondary school teachers who had taken a special interest in them. For example, Cher explained that when she was having trouble in her ninth-grade English class, her teacher "just kept pushing [her] and pushing [her] and finally [she] got a good grade." Similarly, Sabrina reported that her division teacher "never let up on her" and was "determined to make [her] a better student."

Tina did not receive this kind of in-school "care" until she met Mr. Shils in the seventh grade. She explained:

> [Mr. Shils] pushed me and told me I could do better when I didn't do as well as I could in school. He really boosted my energy, you know, told me to do—he told me you got a talent, you smart. So that's when I really decided, you know, I'm good at this school thing and that's when I really started trying.

Tina continued to receive instrumental academic assistance from teachers when she entered high school. There was her business teacher who pushed her as Mr. Shils had done, and her music teacher who was willing to "help her with [her] work" when she "didn't understand what was going on." But while quasi-optimistic Tina had received less academic assistance than the optimistic young women, she had received far more support than those who were pessimistic about their life chances and had only known academic mediocrity or school failure.

The pessimistic youth had GPAs of 0.27 (Benita), 0.52 (Collette) and 0.86 (Janine) and ranked 272nd, 226th, and 168th in their sophomore class. During their sophomore year they were enrolled in a number of remedial classes (Applied Mathematics, English with Support, General Science, Physical Science) and expected to take only those courses that were required for high school graduation (one year of science, two years of math, and no foreign language). These girls reported that in grammar school their performance was never higher than "satisfactory" and they often received "unsatisfactory" ratings or D's in school. Unlike the optimistic young women, these girls had not received an academic head start from their families. Benita reveals how this would necessarily place them at an academic disadvantage:

> I think some kids when they smaller their parents they work with them. You know, they don't let their child—some people their parents when they growing up they don't teach them nothing—they just wait till they get in school and just let the school do everything. And when they come home from school they don't work with them and they have to do their homework by theyself or don't go over the points. They don't have no time with them.

There was no absence of care on the part of these caretakers. But unlike those who surrounded Cher and Sabrina, these parents/guardians and their extended kin might not have retained the academic knowledge necessary for supporting the schooling activities of these children or may have been unaware that this was a role they should assume.

The work of Pierre Bourdieu (1977a, 1977b; Bourdieu and Passeron 1977) offers us insight into why these caretakers might not have assumed a more active role in the education of their children. Through his concept of cultural capital, Bourdieu maintains that the norms and expectations of schools (as they are revealed through pedagogy and curriculum as well as rules of social order and interaction) are consistent with the culture of the middle class. Low-income and working-class students who draw upon other social and cultural resources are therefore at a decided academic disadvantage in school. In accordance with Bourdieu's theory and findings, low-income and working-class parents, who are often less educated than their middle-class counterparts, are less familiar with the knowledge structures and linguistic patterns that are privileged in schools and are therefore less able to provide their children with the cultural capital necessary for accessing school knowledge. Annette Lareau (1987), building on Bourdieu's notion of cultural capital, revealed that the culture of a social class prescribes norms for how parents should participate in the education of their children. She found that in contrast to the cultural norms of the middle class, low-income and working-class parents are more apt to turn over the responsibility for educating their children to the schools. "Just as they [depend] on doctors to heal their children, they [depend] on teachers to educate them" (Lareau 1987, 81).

In sum, the optimistic students had the most robust indications of their capability to do well in school because they had received the social support necessary to have developed a track record of academic success. They had family members whose cultural knowledge and presumptions enabled them to develop their cultural capital in ways that were consistent with the norms and expectations of schools and facilitated their academic achievement. Additionally, they encountered teachers who established high expectations for their performance and provided them the necessary pragmatic assistance to meet these expectations. In direct contrast, the pessimistic youth, unable to rely on kin or school to support their academic performance, knew nothing but academic mediocrity or school failure and had the least evidence that they could meet the educational obligations that were associated with their ambitions. Thus, like Benita who did not believe she was "smart enough" to go to college, Janine stated that she didn't "know if [she could] hang" in college—"if [she] had what it takes." Similarly, when I asked Collette what were her chances of going to college, she responded, "You got be real smart to go to college" and left it at that.[11] These data support the relationship between capability beliefs and future expectations. However,

Tina's case reveals that while the development of strong capability beliefs may contribute to optimism toward the future, it does not ensure high expectations.

In contrast to these pessimistic students, quasi-optimistic Tina did not express insecurity about her academic ability. Because she did not know academic success until relatively late in her schooling career compared with the optimistic girls, she may not have developed as robust evidence of her capabilities. Nevertheless, the evidence she did receive as a consequence of teacher sponsorship seemed sufficient for her to believe that she personally had "what it takes" to realize her aspirations. But while Tina may not have questioned her ability to meet the tasks and demands associated with attending college, she worried that she would not be able to afford college. Thus her optimism was constrained by her inability to imagine how she could manage an external constraint.

Tina, like the optimistic youth, received information on how she could navigate the college admissions process. However, she had not received any insight into how she could overcome the single obstacle that she believed stood between her and her life aspirations: lack of money in the family. The optimistic girls, however, had significant others who provided them with pragmatic insight into how they could navigate mobility pathways and circumvent obstacles to social upgrading. With an ability to imagine how they could organize toward the future and pursue a realistic path toward their goals, these girls could interpret their aspirations as attainable.

Navigating Pathways to Upward Mobility

Sabrina vividly recalls the assistance provided by her division teacher:

> [Ms. Carter] made me take courses that she think good for me. When I—me and her will argue like around the time you picking your program. I mean your classes for next year. Me and her will argue for about two weeks . . . I wind up taking the classes anyway. Because, OK, like when I was in geometry I told her I didn't want algebra-trig. She told me it's good for me. It look good on my résumé for college. I was like I still don't want to take it because I don't want to be no sophomore all my life. And she was like go on and take it. And I was like I don't want to—I don't want to—I winded up taking it anyway. Now we arguing about ahm—they don't have calculus here no more so we arguing about analytical algebra/geometry. Now, I didn't want to take that. This make . . . four years of math. I told her ain't three good enough? She said it's three years required but four would look real good. I said OK.

The "push" provided by this teacher communicated her belief that Sabrina was academically able and should be college bound. Hence the mobility expectations of Sabrina's family were reinforced, and Sabrina's sense of efficacy and academic motivation was presumably strengthened. However, this "push" additionally communicated information that would facilitate Sabrina's admission to college and, therefore, her upward climb.

In most instances, admission to four-year institutions requires the high school applicant to have completed at least four years of English and history, three years of math and science, and two years of a foreign language. The applicant is also expected to take one of two college admissions tests: ACT or SAT. Sabrina's division teacher had not only informed her of the academic prerequisites for college and coerced her into taking a college prep curriculum, she also directed Sabrina to take an ACT preparation course that was being offered at the school. Additionally, she discussed financial aid options with her. According to Sabrina, Ms. Carter "got all down into it" and "told me about how I could get scholarships, and loans and a package and stuff." So though Sabrina rated the "amount of money in the family" as being "important" for getting ahead in America "because some parents don't have enough to pay your way to college," she, unlike Tina, did not worry that the financial limitations of her household would hinder her personal chances of "making it."

Cher relied on her family as opposed to school personnel for information about college admissions and financing. I asked her whether she had "talked to a teacher, counselor, or anyone about what you would have to do to get into college," and she responded:

> A lot of people in my family already done told me what classes to go on and take. Who to talk to. Go on and try and get in some [extracurricular] programs and stuff. And they told me to start taking a class for the SAT.

As a consequence of this information, Cher was participating in the ACT preparation course that was being offered at Burnside. She had participated on the track team during her freshman year in high school and was now trying out for the pom-pom squad. She also was taking a college prep curriculum.

Cher also required guidance as to how she could overcome the financial limitations of her household and afford college. She had a cousin who was attending Notre Dame on an academic scholarship and, therefore, was familiar with this method of financing a college education; but she had already realized that her grades might foreclose this as an option. However, she had one cousin who was using the G.I. bill to help finance his education at North Central State and another who was working on her B.A. while she was enlisted in the military. Having used the military as a means for accessing higher education and paying for college, these cousins, in turn, advised Cher about this financing strategy. Thus while Cher's cousins had not given her the depth of information on financial aid that Sabrina's teacher provided, Cher did not despair because she had an alternative strategy to realize her aspirations. Cher explained:

> I don't think I'm going to go [straight] to college for the money problems and stuff. And plus when I was in grammar school I always talk about yeah I'm going to get scholarships and all this, but then when I got to high school I didn't get all A's in my first year and I ain't getting all A's now—I'm like mostly A's and B's and plus I don't do too many sports activities. I ran track last year. I didn't get on the track team this year. So I was thinking, you know, I probably go to the army like my cousin. One he in the reserves and the other one she you know she making it. Other people be like that's just the white man's place that ain't no place for nobody black. And they right in a way 'cause why you fighting for people that don't treat you right. But you know they getting a lot of benefits you know they paying for them to go to school and stuff and they making it.

Cher realized that "by going through the army" it was "going to take longer to get through college." But she believed that she would "eventually get through."

In sum, there were critical differences in the information Cher and Sabrina received regarding how they might overcome the financial limitations of their households and pursue college. Sabrina's school sponsor communicated a greater breadth of knowledge on this matter. Both girls, nevertheless, imagined (albeit by referencing different strategies) that this constraint on their mobility could be negotiated.

In contrast to the optimistic youth, quasi-optimistic Tina had *only* received information on college admissions. One of her teachers was the coordinator of the ACT preparation course and had encouraged her to take it. Another had shown her a college catalogue that contained information on college prerequisites. Unlike Sabrina, Tina had no one pushing her to take the most rigorous course schedule. She was only enrolled in Honors U.S. history. She took "regular" English, "regular" geometry, "regular" chemistry, and no foreign language. However, she indicated that she was prepared to take a total of three years of science and four years of math. If she completed her anticipated academic course, she would still qualify for some four-year institutions.

No one helped Tina think through available options to meet the cost of college. In her words, "Money—that's about the only thing [stopping me from going to college]. Will I be able to afford college?" When I later asked her what did she think were her chances of getting the money to go to college, she responded in a very quiet voice that nearly trailed off into a whisper:

> I don't know—you know. I can't say if my grades are good enough for a scholarship, but I do know my mother ain't got the money to send me to college. I don't know.

She quickly added, however, "I'm going to finish high school even if I don't go to college." And as stated earlier, she felt that this alone would allow her life to be better than the one her mother had lived.

In contrast to Cher, Tina, and Sabrina, the pessimistic students had received almost no information on college admissions. When I asked them whether they had talked to anyone about what they needed to do to get into college, they all indicated that they had not. When I made inquiries about whether they had planned to take the SAT or the ACT, Collette said, "I don't know what that is." Benita responded "I took the SAT—I think this year—we take it every year." She, however, was confusing the SAT with the Test of Achievement Proficiency (TAP), which is given to Chicago's high school students each spring. And though both Janine and Benita discussed external barriers to realizing their aspirations, they had no idea how to navigate these obstacles and had received no advice.

Janine, who had expressed interest in becoming a registered nurse, explained that a second reason why she "probably wouldn't make it to college" was because "even before [she] even think[s] about going to college [she would] have to get a baby-sitter to watch [her kids] while [she went]." She was already having difficulty finding care for her children. Though Burnside had a child-care facility, it only accommodated twenty to twenty-five children at one time. In a school where more than forty female students become pregnant each year, there was no room for Janine's babies. Janine could not afford private care, and though her mother "helped out," she suffered from seizures that were getting worse as she got older. Janine did not think her mother would be able to help her out "much longer."

Janine, like Benita, also believed that the "amount of money in the family" mediated the individual's life chances. They both mentioned that economic privilege improved individuals' chances of getting ahead because it increased their access to college. After all, "it cost money to go to college." They knew of academic scholarships, but they both were aware that their current level of academic performance placed them out of the running for these awards. Benita indicated that she could probably "find the money" to attend a junior college, but she didn't want to attend "run-down colleges like Malcolm X [a local junior college]". She wanted to go to "a university." These girls were aware that if they maintained their current level of academic performance, they would be "lucky" to graduate from high school. However, even if they were to graduate, they had no insight into how they would negotiate those obstacles that hindered their access to the postsecondary education necessary to achieve their ambitions.

The constraints these young women discussed were not all tied to college matriculation. Benita recognized constraints that were more directly tied to the nature of the profession to which she aspired. She explained:

> You got to know how to get where you want to go cause nobody just ain't putting you there. . . . Well I want to be an actress but that don't really feel like a choice 'cause I don't know how to go about breaking into it or nothing.

Ironically, it was one of Benita's elementary school teachers who sarcastically suggested she should consider a career in acting because she "was a liar." Benita preferred to refer to her lying as "fantasy."

None of the pessimistic girls knew how to get where they wanted to go. They did not know how to navigate the pathways to their dreams and negotiate obstacles that inhibited their upward climb. Benita and Janine were desperate for strategies that would facilitate their mobility. They therefore concocted and pursued unrealistic mobility strategies. Benita, having stated that knowing the right people was important when it came to getting ahead in America, reported:

> [My chances of knowing the right people] ain't too good . . . I don't know the right people now. But I like to go to museums and all that stuff and I guess you could meet people through there. And I like going places so maybe I could overhear somebody talking about this job or something and I could just go in.

Janine similarly explained:

> Well, the one [volunteer job I had] at the hospital—I was looking at TV one day on the news and they was showing about girls—these girls and boys who had volunteered. And they showed one girl who had volunteered—and she had volunteered at a hospital and she was in a pharmacy part—they had her in the pharmacy part. And then when the summer came they had gave her a job because she had did it so well

and they felt as if she should be getting paid for what she was doing. And I was kind of hoping on something like that.

Their life stories also revealed that illegal mechanisms for acquiring the material trappings associated with social upgrading had also become attractive to them:

> INTERVIEWER: Last time we spoke you said that you were hoping to be a little less "negative"[12]—not doing auto theft and all that—how have things turned out?
>
> JANINE: Well I ain't do anything like that for a couple of months now. I'm trying to cut down. Cause I don't want my kids taken away or nothing—like with my mom.[13] But, you know, if that end up being the only option I got, what am I going do?
>
> INTERVIEWER: How much money do you make doing auto theft?
>
> JANINE: Like $150 to $200 a day.

Janine had been brought into the "auto theft trade" by her older brother, and she explained that this was one thing she "was real good at." If she could not imagine herself realizing any degree of mobility (much less all that she had hoped for) because she was not receiving adequate academic support or even sufficient child care to complete high school, what other options did she have? She and the other girls in the study were no different than most Americans in their desire for material things. Janine was clear in stating, "I like nice things and I like to have a lot of money in my pocket." She was aware that "that once a month check [i.e., welfare] wasn't nothing" and explained "you ain't getting no good paying job without a high school diploma—you barely finding work with a diploma." If Janine lacked the social support necessary to realize her mainstream notions of "making it," she like so many others would find alternative ways of becoming self-sufficient.[14]

Summarizing the Significance of Individual Sponsorship

The relationship between high academic achievement and high expectations for the future has been well documented (Carpenter and Fleishman 1987; Epps and Jackson 1988; Manski and Wise 1983). These case studies reveal that the differences in the girls' expectations for the future were not only associated with the types of support they received (or failed to receive) but the quality of that support (House 1987, 1988). The life stories of these six young women show that the girls only interpreted their aspirations as realizable when individual family members and teachers had supported their ability (both perceived and real) to achieve them. But the stories also illustrate the extent to which sponsorship is accidental. Chance encounters with caring teachers and birth into families with greater middle-class cultural capital distinguish the life stories of the optimistic young women. Moreover, the life stories of these girls conveyed that this mode of sponsorship may have operated via "cumulative advantage" (McLelland 1990). That is, those who were "lucky enough" to experience individual sponsorship early on may have been more likely to evoke sponsorship from others as they moved through time, because their early sponsorship enabled them to express the cultural capital that "marked them" as worthy of further support. The academic "head start" Sabrina and Cher received from kin may have made these students appear more "able" in school and, therefore, more deserving of teacher sponsorship.[15] As Cher said, "[My elementary school teachers] had me in programs [i.e., extracurricular and academic] and stuff and always wanted to help me because I always was smart and got good grades."

The role of chance is troubling here. These young women had been raised by individuals with limited levels of education and had grown up in areas of concentrated poverty. The odds were not good that they would develop intimate and sustained contact with individuals who could afford them the psychological, cultural, and informational resources necessary to facilitate their optimism. Both ethnographic and survey studies reveal that poorly educated individuals who reside in racially and socially isolated communities (1) often express limited expectations (though not aspirations) for their children because they are cognizant of the barriers that may inhibit their children's mobility; (2) are more likely to develop a cultural repertoire that is not only inconsistent with but also often generated in opposition to the norms and expectations of schools (e.g., Fordham 1988; Ogbu 1987); and (3) are less likely to have knowledge of opportunities and strategies that are likely to facilitate mobility in mainstream society (Sosin 1991; Wilson 1987, 1996). Consequently, it is luck that governs whether poor children growing up in poor neighborhoods have an opportunity to develop relationships with individuals who have extensive knowledge of work- and education-related resources necessary for sponsoring their upward mobility. In this context, the failure of most inner-city youth is assured. Public institutions, including schools, must assume the responsibility of providing these youth with the requisite support for maximizing their life chances. But do they? The climate and organization of Burnside High School—the formal institution that all six youth attended—could not support the aspirations of these young women.

The Failure of Institutional Support:
The Case of Burnside High

When visitors enter Burnside High School, they are greeted by the following sign:

> Hold Fast to Your Dreams for if Dreams Die
> Life is a Broken Winged Bird that Cannot Fly.
>   Langston Hughes
> Work to Achieve your Dreams

Burnside High School is a small, comprehensive, public high school in Chicago. It has fewer than one thousand students. Because it is a neighborhood high school, many of the community's "gifted" (those who perform well on standardized achievement tests) have been siphoned off by the city's magnet schools. The students are poor and with the exception of one Hispanic youth, they are all African-American. The school's mobility rate is over 50 percent. Average daily attendance is less than 70 percent, and almost 20 percent of the student body is chronically truant. More than three-quarters of the student population scores below grade level on standardized achievement tests, and the graduation rate hovers near 30 percent. In the 1992–1993 academic year, over 10 percent (more than forty cases) of the school's withdrawals were due to pregnancy.

In the following sections, I discuss how particular aspects of the culture and organization of Burnside High School were unlikely to facilitate high expectations for mobility. More precisely, there was little evidence that the disposition of the instructional staff, the structure of teachers' work, and the operation of the counseling programs could systematically support the ambitions of these young women.

The Instructional Climate and the Teachers

The instructional staff at Burnside consists of fifty-five classroom teachers, four guidance counselors, and one librarian. More than half of the instructional staff has taught for more than twenty years, and nearly two-thirds of the faculty have been assigned to Burnside for more than fifteen years. Eleven teachers reported to me that they had been in the school since the late 1960s. More than one-third of the faculty is white. With the exception of one staff member who is East Indian, the rest are African-American.

Like teachers in other urban schools, the faculty expresses frustration over student attendance, tardiness, and work habits. They are dismayed that some students don't even bring a pen or pencil to class. Repeatedly, they describe the students as "lazy" and "disrespectful." A few faculty members are more extreme in their comments—characterizing the youth as "animals." Both staff members and students report that one white faculty member has referred directly to the students as "niggers."

Those who taught in the school before the 1970s explain that Burnside was once a "good school." They report that "back then" the school was "integrated"; in addition to blacks, there were Greeks, Italians, and Jews, and the teachers received more "cooperation from the parents." The teachers attribute the school's decline to its "changing population." I was often told that the students "now" come from "single-parent households" and "broken homes" and are the products of "younger parents." The teachers blame the parents for the students' academic orientation, poor scholastic performance, and "inappropriate attitudes."

The students, in turn, complain that most of the classes are boring, few teachers allow them to actively participate in the learning process, and some teachers have so little control of the classroom that little instruction occurs. The youth also identify some teachers as racist and classist. They explain that these teachers stigmatize them and express low expectations because the students are African-American and overwhelmingly reside in "the projects." Many complain that most of the teachers are only there to get a "paycheck." Students do, however, report that individual teachers do try to make a difference. According to Tina:

> [Burnside] got some teachers who care, who will give you that extra help you need with your work when you don't understand or talk to you about personal problems, stuff like that. But most of them don't even care.

In a focus group interview with six juniors (four of whom had attended Burnside since their freshman year) I asked, "If you could change one thing about [Burnside] what would it be?" Without hesitation, one student responded:

> The teachers. They don't care. They don't want to teach. And some of them don't even have basic skills. Can't spell. Can't read. How you going to be teaching us what we need to know and you don't know yourself?

The other students sitting around the table responded by nodding their heads, offering "Amens" and other expressions of agreement.

The principal, a young black male, is also concerned about the attitudes and practices of his teaching staff. He walks Burnside's halls trying to ensure that his teachers are teaching. He worries that his teaching staff is "old and resistant to change," and he is anxious about what he perceives to be their poor class preparation. He provides financial and emotional support to those teachers who are attempting instructional innovation, and he haunts those classrooms where he suspects little instruction is taking place. He is also actively recruiting young black faculty members, hoping that they will be more "committed" to the student body and will bring enthusiasm and creativity to Burnside. The principal stated that many of his staff members were "in need of professional development," but he maintained that one of the factors that particularly hindered their performance was that they believed they were teaching "content" when they needed to understand that they were teaching "students." He explained: "Our kids need to be coerced into doing a job and coerced into doing the job well."

In the case studies of Cher, Sabrina, and Tina we recognize the significance of "coercion." We need only recall how the academic "push" they received from teachers facilitated their scholastic success. But few teachers at Burnside were committed to coercing Burnside students into doing a job and doing it well. They had low expectations of the students and did not believe it was their job to sponsor these youth this aggressively. Although the principal was making strenuous efforts to improve the instructional climate of the school, the culture at Burnside currently made it unlikely that students like Collette, Janine, and Benita, who entered high school at a disadvantage, would receive the academic support they required. They, therefore, had little chance of developing hard evidence that they were capable of meeting the educational demands that were commensurate with their life goals. But while the attitudes of the teaching body may have been wanting, we also must consider how the structure of teachers' work may have inhibited some teachers' ability to provide adequate support to a population that required substantial assistance.

The Structure of Teachers' Work

Research on restructuring efforts that improve student achievement has established a relationship between teacher collegiality and student performance. This research has shown that teacher collegiality that can be fostered via the development of smaller academic units, group planning, team teaching, and double-staffing (1) increased opportunities for students, particularly low achievers, to receive individualized or small group instruction (Glenn 1981; Levine and Eubanks 1989; Levine, Holdsworth, and Aquila 1987; Mamary and Rowe 1985; Venezky and Winfield 1979)and (2) facilitated teachers' commitment to improve student achievement (Glickman and Pajak 1986; Newmann 1981; Purkey and Smith 1983; Wynne 1980) and "carry out more substantial (and difficult) innovations that affect instruction" (Louis 1992, 141; see also Little 1982). Though most of these studies were conducted at the elementary level, case studies on effective intermediate and secondary schools serving at-risk populations found that the institutionalization of alternative types of learning arrangements that included schools-within-school, minischools, and reduced departmentalization were particularly beneficial to low achievers, who demonstrated substantial academic growth under these more intimate conditions (Levine and Eubanks 1989; Levine, Levine, and Eubanks 1984; Levine and Lezotte 1995). In sum, the research suggests that at-risk youth learn best when they work with a community of teachers who know them well and can provide them with the academic assistance they require.

Despite such findings, Burnside teachers, like most teachers in the United States, worked in isolation (Little 1990; Lortie 1975). There was no team teaching, nor was the school divided into smaller "academic houses" where teachers had the opportunity to know their students on a more intimate basis and to work cooperatively with other colleagues to improve instruction. Instead, the teachers were individually responsible for five classes each day. With a mean class size of twenty-one students, each teacher was responsible for personally meeting the needs of more than a hundred students per day. Under these circumstances, even the most well intentioned teacher could not adequately support the needs of each and every child in the classroom. In the following exchange, Benita recounts how some students—particularly those like herself who are academically underprepared—get lost when teachers' work is structured in this way:

> INTERVIEWER: You talked about peer pressure. Are there any other things that can prevent students from doing well in school?
> BENITA: Teachers. If the teachers downing [i.e., criticizing] the students and don't have enough interest in the students, you know, they down. And I feel as though public schools got too many students in one class, and kids don't have enough one-on-one attention. 'Cause they got twenty students or thirty students in one class, somebody going to be over here talking and somebody going to be over here playing cards and somebody over here going be sleep. But like the school I wish I could go to—the military school—they only got seven to like ten kids in one class and I feel as if you can get one-on-one attention and the teacher can look straight, you know, and if you over here sleep the teacher can wake you up. But by you having all those kids in the classroom it can really make it boring.
> INTERVIEWER: When you were in school, did you feel you weren't getting enough attention?

BENITA: Yeah. Because like when you have a problem on your paper and you need help and you be raising your hand for like thirty minutes. And the teacher be taking all day. They have to do this and this and this. If they got seven students in one class, they can get to you faster and do it there. Because I be getting like frustrated. And you don't always like to feel you can't do the work and then you ain't getting no help. So you don't want to just sit there feeling stupid. And then they got all them other students and don't really have time to help you.

Given the constraints of working in an environment where teachers function in isolation and the demands of the populations are great, many teachers must make unenviable choices. One teacher explained:

These kids have so many needs, and no one person has that much energy and time to give. I would be burned out if I tried to realistically touch each and every one of them—and then I wouldn't be good to any of them. So though it's terrible to say, I bet on the ones who look like they have a chance and give them all that I know how to give.

According to Lipsky (1980), this is the dilemma of the street-level bureaucrat. Teachers and other agents must carry out the duty of public bureaucracies (e.g., schools, social service agencies, police precincts) and dispense services while operating under considerable constraints (e.g., tremendous need, insufficient time, limited human and material resources). To deal with the difficulties and indeterminacies of their role, they often "develop routines to deal with the complexity of their work tasks" (Lipsky 1980, 83). Often bureaucrats ration services in accordance with the logic of triage—withholding services from those who presumably have a lower *probability* of benefiting from the expenditure of already limited resources (Lipsky 1980). But because street-level bureaucrats are afforded considerable discretion in meeting their roles and obligations, their assessments of who has a lower probability of benefiting from their intervention is not patterned after official guidelines and is subject to "occupational and personal biases, including prejudices that blatantly and subtly permeate the society" (Lipsky 1980, 85). Consequently, it "should be no surprise that self-fulfilling prophecies run throughout street-level bureaucracies" (Lipsky 1980, 114). But what are the cues by which teachers ration their services? How do they determine the probability by which individual students will benefit from the expenditure of scarce time and resources?

In light of the data already discussed, the teachers at Burnside High School may have been more apt to provide academic help to students like

Cher, Sabrina, and Tina who, as a consequence of previous home tutelage and/or teacher assistance, displayed scholastic skills that made them "look like they had a chance" to "make it." Conversely, the academic disadvantages that Janine, Benita, and Collette displayed made it less likely that teachers would "bet on" them and provide the substantial academic support they required to develop capability beliefs that were consistent with their ambitions. In the absence of such sponsorship, these young women were unlikely to develop high expectations for their futures.

But it was not only the instructional climate and the structure of teachers' work that inhibited these girls' ability to imagine that they could realize their dreams. The counseling program was not designed to provide adequate support for those who imagined themselves as college bound and aspired to middle- and upper-middle-class occupations.

The Counseling Program

Each incoming class at Burnside High School was assigned to a counselor who was responsible for following these students as they moved through their academic career at the school. Administrators presumed that this structure would allow counselors to better know their advisees and develop a more precise gauge of students' individual needs and interests. Therefore, each student would be afforded the supervision and guidance they required to make "successful transitions" to further education and employment. But these opportunities for "one-on-one" counseling were also supplemented with a group guidance program that targeted "study skills" in grade 9, "careers" in grade 10, "college prep" in grade 11, and "postsecondary planning" in grade 12.

Because the students featured in this chapter had been interviewed during their sophomore year, none of them had had the opportunity to attend the college prep seminar. But neither had they benefited from individual counseling. While we might presume that the poor attendance of Benita, Janine, and Collette circumscribed the opportunities they would have had to meet with their counselor, the three students who attended school regularly and were doing well academically indicated that their counselor, Mr. Donlevy, had not provided much guidance on how they could make the transition to college.

Sabrina stated that Mr. Donlevy had "given her some information—some [college] brochures and stuff," but he "didn't really get down into it" (i.e., into college admissions and financing) like her division teacher had done. When I asked Cher whether she had received any help from the counseling office, she responded, "he ain't no help." Tina reported that during division, counselors sometimes dropped off "papers" on college (i.e., college brochures). However, there were no structured opportunities to follow up on these notices:

> TINA: It's just like they drop the papers off, you know, and then we'll just pass them out and then they explain if you have questions you know we can go and talk to them about it.
>
> INTERVIEWER: Have you ever received information that was passed out and then later gone to talk to the counselors?
>
> TINA: No. To tell you the truth I ain't never been to see my counselor. I know what he look like, but I ain't really never talked to him or nothing, and it ain't like he came looking for me or nothing.

Although some of Donlevy's inability to effectively guide his advisees might be attributed to incompetence,[16] his work was also hampered by the size of his counseling load. No individual counselor could have provided adequate supervision and guidance to 335 students. And because Burnside's counselors were overloaded, program officers regularly scheduled students for classes without counselor input and without sufficient insight into the students' academic needs or personal aspirations. As revealed by the following exchange between a program officer and a student who was transferring in from a high school for pregnant girls, this counseling structure made students exceptionally vulnerable in a climate and culture that had already established low academic expectations for the student body. I sat in on one meeting:

> STUDENT: Do I need to take chemistry?
>
> OFFICER: No, but if you want to go to college, you'll have to take a second lab. You only have biology now. Do you want to take it?
>
> STUDENT: No.
>
> OFFICER: OK. Well you can take Home Economics, Fashion, Food 1, Food 2.
>
> STUDENT: Food 1, What's that?
>
> OFFICER: Cooking—preparing food. You might want to be a chef at McDonald's [not in a fully serious tone].
>
> STUDENT: Chef at McDonald's—I didn't know there were chefs at McDonald's. [turns to me and smiles].
>
> OFFICER: You also need some consumer education. You can take sales.
>
> STUDENT: What's sales?
>
> OFFICER: I think you'll prefer sales—accounting has a little math in it.
>
> STUDENT: No, I don't want that.
>
> OFFICER: [Continues checking that student has sufficient credit in the other academic areas] OK, we're done.

With a counseling structure that failed to provide adequate supervision and guidance to even those who attended school on a regular basis and did well, students like Collette, Janine, and Benita had little hope of receiving guidance. While these young women may have had big dreams for the future, they had little reason to interpret their aspirations as realistic. And even if we entertain the thought that the ambitions of these young women were unrealistic, given their long histories of academic mediocrity and failure, there are two questions with which we must wrestle.

First, who must assume accountability for their poor performance in school? When we consider the cultural capital that is privileged in schools and the limited likelihood that these girls would have been able to develop such capital in their homes, who is responsible for affording them with the skills and knowledge they require for academic success? Second, if we maintain that the girls' ambitions were in fact unrealistic, what were the chances that they would receive the advice required to pursue alternative career options? And how realistic would such options be if they were not afforded the academic assistance necessary for graduating from high school? In sum, Collette, Janine, and Benita, unlike the more optimistic young women, were at an alarming disadvantage in developing high expectations for their future.

Summary and Conclusion

This analysis revealed that students cannot hold fast to their dreams without sufficient sponsorship. Sponsorship, or the lack thereof, affected the future expectations of six women who shared comparable background characteristics and expressed similar educational and occupational ambitions. Despite growing up in poverty, two of the young women expected to realize their aspirations to attend college and assume middle-class professions. Their optimism was associated with contact with individuals who (1) established high expectations for their mobility, (2) provided them with the assistance they required to achieve academic success that would facilitate their educational attainment and enhance their capability beliefs, and (3) afforded them knowledge of how they could negotiate external constraints on making it. But the opportunity for individual sponsorship in the lives of these young women was a consequence of chance. More often than not, young people growing up in these circumstances do not develop relationships with such individuals. It was not surprising that the remaining young women featured in the chapter had not received the kind or degree of support that had been afforded the optimistic young women. Instead, these girls had limited expectations for the future because others had (1) conveyed ambiguous or limited expectations about their prospects for upward mobility, (2) provided them with little or belated assistance in developing academic skills and knowledge that would facilitate their educational success and social upgrading, and (3) failed to afford them insight into how they could negotiate external barriers that stood between them and their life goals.

Given that the odds of encountering individual sponsors do not favor those who are poor and reside in areas of concentrated poverty, one would hope that public institutions such as schools would provide the support such young people need to develop high expectations for mobility and an ability to organize toward that end. However, a secondary analysis revealed that particular aspects of the climate and organization of the high school the girls attended made it unlikely that without very good luck, they and others like them would receive the sponsorship they needed.

Burnside teachers expressed low expectations for the students, and the structure of teachers' work seemed to prevent even the most "committed" Burnside teachers from providing their students with adequate academic support. Burnside teachers operated in isolation. In a context where students' needs are high and human resources are scarce, teachers who work in isolation are more apt to operate with a system of triage, providing intervention to those students who look like they will make it. Under this system, those who enter high school with significant academic disadvantages will be the least likely to receive the assistance they require. They will be more susceptible to developing low expectations for their own mobility because they have not had sufficient opportunity to develop evidence that they are capable of meeting the tasks and demands associated with their ambitions.

Finally, the counseling structure at Burnside High School magnified the likelihood that its students, particularly those who were already doing poorly in school, would develop low expectations for their future. Counselors were overloaded and could not reasonably meet the needs of all their charges. Students were not systematically provided with information on how they could organize toward their dreams or even pursue alternative life options.

These findings suggest that if we are to enhance the future expectations of inner-city youth and maximize their life chances we must (1) explore different processes (including teacher preparation, training, and recruitment) by which we might raise the expectations teachers have for these youth; (2) reexamine how we might best reorganize the structure of teachers' work to give them more space, time, and energy to offer disadvantaged students greater and more effective social and academic assistance; and (3) develop alternative mechanisms for providing youth with adequate academic, college, and career counseling, given shrinking city budgets that prevent us from hiring additional school counselors. In sum, if we are to improve the life chances of poor children growing up in the inner city, we must continue to examine how teacher dispositions, the structure of teachers' work, and counseling structures can function in concert to provide the disadvantaged with a more consistent and reliable system of sponsorship that would enable them to hold fast to their dreams.

NOTES

1. With the exception of Cher, all of them lived in the same west-side public housing development. Cher lived in a public housing development on the south side of the city.

2. Hochschild (1995) also argues that the actions of poor African-Americans are often inconsistent with their articulated belief in the American dream because some simply acquiesce to the dominant ideology while others express "unwarranted optimism." These findings are not, however, relevant to these six women as most were not optimistic about their futures and those who were optimistic did not express unfettered renderings of the dominant ideology (see O'Connor 1997 for more discussion on these matters).

3. Less than a quarter of the respondents ($n = 11$) had a parent or guardian who had received postsecondary school training or education, and more than a third ($n = 16$) indicated that their caretakers had received neither a high school degree nor its equivalent. In more than half of the cases the head of the household was either unemployed ($n = 18$) or working low-skilled and minimum-wage work ($n = 6$; e.g., stock clerk, short-order cook, baby-sitter, paid parent volunteer). Some "parents" ($n = 9$) had semiskilled, nonunion jobs (e.g., nurse's aide, office clerk, bartender, steelworker, security guard) while others ($n = 13$) were skilled or civil service employees (e.g., LPN, typist, keypunch operator, bookkeeper, school bus driver, postal worker, Board of Education janitorial or cafeteria worker). Despite the range in "parents'" employment statuses, the economic constraints on the students' households are evident from the fact that they all qualified for free or reduced lunch.

4. For each month that school was in session during the period of data collections (i.e., March, April, May, June, September, October, and November of 1993), both schools received a minimum of two site visits per month. There were, however, periods of concentrated visits to each school where the focal school was visited anywhere from one to three times per week for two months in the spring and one month in the fall. Although no site visit was designated solely for observation (i.e., each visit allotted time for staff and student interviews), field observation notes were generated for each visit to the school. In most cases, a specific topic (e.g., student behavior during passing; students entering or leaving school building; classroom activity during the first fifteen minutes of a period; local school council meeting; physical appearance of the building; report card pickup) or school area (e.g., lunchroom; counselor's office; attendance center; library; bathrooms) and the commensurate activity was targeted for observation. Serendipitous observations also were included in the field notes.

5. At one site (i.e., Burnside High School), I also conducted interviews with the principal and members of the local school council as well as observed local school council meetings as a consequence of my work on a second project that explored school-based management in Chicago.

6. High achievers were defined as students who had a grade point average (GPA) of 2.5 or greater and ranked within the top 5 percent of the sophomore class; low achievers were defined as having a GPA of 1.5 or less and preferably ranked in the bottom 25 percent of the sophomore class. In the first school, the sophomore class was comprised of 335 students. The highs in this school ranked within the top 18 and had GPAs that ranged from 2.5 to 3.33 with a mean of 2.90. The lows ranked between 141 and 314 and had GPAs that ranged from 0.00 to 1.01 with a mean of 0.47. In the second school, the sophomore class was comprised of 441 students. The highs were ranked within the top 19 in the class and their GPAs ranged from 2.61 to 3.77 with a mean of 2.93. The lows' GPAs ranged from 0.38 to 1.14 with a mean of 0.89. Grades indirectly capture students' willingness to work hard in and accommodate to the norms and expectations of school (Jackson 1968). Thus while in absolute terms many of the high achievers seemed to exhibit modest academic achievement (i.e., 14 of the 23 had less than a 3.00 average), their GPAs suggested that relative to the low achievers in this study they were putting considerable time and energy into school. The interviews confirmed that the low achievers often did not try in school and had poor attendance records.

7. In the context of this paper, "nontraditional" occupations refer not only to those occupations associated with the sports and entertainment industry, but also, in the case of women, to traditionally male occupations (e.g., computer science, business administration).

8. The following represent the statistical distribution of the risk factors: mode = 3; mean = 4; median = 4; range = 2–8.

9. Benita also indicated that "trying" to get that far in school may not be worth the effort because "they going to give the white man the job before they give the black man." I have previously reported (O'Connor 1996) that unlike optimistic respondents, Benita and other pessimistic youth were less likely to have had intimate and sustained contact with black individuals who had achieved high levels of educational and occupational attainment and, therefore, seemingly defied racial (if not more profound constraints) on "making it." Without "concrete" evidence that individuals like themselves had the potential (though a less than equitable chance) for social upgrading, youth like Benita had little reason to imagine that upward mobility was within the realm of that which was possible. These models of upward mobility, however, "influence ego indirectly though their own aspiration and level of attainment" (Haller and Portes 1973, 71). Consequently, they are not discussed in this chapter, which is concerned with sponsorship—an animated, proactive, and conscious effort on the part of some to facilitate directly the mobility of others.

10. The only exception to this was Cher, who reported the following: "I always got good grades except for in fourth grade I almost failed cause, you know, because at that time I was getting picked on and stuff—wouldn't fight back for myself. I had gotten picked on first on up to sixth because I ain't dress like the other kids did. I didn't have all that they did. And I wouldn't fight back for myself."

11. At an earlier point in the interview, Collette indicated that her mother had told her that she had to stop saying that she was "stupid."

12. I used the term "negative" because this is how Janine had described her engagement in auto theft.

13. Cher explained that her mother had been "a big-time drug dealer." After she was arrested for drug dealing, the Department of Child and Family Services determined that she was unfit to care for her children and custody was temporarily ceded to Cher's aunt. Cher lived with her aunt between the ages of ten and fourteen.

14. Benita informed me that she had already been arrested for robbery. She and two of her friends had snatched a purse because they "needed some money."

15. Werner and Smith (1992), referencing Scarr and McCartney's (1983) work on how individuals evoke supportive environments, provided evidence that individuals who were "intelligent" were more likely to receive the support necessary for facilitating their educational resilience.

16. In my interviews with three Burnside teachers, they indicated that Mr. Donlevy "didn't know anything." They explained that he provided "lump-sum orientations to freshmen" and sometimes held "class meetings" but failed to provide "real one-on-one college or job guidance."

REFERENCES

Allen, W. R. 1980. "Preludes to Attainment: Race, Sex, and Student Achievement Orientations." *Sociological Quarterly* 21:65–79.

American Association of University Women Educational Foundation. 1992. *How Schools Shortchange Girls.* The AAUW Report, Executive Summary.

Bandura, A. 1982a. "Self-efficacy Mechanism in Human Agency." *American Psychologist* 37:122–47.

———. 1982b. "The Self and Mechanisms of Agency." In *Psychological Perspectives on the Self, Vol.1,* ed. J. Suls, 122–47. Hillsdale, NJ: Erlbaum.

———. 1986. *Social Foundations of Thought and Action: A Social Cognitive Theory.* Englewood Cliffs, NJ: Prentice-Hall.

Berman, G. S. 1975. "Occupational and Educational Goals and Expectations: The Effects of Race and Sex." *Social Problems* 23 (2): 166–81.

Bernstein, B. 1971. *Class, Codes, and Control.* London: Routledge.

Bourdieu, P. 1977a. "Cultural Reproduction and Social Reproduction." In *Power and Ideology in Education,* ed. J. Karabel and A. H. Halsey, 487–511. New York: Oxford University Press.

———. 1977b. *Outline of a Theory of Practice.* Cambridge: Cambridge University Press.

Bourdieu, P., and J. Passeron. 1977. *Reproduction in Education, Society and Culture.* London: Sage.

Bowles, S., and H. Gintis. 1976. *Schooling in Capitalist America: Education Reform and the Contradictions of Economic Life.* New York: Basic Books.

Carpenter, P. G., and J. A. Fleishman. 1987. *Youth Achievement and the Structure of Inner-City Communities.* Chicago: University of Chicago Press.

Chunn, E. W. 1989. "Sorting Black Students for Success and Failure: The Inequity of Ability Grouping and Tracking. In *Black Education: A Quest for Equity and Excellence,* ed. W. D. Smith and E. W. Chunn, 93–106. New Brunswick: Transaction Publishers.

Crowley, J. E., and D. Shapiro. 1982. "Aspirations and Expectations of Youth in the United States, Part I Education and Fertility." *Youth and Society* 13 (4): 391–422.

Dawkins, M. P. 1981. "Mobility Aspirations of Black Adolescents: A Comparison of Males and Females." *Adolescence* 16 (63): 701–10.

Delpit, L. 1995. *Other People's Children.* New York: The New Press.

Dusek, J. B., and G. Joseph. 1985. "The Bases of Teacher Expectancies." In *Teacher Expectancies,* ed. J. B. Dusek, 229–50. Hillsdale, NJ: Erlbaum.

Eckstrom, R. B., M. E. Goertz, J. M. Pollock, and D. A. Rock. 1986. "Who Drops Out of High School and Why? Findings from a National Study." *Teachers College Record* 82 (2): 356–73.

Epps, E. G., and K. W. Jackson. 1988. "The Educational Attainment Process among Black Youth." In *Desegregating America's Colleges and Universities: Title VI Regulation of Higher Education,* ed. J. B. Williams III, 137–58. New York: Teachers College.

Fine, M. 1991. *Framing Dropouts: Notes on the Politics of an Urban Public High School.* Albany: State University of New York Press.

Fine, M., and P. Rosenberg. 1983. "Dropping Out of High School, the Ideology of School and Work." *Journal of Education* 165:257–72.

Fine, M., and N. Zane. 1989. "Bein' Wrapped Too Tight: When Low-Income Women Drop Out of High School." In *Dropouts from School: Issues, Dilemmas, and Solutions,* ed. L. Weis, E. Farrar, and H. G. Petrie, 23–53. Albany: State University of New York Press.

Ford, M. E. 1992. *Motivating Humans: Goals, Emotions, and Personal Agency Beliefs.* Newbury Park, CA: Sage.

Fordham, S. 1988. "Racelessness as a Factor in Black Students' School Success: A Pragmatic Strategy or Pyrrhic Victory?" *Harvard Educational Review* 58 (1): 54–84.

Glenn, B. 1981. *What Works? An Examination of Effective Schools for Poor Black Children.* Cambridge, MA: Harvard University Center for Law and Education.

Glickman, C. D., and E. F. Pajak. 1986. *A Study of School Systems in Georgia Which Have Improved Criterion Referenced Test Scores in Reading and Mathematics from 1982–1985.* Athens, GA: University of Georgia, Department of Curriculum and Supervision, ERIC, ED 282 317.

Haller, A. O., and A. Portes. 1973. "Status Attainment Processes." *Sociology of Education* 46:51–91.

Han, W. S. 1969. "Two Conflicting Themes: Common Values versus Class Differential Values." *American Sociological Review* 34:679–90.

Hanson, S. 1994. "Lost Talent: Unrealized Educational Aspirations and Expectations among U.S. Youths." *Sociology of Education* 67 (3): 159–83.

Hochschild, J. L. 1995. *Facing up to the American Dream: Race, Class, and the Soul of the Nation.* Princeton, NJ: Princeton University Press.

House, J. S. 1987. "Social Support and Social Structure." *Sociological Forum* 2:135–47.

———. 1988. "Structures and Processes of Social Support." *American Review of Sociology* 14:293–318.

Jackson, P. 1968. *Life in Classrooms.* New York: Holt, Rinehart.

Kerckhoff, A. C. (1976). "The Status Attainment Process: Socialization or Allocation." *Social Forces* 52 (2): 368–81.

Lareau, A. 1987. "Social Class Differences in Family-School Relationships: The Importance of Cultural Capital." *Sociology of Education* 60 (2): 73–85.

Levine, D. U., and E. Eubanks. 1989. "Organizational Arrangements at Effective Secondary Schools." In *Organizing for Learning,* ed. H. J. Walberg and J. J. Lane, 41–49 Reston, VA: National Association of Secondary School Principals.

Levine, D. U., S. Holdsworth, and F. D. Aquila. 1987. "Achievement Gains in Self-Contained Chapter I Classes in Kansas City." *Educational Leadership* 44 (6): 22–23.

Levine, D. U., R. F. Levine, and E. E. Eubanks. 1984. "Characteristics of Effective Inner-City Intermediate Schools." *Phi Delta Kaplan* 64 (10): 707–11.

Levine, D. U., and L. W. Lezotte. 1995. "Effective Schools Research." In *Handbook on Multicultural Education,* ed. J. Banks and C. M. Banks, 525–47. New York: Simon & Schuster.

Lipsky, M. 1980. *Street-Level Bureaucracy: Dilemmas of the Individual in Public Services.* New York: Russell Sage Foundation.

Little, J. W. 1982. "Norms of Collegiality and Experimentation: Workplace Conditions of School Success." *American Educational Research Journal* 19:325–40.

———. 1990. "The Persistence of Privacy: Autonomy and Initiative in Teacher's Professional Relations." *Teachers College Record* 91 (4): 509–36.

Lortie, D. C. 1975. *Schoolteacher: A Sociological Study.* Chicago: University of Chicago Press.

Louis, K. S. 1992. "Restructuring the Problem of Teachers' Work." In *The Changing Contexts of Teaching: Ninety-first Yearbook of the National Society of the Study of Education, Part I,* ed. A. Lieberman, 138–56. Chicago: University of Chicago Press.

MacLeod, J. 1987. *Ain't No Makin' It: Leveled Aspirations and Attainment in a Low-Income Neighborhood.* Boulder, CO: Westview.

Mamary, A., and L. A. Rowe. 1985. "Flexible and Heterogeneous Instructional Arrangements to Facilitate Mastery Learning." In *Improving Student Achievement though Mastery Learning Programs,* ed. D. U. Levine, 203–22. San Francisco: Jossey-Bass.

Manski, C. F., and D. A. Wise. 1983. *College Choice in America.* Cambridge: Harvard University Press.

Marini, M. M. 1984. "Women's Educational Attainment and the Timing of Entry into Parenthood." *American Sociological Review* 49:491–511.

Marini, M. M., and E. Greenberger. 1978. "Sex Differences in Occupational Aspirations and Expectations." *Sociology of Work and Occupations* 5 (2): 147–78.

McLelland, K. 1990. "Cumulative Disadvantage among the Highly Ambitious." *Sociology of Education* 63 (April): 102–21.

Merton, R. K. 1968. *Social Theory and Social Structure.* New York: The Free Press.

Mickelson, R. A. 1990. "The Attitude-Achievement Paradox among Black Adolescents." *Sociology of Education* 63:44–61.

Newmann, F. M. 1981. "Reducing Alienation in High Schools: Implications of Theory." *Harvard Educational Review* 51:546–64.

Oakely, A. 1981. "Interviewing Women: A Contradiction in Terms. In *Doing Feminist Research,* ed. H. Roberts, 30–61. London: Routledge.

Oakes, J. 1985. *Keeping Track: How Schools Structure Inequality.* New Haven, CT: Yale University Press.

O'Connor, C. 1996. "Optimism Despite Limited Opportunity: Schooling Orientation and Agency Beliefs amongst Low-Income, African-American Students. Unpublished diss., University of Chicago, Chicago.

———. 1997. "Dispositions Toward (Collective) Struggle and Educational Resilience in the Inner City: A Case Analysis of Six African-American High School Students." *American Educational Research Journal* 34 (4): 593–629.

Ogbu, J. U. 1974. *The Next Generation: An Ethnography of Education in an Urban Neighborhood.* New York: Academic Press.

———. 1987. "Variability in Minority School Performance: A Problem in Search of an Explanation." *Anthropology and Education Quarterly* 18 (4): 312–34.

———. 1994. "Racial Stratification and Education in the United States: Why Inequality Persists. *Teachers College Record* 96:264–98.

Passmore, D. 1987. *Employment of Young GED Recipients.* American Council on Education, Research Brief No. 14, September 1987.

Porter, J. N. 1974. "Race, Socialization and Mobility in Educational and Early Occupational Attainment." *American Sociological Review* 39:303–16.

Portes, A., and K. L. Wilson. 1976. "Black-White Differences in Educational Attainment." *American Sociological Review* 41:414–31.

Purkey, S. C., and M. S. Smith. 1983. "Effective Schools: A Review." *The Elementary School Journal* 83 (4): 427–52.

Rosegrant, J. K. 1985. "Choosing Children." Master's thesis, Harvard College.

Scarr, S., and K. McCartney. 1983. "How People Make Their Own Environments: A Theory of Genotype-Environment Effects." *Child Development* 54:424–35.

Sewell, W. H., A. O. Haller, and G. W. Ohlendorf. 1970. "The Educational and Early Occupational Status Attainment Process: Replication and Revision." *American Sociological Review* 35:1014–27.

Sewell, W. H., A. O. Haller, and A. Portes. 1969. "The Educational and Early Occupational Attainment Process." *American Sociological Review* 34:82–92.

Sosin, M. R. 1991. "Concentration of Poverty and Social Isolation of the Inner City Poor." Presentation provided at the Chicago Urban Poverty and Family Life Conference, cosponsored by the Irving B. Harris Graduate School of Public Policy Studies at the University of Chicago and the Social Science Research Council of New York.

Venezky, R. L., and L. F. Winfield. 1979. *Schools That Succeed Beyond Expectations in Teaching Reading.* Newark: University of Delaware, ERIC, ED 177 484.

Werner, E. E., and R. S. Smith. 1992. *Overcoming the Odds: High Risk Children from Birth to Adulthood.* Ithaca, NY: Cornell University Press.

Willis, P. E. 1977. *Learning to Labor.* Aldershot: Gower.

Wilson, W. J. 1987. *The Truly Disadvantaged: The Inner City, the Underclass, and Public Policy.* Chicago: University of Chicago Press.

———. 1996. *When Work Disappears: The World of the New Urban Poor.* New York: Vintage Books.

Wynne, E. A. 1980. *Looking at Schools: Good, Bad, and Indifferent.* Lexington, MA: Heath.

CHAPTER 6

On the Outside Looking In: Low-Income Black Men's Conceptions of Work Opportunity and the Good Job

Alford A. Young Jr.

> If you know a place that's applying, taking applications for secretary, and you know you can't type twenty-five words a minute, but you can type some words within a minute's time, I mean what is it going to hurt to go fill out that application. Nine times out of ten you might get the job. They might say, "Well look, we'll find someone to do the typing," or the boss might be able to type better than you. He do his own typing and you could do the rest of the work. See, just do it. That's what I mean.

These are the remarks of Joseph,[1] a twenty-three-year-old black man from the ABLA Public Housing Development on the west side of Chicago.[2] Joseph has held two full-time jobs in his life: one as a message courier, the other at McDonald's. Neither of the jobs lasted more than a few months.[3] He explained that when he was not working, he spent his time trying to find odd jobs in order to save money so that he could return to school. Thus far his efforts have borne no success.

For individuals who have experienced consistent employment, Joseph's remarks might seem absurd. He displays little understanding of how prospective employees are evaluated and how duties are assigned in the workplace. When considered in the context of his life experiences, however, his comments reflect the thinking of many young adults who have little or no formal employment history. Their lack of experience prevents them from developing sufficient insight into employer-employee relations and assessments of competence for employment.

Like Joseph, the other twenty-five young black men discussed in this chapter have spent almost all of their adult years outside the workforce. Yet they have resolute notions of what constitutes the "good job." This chapter argues that for these men the attributes of a good job are not limited to a secure and satisfactory salary, but also include qualities such as autonomy, fringe benefits, respect at the worksite, and prospects for advancement. These men are also clear about the site for good jobs—the blue-collar industrial sector, which contains the manual skilled employment options most of these men consider to be their most appropriate and desired jobs. However, this is the very sector of the urban occupational sphere that has been displaced by the white-collar service sector as a site for delivering the kinds of rewards that they desire from the good job. Consequently, the returns they desire from good jobs can best be attained in the employment sector they are least prepared to enter.

To understand the degree to which increased exposure to employment prospects may help Joseph and men like him to make more accurate assessments of the work sphere, we must assess the preparedness of unemployed black men for immersion into the contemporary urban labor force. A crucial first step is to document their notion of the good job and their understanding of the work conditions, employment opportunities, and rewards of the various occupational sectors. This includes exploring their understanding of the appropriate avenues for entering certain jobs, and the resources essential for success in those jobs.

Usually, the investigation of the cultural dynamics of black men's relationship to employment is reduced to an emphasis on their work-related values or their reactions to being on the margins of the world of work. At the simplest level, these investigations explore whether or not these men desire to work, and what sectors or niches in the world of work they most prefer. As shown in prior research, these are important areas of inquiry. For instance, in his classic study of black men on a Washington, D.C., street corner, Elliot Liebow (1967) elucidated how men orient themselves psychologically to the types of work most readily available to them. He argues that the men he studied contemplate whether such employment is fruitful for them, and whether they believe themselves to be efficacious at performing on the job. While this chapter looks at how men understand employment, it also considers how men make sense of the structure of work opportunity in their municipality, and the way they believe they can relate to that structure.

The overarching goal of this chapter is to move beyond the question of whether low-income black men desire or are motivated to work. Unlike earlier work that privileges values or psychological dispositions, this chapter emphasizes beliefs or worldviews as a focal point for cultural analysis. It asserts that a more extensive cultural examination of low-income black men must include an assessment of their beliefs and worldviews about the employment sphere because it is those beliefs and worldviews that establish their bases for action or inaction.

The Research Context: Theoretical and Empirical

The data for this chapter consist of the views and opinions of low-income black men from contiguous west-side Chicago neighborhoods. These findings are connected to the changing nature of the urban occupational sector in Chicago and build on a general finding that has endured throughout decades of research on the African-American urban poor—that a lack of consistent work experience leaves individuals increasingly unable to adjust to the world of work (Anderson 1978; Hannerz 1969; Liebow 1967; Wilson 1996). Among the litany of social problems faced by the African-American urban poor, the employment status of young black men remains perhaps the most crucial concern (Bound and Freeman 1992; Bound and Holzer 1993; Braddock and McPartland 1987; Johnson and Oliver 1992; Moss and Tilly 1991; Sampson 1988; Sum and Fogg 1990; Wilson 1996). Analyses of the structural dimensions of this plight abound. The most common conclusions are that low-income black men either lack the human capital requisite for success in a changing urban labor market structure or reside too far from available employment opportunities that match their human capital attributes.

In addition to depicting the value systems of black men concerning work, a portion of this literature has also explored how they have contemplated and responded to unstable employment (Anderson 1978, 1990; Hannerz 1969; Liebow 1967; MacLeod 1995; Williams 1989; Wilson 1996). This work finds that the reactions to unemployment or erratic employment include despair, hostility, and insecurity about their prospects of functioning in traditionally defined masculine roles such as breadwinner or head of household. Researchers in this area also suggest that the availability of better jobs would allow most of these men to function more efficaciously in other aspects of their lives. Finally and most importantly, studies of black males affirm that they do want to work. This chapter does not dispute these claims, but attempts to move beyond research that has focused on the psychological consequences of unemployment or the value systems of low-income black men to ask the insufficiently explored question of how young black men conceive of the structure of work opportunity.[4]

To assert that gainful employment will help these men improve other dimensions of their lives is true, but simplistic. It implies that easier access to what they consider to be "good jobs" would largely solve their problems. The process of finding adequate employment is more complex for these men than one might think. To explore the barriers to employment, I shall look closely at two questions: the first is whether and how they make sense of the changing nature of the urban employment arena. The second is what attributes they feel they can offer to the work sphere.

The City, the Neighborhood, and the Design
of the Study

For many of its low-income black American residents, Chicago is a site of urban decline (Wacquant and Wilson 1989a, 1989b; Wilson 1987, 1996). From 1970 to 1980 (the early childhood years for the men in this study), the population living in Chicago's poverty areas increased by 62 percent. During the same time span, the population living in extreme poverty areas increased by 162 percent (Wacquant and Wilson 1989b).[5]

These developments are the result of both an out-migration from inner-city neighborhoods of wealthier residents and a decline in the economic fortunes of residents who remained in the communities. The proportion of black Chicagoans living in extreme poverty areas went from 24 percent in 1970 to 47 percent by 1980. Moreover, the black male employment rate in Chicago declined from 62 percent to 48 percent during that decade. A contributing factor to the loss in employment was the closing of 38 percent of Chicago's 8,455 factories between 1967 and 1982 (more than 3,000 of those closings occurring after 1970) and the decline in manufacturing jobs from 390,000 to 172,000 from 1958 to 1982. Retail trade lost 64,000 jobs during that time span, and wholesale trade lost 47,000 jobs (Wacquant 1989; Wilson 1987). It takes little imagination to consider how the socioeconomic changes in Chicago affected the institutional apparatus of low-income communities, as support for banks, stores, community groups, and civic organizations diminished during this time.

The decade of the 1980s saw the further deterioration of the manufacturing employment sector in Chicago. Between 1970 and 1987, Chicago lost nearly 250,000 manufacturing jobs, and the service sector surpassed manufacturing to become the major employment arena in the city (Israilevich and Mahidhara 1990). Service-sector employment went from 0.62 million jobs in 1970 to 1.12 million jobs by 1987, while manufacturing jobs declined from 0.95 million to 0.66 million during that same time span (Israilevich and Mahidhara 1990). Not all of the newly created service-sector jobs were high paying, nor were they necessarily higher paying than some manufacturing positions. However, as will be explained in more detail later, the great crisis for the men in this study was not the increase in lower-paying service-sector jobs, but the decrease of jobs in the very sector of the labor market for which they felt most suited and in which they most desired to be employed.

These historical patterns and trends circumscribe the labor market prospects that the men in this study have been exposed to since their adolescence. This steady disappearance of manufacturing jobs has left most of them witnessing successive cohorts of neighbors and associates with fewer job prospects. Moreover, the changes in the quality of life of their residential location—the Near West Side community area in Chicago—has shaped not only the structure of the labor markets to which they have been exposed but also their capacity to consider what tenable labor prospects currently exist or might exist in the future. There is no strong employment sector in the community, nor do many people work. Therefore, employment opportunities are not visible to residents, and they have few strong ties to people who work consistently in secure and well-paying jobs. Much of the infrastructure consists of large-scale public housing developments, built between 1938 and the 1960s, which now comprise approximately 20 percent of the housing stock and provide shelter for a major segment of the African-American population.

The men discussed here were reared, for the most part, in one of the two major housing developments in the Near West Side community area. About a mile separates the two developments, with low-income and working-class African-Americans residing in the area between them. One development, Henry Horner Homes, is comprised of nineteen buildings with 1,774 units, almost all of which are occupied by African-Americans (Chicago Housing Authority 1992). Over 85 percent of the households receive public assistance, and only 8 percent of the households are supported solely by the employment of one of its members (Chicago Housing Authority 1992). The other development, ABLA Houses, contained 160 buildings and 3,505 units. It also is almost completely populated by African-Americans. Over 75 percent of the households in ABLA receive public assistance, and slightly more than 8 percent of the households are supported solely by the employment of one of its members.

The findings of this chapter emerged from an analysis of structured, open-ended interviews with twenty-six low-income black men between the ages of twenty and twenty-five.[6] This age category was chosen because black men in this age bracket were deemed in public and academic discussion to be in a state of crisis (Gary 1981; Gibbs 1988; Herbert 1994; Majors and Gordon 1994; Staples 1982). Although researchers recognize that the crisis exists for reasons that extend beyond employment status, employment remains a crucial part of their predicament and is inextricably linked with other problems such as lack of education, criminal records, and victimization. This age category also encompasses individuals who, although still young, have come into full adulthood experiencing socioeconomic disadvantage. Thus, men in this age bracket are further cemented into structural positions of deprivation than are younger black males because as adults they have now become their own primary agents for changing their situation (younger males may still rely on parents or guardians).

My respondents were selected by a modified snowball sampling approach, which began with my developing ties to a community organizer and a social service provider, each of whom worked in the Near West Side community area of Chicago. Each of them made office space available to me so that I could hold interviews within the community boundaries, and each introduced me to a few men who fit the age category for the project. Other men approached me after learning about the project from peers who had already been interviewed, from neighborhood associates who informed them of my work, from other respondents, or after some cursory observation of my research-related activities in the community.

Although I engaged in some social interaction with respondents and others in the facilities where these offices were located, I interviewed each of the respondents in a one-on-one interactive format. The formal interview lasted from one to four hours. The preinterview and follow-up discussion sequences (included in every interview) took place over a series of days even if the formal interview was completed within a day's time. For almost all of the men, my interviews disrupted their daily pattern of idleness and street-corner association interspersed with mostly futile attempts to find work.[7]

Family

The men in the study were unmarried at the time of the fieldwork. Only three of them were heads of their own household (meaning that they maintained primary responsibility for the upkeep of the domicile). All of them lived within a mile of their mother's home. Fourteen of the men gave their mother's or grandmother's home as their current residence. Nine others regarded their mother's homes as their permanent address, although they lived with girlfriends or other friends over long intervals of time. Twenty-one of the men were fathers (seventeen men had one or two children, and four had from three to eight). Only three (Butch, Devin, and Ted) resided with their children.[8] With the exception of those three, none of the other men had legal or de facto custody of their children.

Some understanding of the distance that separates these men from formal employment markets can be provided by considering their family backgrounds. Only four of the men grew up with their fathers in the home, although not consistently.[9] In three other cases, a stepfather or mother's boyfriend resided with the men, although in each case not for more than three years. All but seven of the mothers (or maternal guardians) were employed during most of their sons' childhood. Those who were not usually employed were recipients of public aid. The nineteen regularly employed mothers generally did such blue-collar-type labor as school security work, store cashier, short-order cook, and home attendant. Two of the mothers received associate's degrees sometime after the early childhood of the men. Fourteen of the mothers received high school diplomas. All other parents (or parental figures) left school sometime between the completion of eighth grade and the final year of high school.

Schooling

Nine of the men did not complete high school or receive a General Equivalency Diploma. None of the men completed programs of study beyond high school.[10] Most of the men explained that the schooling years were disappointing due to an amalgamation of factors both beyond and within their control. Many of the men spoke of school as a site for physical conflict, promoted either by gangs or by students reacting to life in situations of socioeconomic disadvantage.[11] Even those who did not participate in violent activity needed to negotiate a violent terrain; learning was often less important than attempting to secure an emotionally and physically safe space.

As Lester recalled:

> I liked everything about that school [elementary school] except everybody in there wanted to fight man. By me living in that rough neighborhood everybody was fighting every day. Every day. [Interviewer: What do you think caused that?] Gangs, that's the only thing that causes it man, gangs.

School was often a site of conflict and tension. Although the men reported that violence was not a daily occurrence, they functioned with the perception that it could randomly occur. Thus, these men did not depict their schooling experiences solely or even primarily in terms of the academic context. Indeed, for some of the men the portion of the school day that received the most attention was the time they spent getting to and from school, crossing gang boundaries.

Regardless of whether the men blamed their deficient schooling on themselves, the institutions, or both, each of them was aware of the detrimental impact of their school experience on their present circumstances. Most of the men stressed that their mothers, fathers, or guardians had informed them of the value and necessity of education. Furthermore, they reported that their parents or guardians often pointed to their own lives as examples of the consequences of a lack of proper schooling. However, these messages provided the young men either with a false sense of the educational prerequisites for leading a successful adult life or with no realistic sense of how to pursue educational options in a way that would optimize their mobility chances. In fact, these men reported few, if any, in-depth discussions about the public school system that all but two of them attended for the entirety of their schooling.[12] Their recollections of school involved little or no commentary on learning that pertained to preparation for future employment.

Friends and Peers

Nearly all the men stated that their closest friends shared their status near the bottom of the socioeconomic scale. Deprived of significant peer associations with socioeconomically mobile individuals, the men I interviewed were not socialized into networks of people who had access to and pursued options that could benefit them in the future, nor did they have experiences that might have led them to develop a commonsense orientation to life that included explicit consideration of the future. Instead, a consistent theme in their comments was how little help they and their friends could provide for each other. As Conrad stated:

> (M)ost of my friends . . . they either been in jail or, you know, or they "The Man" out here. They selling, you know, doing that, so I guess if they going to get ahead they going to get ahead in a game and not as far as jobs or anything like that.

Conrad could not recall any serious discussions with his friends about getting ahead in life. He said, "There ain't nothing we talk about like every day. We just, we just be hanging out, just kicking it. We talk about females, or if a tournament going on, we'll talk about the tournament or something like that, basketball, that's all."

Furthermore, a third of the men said that they did not recall having regular serious conversations with anyone in their community except family members. Some of the men said that they were not comfortable enough with their neighborhood peers to engage in serious discussion with them. Barry responded to my question about whether his close friends desired to get ahead in life or not as follows:

> I don't know. Everybody, I guess everybody desires but I don't know. . . . Really I'm a, really I'm a loner, to tell you the truth. . . . (If) We do talk about something we talk about, just talking like, you know, just talking. It don't be nothing, nothing really serious. Everybody be

trying to keep they business to theyself. I'm a loner, that's why I really can't answer that.

Others said that they simply did not raise such questions with their friends and associates. As Joseph said in response to a question concerning his friends' attitudes about getting ahead, "I can't answer that because I don't know what they are."

Even those men who had ventured out of Chicago for some part of their lives lacked sustained encounters with more mobile individuals. These men stated that wider social exposure created a means for them to evaluate more critically some aspects of their lives and to experience different patterns of social relations, but in the end it was not pivotal to creating better job prospects for them.[13]

This overview reveals a number of important points. First, the men's families could not transmit to their sons the requisite capital to navigate schooling in a way that would be conducive to getting ahead. Second, their peer networks and associations did not cultivate and transmit appropriate information and other resources that could facilitate upward mobility. Instead, such networks sometimes helped some of the men navigate the local public space, while often simultaneously preventing them from accessing other resources.[14] Third, the lack of employment prospects created a limited exposure to and involvement with wage earners who regulated their daily lives in accordance with the demands of work. The men did not have to coordinate a variety of daily activities, thus diminishing their capacity to integrate successfully into the workforce if the opportunity presented itself.

As the accounts of their life experiences make clear, the men had little capacity to relate to the world beyond the local context. It was not simply the cultivation of certain norms and values that prevented the men from being positioned for work opportunities. More fundamentally, as we shall see below, their encounters with the everyday realities of socioeconomic disadvantage shaped their commonsense understandings of how to function in the economic sphere.

Contemplating the World of Work

Almost all the twenty-one fathers in this group reported that they were motivated to begin taking stock of the consequences of being (or soon becoming) non-wage-earning adults when their first child was born. They then first took seriously the prospect of experiencing a long-term future as a socioeconomically disadvantaged person. Earlier they had functioned as dependents in the households of their parents or guardians. As one father, Conrad, explained:

I realize that I ain't just living for myself no more. I got my daughter and my son to live for, you know. I don't want to be like my father was to me. I never want to desert my son or my daughter. So I feel like I got to get a job because nowadays, you know, people are dropping like flies. And I feel like, you know, if I go, I want my son and my daughter to have something, you know, to collect something from me, because if I go now, they ain't going to get nothing, you know what I'm saying.

For the most part, these men regarded the birth of their children as a transformative life event. Throughout the interviews most of the men emphasized that having reached their early twenties they were beyond the crisis years of late adolescence. They considered the teenage years to be the high point of gang involvement and/or susceptibility to random violence.[15] Despite their acknowledgment of the unpredictable, yet pervasive, violence in their communities, the men felt that they had reached a point in their lives where they would begin to interact in less volatile contexts. Believing that this would minimize their exposure to life-threatening circumstances, they began to accept the notion of a longer life expectancy than they imagined at earlier points in their lives. However, the men still had very few consistent or long-term employment experiences, and no clear sense of any emerging ones. None of them were employed at the time of my interaction with them, nor had any held a job for more than a few months at a time. The lone exception was Jordan, who at one point was employed at a funeral home for nearly two years before being released due to a reduction in staff. Thus, they began to see longer futures for themselves, but not necessarily futures that included secure employment.

In talking about jobs, each man stated that he desired to work in a secure and stable job. Additionally, each said that he would accept any available job that could provide him with what he felt would be an appropriate salary. Although definitions of appropriate compensation varied, most of the men asserted that per diem or informal arrangements were unacceptable. As Dennis argued:

I can't knock a person for selling drugs, I cannot, cause if you ain't got a job to go to, you can't get one, you run around here and they talking about three dollars and fifty cent an hour. One guy told me he was paying thirty dollars a day to paint. I said, "Is you nuts?!" Thirty dollars a day! My skills, I think my skills are worth better than that. He said, "Well, I'll have to see." [I responded] "You ain't got to see nothing. My skills is way better than that." If I'm a lay a roof or do a shingle roof for you, you think you're fitting to pay me thirty dollars you're crazy. You must going to pay me thirty dollars, you know, just to do the roof, and it better not take me no more than four hours. That's how I feel my skills is . . . I ain't went back. I worked a half a day and left. . . . Hey, if you want me to pick up the paint after they [other workers] get through or move paint cloths for thirty dollars that's about all I'm a do. I ain't going to pick up no paint brush and a roller talking about painting if you only talking about giving me thirty dollars. . . . I'm telling you these people is ignorant these days. I feel that is really stupid. . . . People got to survive. And then everybody say "Well it's so wrong, to stick up [commit robberies]." Yeah I think killing is wrong, but it's hard out there, it's hard. Some people say, "Yeah, well get out here and work. Get out here and find . . ." Yeah, you're getting out here. Man, I get disappointed all the time, you know what I'm saying.

Many of the men shared Dennis's view that refusal to work was preferable to unfair compensation. The few men like him who had some kind of work experience, meaning little more than some experience with per diem or short-term work, or who possessed some manual skills, were generally less willing to accept menial labor opportunities than the others. Dennis's situation exemplified a major conundrum for these men in that many potential employers regarded them as a source of short-term, cheap labor, while most of them (although not all) were adamantly unwilling to accept those kinds of opportunities.

The men understood why individuals would pursue illicit activity; indeed, over half of them said that they had done so.[16] However, most of them also knew that such activity would not guarantee a consistent or secure income. In making this point they stressed that violence and incarceration were inextricably linked to such pursuits. Therefore, even those men who had or continued to pursue such options explained that the risks involved either did or were beginning to outweigh the benefits. One former drug dealer, Barry, said:

(W)hen I started using drugs, I started selling drugs, and the fast money led to other shit, and before I knew it I ain't never been back to school. . . . I believe I did that 'cause when I was coming up I could never hardly get hardly what I wanted or didn't hardly have no money, cause my mother was like, she was on aid, and then sometimes she did a little security, so we, we struggled. So when I got out of high school like, man I could get, you know, expensive gym shoes now and all that. It psyched, it tricked me, you know. That fast money tricked me and I regret it now. . . . I was always around it and seeing it, and seeing what they [other dealers] was getting out of it, the ones that was lucky, you know. Thought I'd be lucky too and shit, like that. . . . (T)he key is coming and seeing how everything is going and that ain't no future. First I wasn't even paying no attention to all of that, just, I got this money. Now I ain't got that money, and that's, ah, I wish I had never started. I know that much. . . . I didn't get nothing out of it. . . . It just tricked me, you know. . . . And then when she [his grandmother] passed it seemed like things started happening, police was, I wasn't going to jail but they was on me. And people all of a sudden want to stick me up and beat me up for the stuff. So I just stopped, you know. . . . It got violent.

The other men who reported involvement in illicit activities had similar points of view. While monetary rewards were plentiful at certain periods, they had begun to question whether a long-term career would provide them the emotional and physical security offered by other forms of employment. The men did not engage in moral posturing while discussing illicit activity. Those who pursued it candidly admitted that it was wrong. They discussed their past and present involvement in matter-of-fact conversational style. They knew that few people over the long-term improved their socioeconomic status through such activity and that the odds were not in their favor. Although at certain points in their lives some of them did attain significant short-term gains through these pursuits, having reached adulthood, the men began to think about the long term, even if they were not in a position to act in their own, long-term best interest.

The majority of the men said that they were always prepared to take advantage of whatever legitimate employment might come up. A minority of the men spoke of specific employment options that they were in the midst. of pursuing.[17] Their comments made it clear, however, that they did not believe that many potentially meaningful employment opportunities existed. As the men reported, there were times when they acted on impulse to pursue employment opportunities. At other times, employment opportunities serendipitously emerged. These circumstances made it virtually impossible to codify coherently any pattern of responses toward employment prospects. Instead, the myriad patterns mentioned here must be understood as part of each man's repertoire of responses to his own circumstances. Peter, a young man who said that he was actively seeking work, said the following:

I've been eagerly pursuing a job. It's almost like they've eluded me. I worked one job that short time with a contractor driving 'cause I have my CD air license. And so I do want a job, and I have searched for a job. I would go back to school but the financial is too much. And then I have a lot of other friends who gone to school and it's not an encouraging thing to see your friends that have gone to school and they're unemployed or they're making $6.00 and they're not even working in the field that they were trained in. It's very discouraging.

The closing of factories in or near their communities of residence diminished the employment sector. In the neighboring community of North Lawndale (which borders the western boundary of the Near West Side community area), a headquarters for Sears, Roebuck and Company, an International Harvester plant, and a Hawthorne Western Electric plant, all reduced staff and eventually closed their doors between the late 1960s and 1984, eliminating more than sixty thousand jobs. This pattern of neighborhood-specific job reduction led to extreme levels of unemployment by the 1980s. By that time, unemployment had become a commonplace feature of community life, exemplified by clusters of men associating on street corners and in open public space.

When asked about pursuing employment, most of the men could not offer definitive strategies or plans for how they or others in the neighborhood could go about finding a job. Instead, they described "trying to stay busy," or "not be idle," as Conrad stated, so that they would have some access to any emerging opportunities. Staying busy often meant little more than being in the streets, interacting in the public—a task that required little orientation to time, and no orientation to "standard time." The men spent daily life in their neighborhoods of residence pursuing activities that did not often necessitate a careful coordination of daily schedules. Some of them cultivated a relaxed attitude toward time, most evident in my efforts to schedule interviews. They would often show up at predetermined sites hours late, or hours early, explaining that they had arrived early because they had nothing else to do that day. They did not expect this to pose any problem for me. In most cases, the men who did not appear at our scheduled times simply waited until I was available to talk to them. In one case, Devin waited more than six hours since he had nothing else to do.

In sharing accounts of how they had acquired and then lost jobs in the past, a number of the men emphasized their desire to be respected or appreciated by their employers. In motivating them both to get jobs and to leave them, respect was usually more important than meeting or failing to meet any requirements for maintaining jobs. Given the kind of jobs they could get, this focus on respect was a virtual guarantee of short-term employment because sensitivity to disrespect in the workplace, or their reaction to perceived disrespect, often encouraged them to act in ways that led to their loss of employment. Tito, a former gang member who had spent some time in prison, told of his experiences during a brief period of employment at a warehouse for a moving company:

> I ain't have to quit, but I couldn't accept what was happening in there because the manager's sister came [to get a job] and two days later she's assistant manager. We trying to move up. How she going to get that spot in front of all of us and she ain't been there, you know. So I kept saying something. I was speaking what I had in my mind. I was speaking my mind. . . . I went to talk to the manager. I said, "Can I talk to you about our positions?" She said, "Yeah, yeah, go ahead." "[I said] Okay, I want to know how can she be a manager?" "[She responded] Well, I don't want to talk about it." "[I said] But you wanted to talk about it before we were . . ." She wanted to talk about it before she found out I want to talk about her sister, you know. I told her I want to talk about her sister and she ain't want to talk about it. So I said, "Man, you know what, man, I quit," because I cursed at her. I think she would have fired me anyway, in the end. . . . She would have fired me anyway I think.

Another example was provided by Felton, a former high school baseball standout who was considered by some minor league organizations but was not good enough to break into the majors:

> . . . (W)hen I was working at Dominick's (supermarket). . . . It was a Caucasian guy, and I'm bagging these groceries, and at Dominick's they tell you to evaluate the load. That means make both bags even in weight. So I'm here bagging his groceries, and by the time he just got his money from the cashier, he just pushed me and said, "Bag my groceries right nigger," like that. And we got to fighting. I mean, you know, I just didn't like what he did. The manager, he's sitting over here. . . . The manager had come over there and he was a white guy, too. He came over there and he broke it up. He was like, "What's all this ruckus for?" I said, "Man, I'm minding my own business. He just pushed me and told me to grab his groceries and 'bag his groceries right nigger.'" And the manager pulled me over to the side and told me the customer is always right. I said, "Fuck you," and got out of there. Excuse my language but that's what I said.

For a handful of the men, brief encounters with work allowed them some exposure to life beyond the confines of the Near West Side of Chicago. These employment experiences enabled them to discern some features of a better life. Dennis, who earlier in this chapter explained his frustration with a job opportunity that offered what he felt was an insufficient salary, provided such an example:

> [On working for McDonald's] It really encouraged me to try an advance because I worked up north for them on Chicago and State [downtown Chicago], and, you know, all the people that you see come back and forth and the way they dress, how they look, and the way they carry themselves, they make you want to dress and look and be like them, you know. I was, you know, I used to see all kinds of walks of life as being out there, then you see the homeless, people that ain't got nothing, and then you look at people that got everything. . . . And that's what made me look like "What I'm doing in a McDonald's job when I could be doing the work they doing," you know. I don't know what they doing, but I know whatever it is, it's an honest living, you know. You see them come in there every morning or every evening for lunch. You know, I know they doing something honest, dress nice, and, you know, that's what I'm saying. Ain't got to sweat. That's what made me look at that.

Dennis was one of the very few men who spoke of having any kind of interaction with businesspeople. As sparse as his exposure to the white-collar professional milieu was, it allowed him to form a sense of that world far beyond what most of other men I interviewed could imagine. Indeed, as the next section explores more fully, the lack of exposure not just to white-collar employees, but to most employment sectors, left most of the men unable to make sense of the transformations that had been occurring since the 1960s in the urban employment arena.

Assessing Opportunity and Mobility in the Municipal Arena

Most people have only a partial understanding of the socioeconomic forces and structures that shape their lives. The men in this study probably understood less than most about the world of work because of their isolation from employment. What is striking in their case is their beliefs about work opportunities in Chicago. Although these men could not grasp the full complexity of the transformation of the inner-city employment sector, their comments show that some of its effects were quite evident to them. First, many of them were aware of the decline in the type of inner-city employment that individuals in their communities had previously acquired. They knew that people in the previous generation had jobs. They also believed that the people of that generation were no different from themselves in terms of education and preparedness for work. Their remarks exhibited their confusion, frustration, and insecurity about the contemporary world of work in Chicago. A sample of their remarks about the availability of jobs makes this clear:

> TRAVIS: I think it's more harder now, cause I know there is a lot of people that's unemployed. I think it's kind of hard now than by for what it was in the early days. . . . 'Cause as far as my family everybody I knew in my family, as far as aunties, uncles, everybody was employed. But I know it seems like my generation it's like harder to get a job. . . . (A) lot of people that I've been involved with or talk to, they, you know, are looking for a job or trying to get a job, or trying to get a better job.
>
> TITO: I think there's less (employment opportunity in Chicago). . . . It's less because it's not, it's like the jobs that was out here back in the days . . . because in those days you could be like, you could be so much. You could be this or you could be that, and get a job easy. But like now, these days, I think you need a high school diploma to be a garbage man, you know, to be driving out there.
>
> JOSEPH: Ain't no reason nobody should be unemployed, but they say they don't have enough jobs for everybody, so. I mean they steady building stuff so quit having people come from the suburbs to the city and working. I mean they making all the city money, and they way out in the suburbs. It don't make sense.

As these comments indicate, most of the men could not decipher exactly what was going on with respect to job acquisition. They only knew that a change had occurred by the time they reached adulthood that made them worse off than their elders. Some of the men, such as Joseph, offered opinions that tapped into current policy debates about inner-city employment. But such critical perspectives were rarely linked to accurate statements about how one might overcome these constraints in order to secure employment.

A comment by Jordan, a young man who spent much of his time in a neighborhood community center and who particularly enjoyed conversing with visitors to the facility, typified the views of many of the men about the increasing credentials needed for employment in the modern urban community. As accurate as Jordan was, his lack of exposure to more upwardly mobile individuals left him only partially able to delineate effective strategies for overcoming this circumstance. He said:

There used to be a time, they used to tell you you couldn't sweep a floor, you couldn't get a job without a high school diploma. Now they tell you you have to go to school to get a bachelor's degree. Now you have to get a higher degree. And after that you still have to go to school for more, more, more, training. And as you look back on all that money you been spending, all that training you can get, there's still nothing out there at all. Every year they tell you, "Well, the market is going up. You need this. You need that. You need this. You need that." And then you're steadily going to school, then the more older you get, and then you get out and apply for such and such a job, and certain jobs ain't out there. And then you're still stuck with that loan. If you don't find a job, you're still stuck with it. That's good way to mess up your credit, and your credit gets messed up the rest of your life. . . . So, therefore, when you get your diploma, your degree, that doesn't mean that job is open in that field, and you're stuck with a piece of paper and you'll be stuck with nothing but the bills still hanging over your head. But they don't tell you that. . . .

Jordan went on to speak of the irrelevance of pursuing higher education given these conditions. His life experience left him unable to identify anyone who had pursued education and overcome these problems. He had no close friends who had attended, much less graduated from, college. When asked to explain how he came to his views about the value of a college education, he said that he developed his point of view from casual conversations with others in the neighborhood. While he accurately assessed the increasing importance of academic credentials for access to jobs, he had no knowledge of the utility of other aspects of a college education for overcoming certain barriers to upward mobility.

Jordan was similar to most of the men in that his interpretations of the world of work were partially accurate. He and most of the others could make sense of some things, such as the need for more credentials to access the kind of jobs historically available to low-income black men in Chicago. But they could not decipher the arenas that were too far from their purview. The tragedy here is that the arenas least accessible to these men were those that were most significant for upward mobility, such as higher education and skilled labor markets.

Although the men knew that credentials were increasingly important to accessing even minimally skilled jobs, they were not as thorough in considering the effects of other recent developments on their prospects for employment. For instance, many of the men spoke of the increasing importance of technology. For them, the term meant anything that had to do with the increased mechanization of the workplace. Their discussion of technology also conveyed how their removal from the world of work affected their ability to interpret it accurately. Jason, another of the men who could be found around the community center mopping floors and running errands in order to make pocket change whenever possible, said the following in discussing the impact of technology on employment opportunity:

> Everybody's going to be the same. . . . It's going to be like first come first serve. That's what things are going to be like. . . . 'Cause the way technology is going. There's more pushing like, everything will be computerized, you know terminals and stuff like that. People will be competing for the same job and you happen to show up a little later and I show up a little earlier I get your job. I think it's going to be more like that. For the person that comes and is eager to work they going to give the job to them.

Gus, a former high-school all-city football player whose addiction to drugs curtailed his potentially promising future in the sport, commented:

> (T)echnology has changed and everything, things have changed and all, the more you're willing to work at it, the more you have to work with now. They're spending a lot of money on things that are going to help make a difference. All you got to do is want to make a difference.

These men understood that technological change was important, but they had little inkling of why. Many argued that technology would diminish the importance of social relations in the pursuit of employment. For them, technological advance was an indication that individual skill and motivation would override considerations such as one's appearance or social ties in the determination of who gets hired. Of course, the evidence of Chicago-area employers' negative attitudes toward hiring black men suggests the exact opposite (Kirschenman and Neckerman 1991; Neckerman and Kirschenman 1991). Many of these men were not fully cognizant of the extent to which being black would hinder their chances for employment, despite technological developments in the workplace.

It was clear, in particular, the men did not realize how changes in the Chicago labor market would exacerbate their isolation from it. They recognized that their past behavior might have created obstacles to employment, but their discussion of these obstacles revealed little comprehension of the forces and dynamics shaping occupational sectors. Exploring another aspect of their views on employment—their notions of the good job—provides additional insight into the consequences of their isolation from the world of work.

The Good Job

The men's conception of the "good job" conveys a lot about how they situated themselves in employment hierarchies. It informs not only what they may aspire to but also what is acceptable to them. Their descriptions of the good job indicate how their values about employment connect to their beliefs about its availability.

Conceptions of the "good job" fell into two categories: the ideal good job and the accessible good job. In their discussion of the ideal good job, the men usually stressed occupations that reflected social power or influence. Here they spoke of business owners, lawyers, doctors, and politicians as possessing the ideal good job. For example, Travis, an ex-convict who expressed an equal measure of bitterness over what he felt was a false conviction and over his distressing experiences in looking for work due to that conviction, argued:

> (A) self-employment job, owning a business would be a good job. . . . I mean, you self-employed then you are your own boss, you know what I'm saying. You know what you got to do for you to keep your business running, you know, you're going to be on your job.

In discussing his ultimate occupational desire to own a construction company, Conrad said, "I ain't got nobody looking over my shoulder trying to tell me how to do it. I can take my timing and do it right, you know what I'm saying. And, you know, I could be my own man, so."

Arthur, a recovered substance abuser who does ad hoc volunteer work for the local alderman's office, had a similar view:

> (I want to) basically own my own business, a shipping business, shipping things overseas. That's what Onassis did, I think. And UPS, that's how they got started. Onassis concentrated on shipping and he just used a boat. And another thing is getting into the music industry like being a concert promoter or something like that. And another thing is opening up a small business. So one of those three things I know I'm a get a chance to do.

These remarks illustrate the men's views on the virtues of self-employment. Almost to a person, they emphasized less the nature of the work than the status. Nor did they discuss any domain-specific goals or objectives. Instead, their sole preoccupation was the extent to which such employment would create for them a measure of control over both their daily time and their means of generating income.[18] Although the content of their views may not differ from those of upwardly mobile individuals, the stress they placed on particular values, and their inattentiveness to others, distinguishes them. For these men, the ideal good job was important precisely for what it offered by way of social standing and socioeconomic independence, not for the duties or obligations associated with it. This is consistent with the priority placed on respect by the men who had very brief spells of employment. It is not surprising, given what we have seen so far, that the men's clarity about what would be the ideal good job was not matched by an understanding of the prerequisites for attaining it.

Peter's extended comment reveals how his intense commitment to business ownership and personal control of his socioeconomic endeavors was detached from an appreciation of the core requisites for achieving this goal:

> I want to go back to work. I want my own business in mechanics, and I have to find a solid job. I don't necessarily want to go through the rigmarole of prerequisites. I want to get my certification. . . . I think the only people in my opinion, everyone has their own opinion, but in my opinion I would not go through a four-year program again unless I was going in a science field, a math field, a field that's technical, because I feel it's a waste. That's my opinion personally. I don't think education is just cluttering your head with a bunch of stuff. I feel personally that the first two years of college for some it might help because they've had, they may not have had a successful four years. But a lot of stuff if you've not gotten it by high school, you're not going to get it in two years or four years of high school crammed in two years. . . . Just to generate revenue that is, first two years of college. The second two years is what you use in your field. And if I'm going to be a social worker, what do I need with math? I know how to add, subtract, multiply, and divide. What do I need with calculus? What do I need with tangents? What do I need with this stuff? It's not related. But nevertheless, so I do want to work, and I'm learning more and more that it's not necessarily what you know but who you know. I know a lot of people who have no degrees who have not even stepped foot in an institution but they make $50,000 a year. Why is this? I don't understand it. And then I begin to understand that as long as a man is subject to another man or has no vision, he'll work for a man that has a vision. And that's why I want to be self-employed. I don't want to work for anybody. I want my own economic base.

It was not the job itself, but what the job indicated about social standing—and more importantly about autonomy, power, and economic prosperity —that they emphasized in their remarks.

Discussing how they reckoned with their situations, the men pointed to personal inadequacies as much as to external factors.[19] Whether the men focused on themselves or on external factors as the primary cause of their poor employment histories, each man was cognizant of the distance between his ideals and more viable prospects. Their accounts of the ideal good job provide a context for locating their remarks on the more accessible good job.

As to more realistic prospects, the men spoke of jobs that emphasized manual skills and physical attributes. More importantly, they also discussed the importance of fringe benefits accompanying these jobs, often stressing the importance of such benefits more than the importance of work conditions. As Barry argued in discussing what he hoped would emerge for him in the near future:

> (A) job like, benefit jobs, jobs that have benefits, not all that you have to be a doctor or policeman, but benefits, you know. . . . It take a lot of load—it's take a load off of you when you know you got something to back you up if you get sick or something, you know.

Earl, who was released from jail a few months prior to our meeting, and who was eager to find work as soon as possible in order to begin putting his life back together, offered the following about his immediate desires:

> There are a lot of good labor jobs, a lot of jobs like working for the city, and just like construction jobs and the good paying jobs, like, well there's a lot of jobs where you don't find a lot of education but a lot of skills, you know what I'm saying. Like I'll say like a bricklayer, you know what I'm saying, you don't need to be, you don't need no computer to lay no bricks, you know, but it's a good paying job.

The men were clear in stating that not just any job would provide sufficient rewards. As Dennis explained:

> I'll say any trade job I think is good. . . . There's a lot of factory jobs and everything. I ain't talking about those little temporary jobs where they halfway work you to death. I mean, you know, something where you can be stable in, financially set if you work every day. . . . Yeah, a trade job, or factory machinist, mechanics, fireman, policeman, every, every trade job I think, you know, not cleaning floors and washing dishes. That ain't no trade, you know. It's a job, but it's not no trade for making money. As far as advancing to me it's not.

These and other comments about the more accessible kinds of employment reveal that these men could have flourished in the kind of employment milieu that was prevalent in mid-twentieth-century urban America. They fixed their interests on unionized factory work and, to a lesser extent, on the moderately skilled municipal service sector such as the postal service. Conspicuously absent in their remarks was a desire for inclusion in the employment sector that continues to be the fastest growing in Chicago—the white-collar service sector (Israilevich and Mahidhara 1990). Only three of the twenty-six men gave meaningful consideration to minimal- to moderate-skill employment positions in that sector (e.g., data entry, mail clerk, etc.), or to the possibility of acquiring training for entry into such positions.

Public discussion often focuses on whether such men desire to work or not, but this analysis reveals that desire is not the issue. The sectors in which they desire to work are the sectors that are most rapidly disappearing from the urban landscape. Aside from employment in local, state, or federal government agencies, for these men the accessible good job was one that involved manual skills, was unionized, and was located in the industrial sphere. And these jobs would best utilize the skills and resources that they thought they could bring to the employment arena.

Self-Inventories of Skills and Resources

Like many people, the men in this study emphasized basic educational credentials, human capital characteristics, and appropriate orientation to the job as the most essential skills for employment. All of the men argued that education was important, not only as a mechanism for certifying general competence, but as a foundation for developing job-specific abilities and skills (i.e., human capital). In discussing positive work orientations, the men used terms such as hard work, discipline, focus, and determination, the vocabulary of self-advancement in American society.[20] The skills that the men claimed to possess ran along a continuum; the more-advanced end included those who mentioned carpentry, welding, plumbing, and car repair (Ted, Casey, Lester, Jason, Dennis, and Peter). While most of the men had received no formal training in these areas (e.g., trade school experience), they spoke of how they acquired these skills and how they made use of them during their very brief periods of employment. The middle of the continuum included those who claimed to have acquired basic drawing or typing skills while in high school (Butch, Barry, Anthony, Damon, and Travis). At the other extreme were those who spoke of being good at social relations, "helping people," and being friendly and hardworking as their principal areas of competence (Leon, Gus, Conrad, Earl, Kurt, Jordan, Felton, Joseph, Devin, Tito, Jake, Arthur, and Donald).[21] Indeed, two men (Roy and Larry) stated that they had never before considered what skills they possessed and could not offer any at the time of our conversations. The consistent reference across these groupings (especially for those who participated in athletics in high school) was to physical competence, or the ability to use one's body well (especially the hands). Interestingly, those who claimed to possess skills like typing were not particularly cognizant of the white-collar service sector as an appropriate site for their skills. The men who mentioned typing did so as if they were simply listing what they knew how to do rather than what they thought would matter for their potential employment. As we shall see, their detachment from employment limited their perceptions of what is valuable to employers.

Leon, one of the men who could claim only diffuse social skills, said, "Particular skills at present? That's a hard question to answer because I'm not sure what my talent is. I know I like working with people in general. That's about the best skill that I could say that I do have."

Along the same lines Donald said the following in response to a question concerning what he felt he was good at in terms of work-related skills, "Not very much. I'm fairly good at working with people on a social basis. . . . Like I say, my upbringing, talking to people, listening and learning."

Gus conveyed the challenge he confronted in trying to ascertain exactly how he might be useful to prospective employers:

I'm just a normal person. I think I have good common sense, pretty much. I do spend time thinking about things before I say it, little things like that. I think I'm a normal person. I don't think I'm too much smarter than nobody. I don't think I'm too much dumber than a lot of people either, but I consider myself being a pretty average guy, you know what I'm saying. . . . I think I'm a fairly hard worker. Compared to others I do believe that I'm willing to work hard. I know that if someone is doing the same job that I'm doing I am willing to do it, to work hard. I do know that . . . I'll do it 'til I can't do it no more. . . . I'm a good listener. I know if I hear something I might need to be doing I know that I will spend that time listening and I hear and I'll do it. . . . I believe I have a great body. I have a short-term goal of starting to maybe getting into modeling or something.

Gus struggled and failed to elaborate his skills, and he completed his comment by eventually turning to his physical capabilities, as a last resort, to affirm what he could offer. Jordan and Joseph provide two additional examples of an inability to articulate specific work-relevant skills:

JORDAN: My skills and talents is to help people and doing all that you can and just being yourself. And once you're yourself you can get in on with what you can, and you give it your best. . . . I think if you know what you're talking about and you can walk and talk like you have a whole lot of degrees on the wall you don't have to have anything at all. You just go by your personality, you know different things. . . . You just have to know. If you know you can do the job to the best of your ability, then you just give it your best. I learned nine out of ten that people aren't looking at how many diplomas you got, how many stuff you got up on your belt. Most of the time people are looking for talent, your attitude, your credibility, how can you do different things, you know.

JOSEPH: Certain talents or skills? I feel as though right now there's nothing out there that I can't do. There isn't. I mean I could work at a steel mill if they put me at a station and they show me what they want done and how they want it done, that's the way it should be done. Right now it don't make a difference [to the kind of jobs he thinks he'll have in the future], whatever the job consists of. There's nothing that a person can't do. The only thing he needs is for someone to show him the one time, or tell him how he want it done. That's it. Go do it. . . .

In contrast, the men who professed to have some definitive skills argued that their lack of certification was detrimental. They believed that formal certification would be an important next step for them to actually get a job. As Jason stated, "Yeah I got a couple of skills. . . . Carpentry, wood work, electrician, plumbing, I could do all that. I need to go to school to achieve more. I just need to go back to get that degree. That's it."

The skill self-assessments reveal the depth of the dilemma confronting these men. Those with at least some labor market experience who professed confidence in their manual skills faced a labor market in which the kinds of skilled jobs they might acquire were rapidly disappearing. Those men who never held a job that required manual skill had virtually nothing they could claim as a legitimate advantage for work prospects. Without additional training, a large number of the men would only be equipped for minimally skilled service-sector positions. Yet it was the more-skilled rather than the less-skilled men who spoke most of additional training, which they equated with certification. The least-skilled men seldom considered the service sector, and had they done so they would have found that jobs there provided far less remuneration than they said they were prepared to accept in the long term, and minimal or no benefit plans. As adolescents, perhaps the men would have found such jobs appealing. As young adults, the men resolved that such opportunities would not suffice.

Conclusion

Ethnographic research to date has uncovered how low-income black men feel about being unemployed or underemployed, their prospects of low-wage employment, and why they do and do not pursue certain jobs. This chapter confirms what prior research has found and moves to explore more substantively the related issues of how men read opportunity and possibility in the contemporary world of work. Earlier research has emphasized norms, values, and psychological predispositions as the analytical vocabulary for considering how black men respond to work. This chapter explored how one class of black men came to their understanding of the work environment in Chicago, and how these men believe they relate to it.

Low-income black men continue to be ill-suited to a work environment that has been changing dramatically over the past two decades. Although they know the work situation has changed and gotten worse, they do not appreciate the specifics of the changes and so cling to aspirations that fit the disappearing but not the rapidly emerging work environment. The men I interviewed do not recognize that their perceived skills and resources will not benefit them in attaining employment in an expanding service sector. Coupled with this is their resolute stance against accepting long-term employment in the most menial occupational niches in that sector. As men who have begun to view themselves as adults with the potential for a long life span, they believe these jobs will not provide them with the financial capital to navigate their lives over the long haul. Essentially, what these men are looking for is not there.

Additionally, this chapter illustrated that the men do not simply lack the requisite skills for success in the white-collar service sector, even for the lower-mobility and lesser-skilled occupations in that sector, but more importantly, they do not even have a coherent understanding of what the essential skills for success are. The gap is wide between the men's ideals and the realities of the segment of the labor market that is closer to their grasp. Some have experienced an inability to adapt to the sporadic employment options that come their way. Others have experienced an absence of employment opportunities altogether. For all of the men, the longer they stay out of work and in the company of others who cannot find work, the more isolated they become from the skills, resources, networks, and means needed to acquire the "good job." This further undermines their employability.

Social isolation does not simply isolate individuals from better prospects, it also denies them the capacity to interpret adequately that which is beyond their social milieu. The men framed a vision of desirable work by connecting what they saw as positive about themselves (i.e., skills with hands, body control) to the kind of work that they knew others did at a time when they had ample visions of others going to work (which for these men meant early in their youth). This helps explain how partially accurate understandings are formed from specific social locations. The men had access to some information (about advances in technology and the disappearance of work in the community) and a history of images (about what work was like in the past). This helped them to formulate whatever was accurate in their portrayals of the world of work. Since they had no jobs and knew of very few people who did, they were inevitably confused about what was going on in the current world of work.

Clearly, the resolution of this conflict necessitates micro- and macrolevel change in the relations of inner-city low-income African-Americans and employment sectors. At the macro level, efforts to augment the employment prospects of low-income black men with benefits and remuneration that will allow them to lead productive lives are a crucial step toward progress. Additionally, initiatives that involve both job training *and* education about the changing nature of the urban employment arena will assist these men in developing more accurate readings of the transformations taking place around them and the ways in which they might adjust to them. Actual change, however, will necessitate some larger-scale transformations in the arrangement of labor opportunities in the inner city. Not only must low-income black men learn to relate better to a white-collar service sector, but, as recent research has shown, that sector must relate better to them (Kirschenman and Neckerman 1991; Neckerman and Kirschenman 1991).

More than thirty years ago, Elliot Liebow carefully looked at how men who associated on a Washington, D.C., street corner responded to the types of jobs that were available to them. He commented, "The streetcorner man wants to be a person in his own right, to be noticed, to be taken account of, but in this respect, as well as in meeting his money needs, his job fails him. The job and the man are even. The job fails the man and the man fails the job" (Liebow 1967, 62–63).

Today many black men are not responding to poor-quality jobs per se, but to the absence of employment prospects altogether. Therefore, much of the contemporary discussion should not be about men and their jobs, but about men's removal from vantage points where they can make even rudimentary sense of the world of work around them. It is this condition, not the question of whether or not men want to work, that demands the attention of those who aim to help the disadvantaged secure better lives for themselves.

NOTES

The author would like to thank the following for helpful comments and suggestions on earlier drafts of this chapter: Renee Anspach, Mark Chesler, David Harris, Howard Kimeldorf, Rick Lempert, Karin Martin, Andy Modigliani, the editors of the volume, and the anonymous reviewers.

1. His name and all others used to identify respondents in this chapter are pseudonyms.

2. Most of the fieldwork for the project that produced this data was conducted in 1994. Thus, all references to age pertain to that year.

3. He left the first job for the second, and the second in order to enroll in a training program for security work. The school that sponsored the program went bankrupt while he was enrolled.

4. At least one other Chicago-based study had a similar focus (Venkatesh 1994). However, it examines an older category of black men, aged twenty-seven to forty-four, and specifically addresses how those men interpret job-specific mobility prospects (what attributes or resources one needs for a good job, and the difficulty the men express in finding work). Unlike the present work, it does not comprehensively address how these men frame an understanding of the structure of work opportunity in Chicago and what specific skills the men feel they can bring to it.

5. Poverty areas are those in which 20 percent or more of the population is poor. Extreme poverty areas are those in which 40 percent of the population or more is poor. The 20 percent and 40 percent barometers are appropriated from census tract measures of poverty rates. The organization of Chicago into community areas allows easy transfer of measures used for census tracts on to the community level (Wilson 1996).

6. The larger objective of this research was to document these men's conceptions of their future life chances, paying specific attention to how they implicated race, class, and gender in their views (see Young 1996). Prior to eliciting their comments on this topic, I attempted in my interviews to capture a specific sense of the life histories and contemporary experiences of the men. The interviews concentrated on past and present interactions within social institutional milieus (labor markets, family, schools, churches, formal and informal peer associations, etc.), and the extent to which the men made use of television, radio, and popular literature as sources of information for the issues at hand.

7. Within a few months in the field, I came to regard these men as the "down but not out" because they were willing to interact with me for both monetary and informational rewards. Each of the men was paid twenty-five dollars for the completion of a formal interview. Aside from the eagerness to earn money (for some of the men this was their only source of earned wages in many months) the men expressed an interest in talking to me as they thought that I might lead them to job opportunities or (in a few cases) so that I might instruct them on how to conduct themselves on job interviews. In the latter case, they inquired about the ways in which the research interview may have paralleled the job-interview setting. This implied that they remained willing to take advantage of opportunities that might benefit them

in some way. Accordingly, their testimonies must be read with the understanding that they are a group of low-income black men who have not altogether given up hope in the possibilities of at least some minimal transformation of their life situations.

8. Included here are two of the men who lived in their own domiciles, Butch, who lived with the mother of his two children, and Devin, who lived with the mother of his child and her three children by other involvements. Finally, Ted lived with his two sons in his parents' domicile.

9. Jason's father was a minister of a store-front church in Arkansas who sent his son to live with relatives in Chicago early in the son's youth. Lester's father was a distributor of contraband who was incarcerated for a large portion of his son's youth. Ted's father was the owner of a small bar that went out of business during his childhood. Larry's father was a manual laborer for the Chicago Housing Authority. In another case, that of Roy, both of his parents lived together (his father was a part-time security guard), but he was raised primarily by his grandmother.

10. Two (Donald and Damon) attended community college for a single academic term and then withdrew. Peter attended a four-year institution and withdrew after one term due to his inability to pay tuition. Two others (Kurt and Casey) attended specialized trade schools in commerce and bricklaying and received certificates upon completing their programs.

11. Five other men explained that their declining attendance and eventual withdrawal were due to involvements in one or more violent encounters.

12. Roy and Kurt attended Catholic school for much of their elementary school education. Kurt could not continue due to a lack of family financial resources. Roy was expelled for disciplinary reasons and subsequently entered and remained in public school from junior high through high school.

13. Some of the men had difficulty in recalling the exact length of their stay outside of Chicago. Altogether, sixteen of them spent substantial time in communities other than their Chicago neighborhood. The range for those who did reside outside of the city was six months to six years. In addition to incarceration (of which there were five sentences in state facilities, and another six who reported spending a day or more in the Cook County correctional facility), the out-of-city experiences included seven cases of temporary family or personal relocation to the homes of other family members (including two men who were born and spent their early childhood in the south and migrated to Chicago before their adolescence), service in the Job Corps (Jordan and Butch), enlistment in the army (Gus), attendance at out-of-city college for less than one academic year (Peter), and residence with a friend who lived out of town (Travis). The count does not add to sixteen as there were some overlapping cases (Earl was born in the south and also was incarcerated, Travis had been incarcerated but also spent time living with a friend who attended a residential college in another state).

14. Gang membership provides the crucial case in point here. While only five men explicitly stated that they had been or continued to be active gang members, several others had siblings who were gang members. In either case, some measure of community-specific security was attained for those men (except, of course, during periods of gang conflict). While gang membership often facilitated security and com-

fort in community-specific public interaction (e.g., mutual protection, etc.), it certainly worked against the men by diminishing their image in the larger public (e.g., interaction with potential employers, police officers, civil servants, etc.).

15. I base this remark not on any objective measures of violence in their community, but solely on how the men explained the tribulations of their adolescent years.

16. While none of the men stated explicitly that they committed an act of violent crime (a few implied their involvement in such activity), many did discuss their involvement in thievery in order to generate income. Others discussed their involvement in drug selling.

17. About one-third of the men asked if they could work for me in any kind of support capacity for this research project.

18. Here this analysis parallels what Jay MacLeod (1995) found in his exploration of the good job for black and white low-income and working-class young men in Boston. Many of MacLeod's respondents spoke of their quest for greater personal freedom and control of time as principal benefits of self-employment.

19. A major objective of the research project from which this chapter emerged was to explore how the life experiences of men from low-income family origins led some of them to conceive of external constraint as a crucial feature in the social mobility process, while others remained focused on individual characteristics as the primary causal factor for mobility outcomes (see Young 1996). Briefly, the extent of consistent exposure to Caucasians, individuals of higher socioeconomic standing, and individuals and institutions that represent social authority (e.g., police officers, correctional facilities) affected the degree to which the effects of external constraint could be elucidated by the men.

20. This discourse is commonly articulated in discussions of what it takes to get ahead in American life (see Hochschild 1995 for a critical review of studies that affirm this finding). Therefore, one might question the extent to which the men actually believed it or were simply forwarding modern-day commonsense perspectives about the process of individual mobility. I suspect that some of both may have been occurring. First, many of the men discussed moments when they were not as focused as they should have been on preparing themselves for a better future (as a consequence of substance abuse, lingering family or personal problems, or various kinds of personal irresponsibility). However, the men also relied on this discourse because in their personal lives there were very few examples of people who did get far ahead. Thus, they had little other than socially legitimated messages—as opposed to concrete examples—to offer by way of explaining this process. Hence, with respect to schooling they could not talk with great confidence or precision about how different patterns of educational acquisition were relevant to certain occupational outcomes. They could only argue the strongly accepted precept in American society— that education matters.

21. One slightly puzzling finding here is that although Kurt reported receiving a certificate from a trade school, he never mentioned any particular mastery of the skills relating to that schooling experience. Of course, it might have been the case that Kurt was victimized by the type of noncredentialed "fly-by-night" trade schools that oftentimes target low-income citizens with the promise of helping them

to transform their life situation by enrolling in their programs and acquiring a trade certificate.

REFERENCES

Anderson, Elijah. 1978. *A Place on the Corner.* Chicago: University of Chicago Press.
————. 1990. *Streetwise: Race, Class, and Change in an Urban Community.* Chicago: University of Chicago Press.
Bound, John, and Richard B. Freeman. 1992. "What Went Wrong? The Erosion of the Relative Earnings of Young Black Men in the 1980s." *Quarterly Journal of Economics* 107 (February): 201–33.
Bound, John, and Harry Holzer. 1993. "Industrial Shifts, Skill Levels, and the Labor Market for White and Black Men." *Review of Economics and Statistics* 75 (August): 387–96.
Braddock, Jomills Henry, and James M. McPartland. 1987. "How Minorities Continue to be Excluded from Equal Employment Opportunities: Research on Labor Market and Institutional Barriers." *Journal of Social Issues* 43:5–39.
Chicago Housing Authority, Office of External Affairs, Department of Research and Development. 1992. "Statistical Profile 1991–1992." The Chicago Housing Authority.
Gary, Lawrence, ed. 1981. *Black Men.* Beverly Hills, CA: Sage.
Gibbs, Jewelle Taylor. 1988. *Young, Black, and Male in America.* Dover, MA: Auburn House.
Hannerz, Ulf. 1969. *Soulside: Inquiries into Ghetto Culture and Community.* New York: Columbia University Press.
Herbert, Bob. 1994. "Who Will Help the Black Man: A Symposium." *New York Times Sunday Magazine,* November 20.
Hochschild, Jennifer L. 1995. *Facing Up to the American Dream: Race, Class, and the Soul of the Nation.* Princeton, NJ: Princeton University Press.
Israilevich, Philip R., and Ramamohan Mahidhara. 1990. "Chicago's Economy: Twenty Years of Structural Change." *Economic Perspectives* 12 (2): 15–23.
Johnson, James, and Melvin Oliver. 1992. "Structural Change in the U.S. Economy and Black Male Joblessness: A Reassessment." In *Urban Labor Markets and Job Opportunity,* ed. G. Peterson and W. Vroman, 113–47. Washington, DC: Urban Institute Press.
Kirschenman, Joleen, and Kathryn Neckerman. 1991. "'We'd Love to Hire Them, But . . .': The Meaning of Race for Employers." In *The Urban Underclass,* ed. Christopher Jencks and Paul E. Peterson, 203–34. Washington, DC: The Brookings Institution.
Liebow, Elliot. 1967. *Tally's Corner: A Study of Negro Streetcorner Men.* Boston: Little, Brown.
MacLeod, Jay. [1987] 1995. *Ain't No Making It: Aspirations and Attainment in a Low-Income Neighborhood.* Boulder: Westview.

Majors, Richard G., and Jacob U. Gordon, eds. 1994. *The American Black Male: His Present Status and Future.* Chicago: Nelson-Hall.

Moss, Philip, and Christopher Tilly. 1991. *Why Black Men Are Doing Worse in the Labor Market: A Review of Supply-Side and Demand-Side Explanations.* New York: Social Science Research Council.

Neckerman, Kathryn, and Joleen Kirschenman. 1991. "Hiring Strategies, Racial Bias, and Inner-City Workers." *Social Problems* 38 (November): 433–47.

Sampson, Robert. 1988. "Urban Black Violence: The Effect of Male Joblessness and Family Disruption." *American Journal of Sociology* 93:348–82.

Staples, Robert. 1982. *Black Masculinity: The Black Man's Role in American Society.* San Francisco: The Black Scholars Press.

Sum, Andrew, and Neal Fogg. 1990. "The Changing Fortunes of Young Black Men in America." *The Black Scholar* 12 (January-February): 47–55.

Venkatesh, Sudhir Alladi. 1994. "Getting Ahead: Social Mobility among the Urban Poor." *Sociological Perspectives* 37:157–82.

Wacquant, Loic J. D. 1989. "The Ghetto, the State, and the New Capitalist Economy." *Dissent* 36 (Fall): 508–20.

Wacquant, Loic J. D., and William Julius Wilson. 1989a. "The Cost of Racial and Class Exclusion in the Inner City." *The Annals of the American Academy of Political and Social Science* 501 (January): 8–25.

———. 1989b. "Poverty, Joblessness, and the Social Transformation of the Inner City." In *Welfare Policy for the 1990s,* ed. Phoebe H. Cottingham and David T. Ellwood, 70–102. Cambridge: Harvard University Press.

Williams, Terry. 1989. *The Cocaine Kids.* Reading, MA: Addison-Wesley.

Wilson, William Julius. 1987. *The Truly Disadvantaged: The Inner-City, the Underclass, and Public Policy.* Chicago: University of Chicago Press.

———. 1996. *When Work Disappears: The World of the New Urban Poor.* New York: Alfred A. Knopf.

Young, Alford A. Jr. 1996. "Pathways, Possibilities, and Potential: Young Black Men and Their Conceptions of Future Life Chances." Ph.D. diss., University of Chicago.

CHAPTER 7

Black Male Employment and Self-Sufficiency

Andrew L. Reaves

Achieving occupational success is a problem for most lower-income and poorly educated people. African-Americans, however, suffer additional obstacles related to racial discrimination; almost all have to deal with racial discrimination in the labor market, and its effects are pervasive throughout their work lives whether or not this discrimination is intentional. They cope with it on a daily basis. Discrimination exists in social organizations, residential housing, and education, but workplace discrimination is the most detrimental. If equal employment and entrepreneurial opportunities existed for African-Americans, they could have more of their own prestigious social organizations and decent residential neighborhoods and educational institutions. In fact, all of the domains of racial discrimination operate reciprocally. Equal education, housing, and social organization opportunities facilitate the ability to earn money, and the ability to earn facilitates other opportunities. Progress in race relations has been slow for African-Americans, and racial discrimination does not change very much for individuals as they move between social and economic contexts (Massaquoi 1996). In the end, occupational racial discrimination is the core of the problem.

This chapter attempts to identify and understand some of the processes that can facilitate occupational success for younger African-American men who are entering the labor force. Many young African-American men do not have a clue as to what it takes to succeed in a postindustrial society. They often do not fully understand the forces working against them, or the many insidious ways in which these forces shape their own employment aspirations. They are uninformed. Identifying problems that older African-American men have confronted—and understanding how they have dealt with them—will provide insight into what must be done to help the current generation and future generations of young African-American men achieve occupational success.

In a succinct and powerful description of racism, Sternberg (1991, 744) posits,

In the United States the essence of racial oppression is a racial division of labor, a system of occupational segregation that relegates most blacks to the least desirable jobs or that excludes them altogether from legitimate job markets.

When unskilled African-Americans look for jobs, they have to either find a company that has affirmative action policies, find a company that is in dire need of labor, or find an African-American employer. Kirschenman and Neckerman's (1991) study of racial hiring preferences among employers identified strong discriminatory hiring preferences. They found that employers preferred to hire white employees. If white workers were not available, employers would hire Hispanics. As a measure of last resort in meeting their staffing needs, they would hire black men.

These overt barriers are reinforced by a set of subtler but equally damaging behaviors that exclude African-Americans from full participation in the workplace. These behaviors can be termed "aversive racism," which Dovidio (1993; Dovidio and Gaertner 1986) distinguishes from old-fashioned overt racism. Overt racists know they hold bigoted attitudes, openly express them, and fairly consistently behave in a bigoted manner. Aversive racism is a subtle form of bias, characteristic of many white Americans who possess strong egalitarian values and believe they are not prejudiced. They may also possess unconscious negative racial feelings and beliefs that they try to disassociate from their image of themselves as nonprejudiced. Dovidio (1993, 57) states:

> Even subtle biases can have consequences that are not so subtle. In fact, the impact of aversive racism is the same as that of old-fashioned racism: restriction of opportunity for certain groups, and support for a system that is believed to be fair in principle but that perpetuates the social and economic advantages of one group over other groups.

Within the workplace, aversive racism is displayed through practices such as favoring white employees, capricious testing and questioning designed to humiliate African-American employees, and denial of social support from coworkers. Treatment like this destroys belief in oneself and faith in the rewards of hard work, necessary for anyone to succeed in a competitive workplace.

In addition to racial discrimination, African-American men face all the problems that confront other Americans. Substance abuse is one of those challenges facing all Americans; its devastating effects are an obstacle to occupational success for a great number of African-American men. Many of the men in this study have successfully coped with substance abuse.

This study suggests that the first step African-American men must take, in striving to overcome barriers to occupational success, is to acknowledge the brutal effects of racism in the labor market. People are very seldom able to deal with these barriers on their own; they must receive a large amount of social and structural support in the process of becoming successful. Social support from both blacks and whites is often also necessary to counteract the large number of obstacles that confront African-American men.

Background and Methods

I interviewed eighteen African-American men whom I either knew very well or who were recommended to me by a close friend. The sample of men interviewed does not represent all African-Americans. It is biased toward the group that Anderson (1990) refers to as "decent people." Consequently, many of the problems faced by "street" people have not been discussed here. Hopefully, this omission has been offset by illustrations of how African-American men overcome some of the problems that are related to becoming "street" people. The sample included ten older men, thirty-six to fifty years of age, and eight younger men, thirty-five years old and under. Some of the men who did not actually know me were initially hesitant to talk about personal and sometimes painful experiences, but they soon learned that I empathized with them and had faced similar obstacles. I conducted unstructured, in-depth interviews that lasted an average of two hours. I told the men that I was interested in their job histories, particularly in things that adversely affected their occupational outcomes, such as problems in school, problems with the police, substance abuse problems, health problems, and problems with racial discrimination. I also told them I was interested in things that facilitated their occupational outcomes, that is, anyone who helped them along the way—family, friends, teachers, employers, a wife or girlfriend, a minister—or any organizations that were helpful in their occupational pursuits.

The men all came from lower-class or working-class backgrounds. All have overcome or are currently facing barriers to occupational success. Most of them live in areas of fairly concentrated poverty, which limits positive role modeling (Wilson 1987). Even when there is heterogeneity of socioeconomic status in a geographical area, segregation by both social class and race prevents significant interaction with people who are successful. Many of the men have had problems in school and/or with substance abuse. Some have been in prison. Some have been homeless. Most of the employed men have overcome at least one barrier to occupational success.

The older men entered the labor market when good jobs were plentiful. The younger men are entering the labor market at a time when good jobs for unskilled workers have essentially disappeared. They face a very difficult job market. However, most of the men interviewed are now regularly employed, contribute financially to their family's support, and are fully functioning in society. They hold full-time jobs, part-time jobs, odd jobs, or multiple part-time jobs; some are entrepreneurs, and some are students who live on scholarships or fellowships. Only a few of the respondents were not regularly employed; they were included to illustrate the problems that some find to be insurmountable.

Men in the older group are thirty-six years of age and over. At the time of the interviews, most were gainfully employed and earning enough money to either take care of themselves or make significant monetary contributions to their families. Only two older men in the study were unemployed. All of the employed men in this group had to overcome substantial barriers to become occupationally successful. Both of the unemployed older men have substance abuse problems. Nine of the ten told horror stories of racial discrimination in the workplace. These men have had remarkably similar experiences of overt racial discrimination. It is interesting and disconcerting to note that five of the eight employed men in this group had to overcome substance abuse before achieving occupational success. Their success stories also illustrate the beneficial effects of social and structural support.

The younger successful men are between eighteen and thirty-five years of age and sufficiently employed to help support themselves and their families. There are six men in this group. None of them are married. They all, at some time, lived in single-female-headed households. They all live either with their mothers or at school. Although the men who live with their mothers are working, they do not earn enough to live independently because jobs that pay a living wage are not readily available to them. Most of those who are not in school have one child who lives with its mother. They pay child support and provide assistance beyond what is required by law. They can pay support only because their mothers share their living expenses. During these interviews I kept asking myself, "What will they do when they no longer have their mothers to depend upon? Will they find mates with whom they can work to survive?" Although currently employed, they are not yet living independently, and their future success will depend on both better job opportunities and a strong, ongoing social support network.

Racial Discrimination in the Workplace

The depredations of racism and the will to overcome them are shown in the story of one remarkable young man, Isaiah. By chance, I had found a young man who exemplified the characteristics and social contexts I had been looking for. Isaiah came from a harsh neighborhood and a single-family home, yet he was doing things that are not expected of young African-American men who live in ghettos. His story illustrates the multiple barriers to African-American occupational success: racial discrimination, destruction of motivation, threats of firing and almost arbitrary firings, limited or non-existent promotions, poor relations with white management, and poor relations with white co-workers. It also shows that to cope successfully with these barriers, one must relinquish the belief that one's work will bring rewards.

Isaiah is a twenty-two-year-old part-time grocery warehouseman and a full-time sophomore at a local university, majoring in computer science. He is unmarried, lives at home with his mother, and has a one-year-old son. He does not have a good relationship with his son's mother; however, he seems committed to and supportive of his son. He feels good about his $9.00/hour job, which provides neither health insurance nor other fringe benefits. He probably feels good about his job because he is doing better than most of his peers. Isaiah has held a large number of jobs for a twenty-two-year-old. His employment experiences chart the developmental progression from an ambitious fifteen-year-old to a twenty-two-year-old who merely tries to stay away from his supervisors.

Isaiah started working at the Hamburger Emporium when he was fifteen years old. Like many adolescents, his motivation for going to work was to save enough money to buy a car. He started working as a cook and in eight months became a crew chief. Of the Hamburger Emporium job, he says:

> It was a pretty nice job; you got along with most of the people you worked with. . . . It was not so much the stress; it was a real fast pace. And you had to discipline yourself, so you could do your job better, learn better techniques. That's what helped me become a crew chief. . . . I got along with most of the managers there. Most of them liked me a lot because I did my work real good.

This is a positive experience for a youngster's first job. His managers showed confidence in him and taught him the skills he needed to do the job well, which, in turn, encouraged Isaiah to perform well, to look for ways to increase his responsibilities and to enlarge his aspirations. Motivated by his success and promotion at the Hamburger Emporium, Isaiah wanted to move to bigger and better things. He says, "I knew I could get a job; hopefully I could get a better job. It was all right for a first job. I stayed there long enough to get some experience."

> I went to the Pizza Palace. I would say it was a job I liked, most part, as far as the people working there. There was a small crew, about fif-

teen people all together. Most of the staff were African-American, as
was the manager, Susan. When I started working there I didn't know
how it was going to be. It was mainly a black staff, a couple of white
people worked there. When I started there I was making $4.25. I was
still going to high school; I was working about thirty-two hours a week.
I was making all right money for me, at the time. . . . The work there,
it was pretty easy. It was pretty OK; I was a good worker there also. I
started on the oven, then I started working as a waiter. Susan, the store
manager, and I were all right; we got along all right, so did me and the
other managers. Working there was more like working with friends; we
could tell jokes. It was a pretty nice place to work. It was perfect working at that store. My one supervisor there, Aaron, he got a promotion
to assistant manager, so he left. My manager, she was real cool, she always liked to promote people and send them out.

The aspects of this job that Isaiah described enthusiastically are significant in what they reveal. Perhaps most important, Susan, the manager,
treated her employees with respect and took an active role in guiding and
promoting them. Isaiah felt valued in this job and saw room to move up. In
addition, he found himself in a comfortable social setting, working with
other African-Americans and a few whites with whom he could relax, joke,
and form friendships. He clearly enjoyed the camaraderie, the sense of being
part of a team.

Both structural support in the form of access to opportunities and social support from his co-workers and supervisors made this job desirable.
But the success of the store under its African-American manager attracted
the attention of the company, which, according to Isaiah, transferred her
and gave her store to a white manager. Isaiah stayed on, but working conditions became unbearable under the new white boss. This is Isaiah's account of the change:

Then the job at the Pizza Palace, it went sour because they were going
to turn that Pizza Palace to a delivery store. The delivery store was supposed to bring a lot more income.
[But] Susan was a black manager so the area supervisor transferred
her to another store and brought in a supervisor from another store to
head this store. The guy who came in brought his whole crew in; they
were all pretty much some bigots. They couldn't stand black people; they
didn't want black people coming out there to that area. It wasn't that far
out in the suburbs; it wasn't way out in the suburbs. When I worked there
before, we had pretty much a half-and-half clientele black and white.
There were never any problems there. Usually, the way he got rid of the

black customers was, when they came there he gave them substandard treatment. Black customers and black workers. He made it so bad for black customers you wouldn't want to come out there again. You would just as soon not want to not come out there just to sit and argue with a cat like this. So all the black customers stopped going out there also. So he turned it into a pretty much white establishment.

Suddenly Isaiah found himself in an unfriendly environment, without the protection of his black manager, confronting overt racism. He was also discovering another facet of racism- that the Pizza Palace did not welcome the patronage of African-Americans. They would rather lose the income than serve black customers. Isaiah continues:

My one supervisor from before didn't go with Susan to the new store. He was a black guy; they gave him hell about everything. He knew his job real well, but they were bigots. They wanted to get rid of him; they worked the dog out of him until they made him quit.

Isaiah did not comment on why or how he himself avoided this treatment, but he clearly learned a bitter lesson as he watched a fellow worker and African-American undergo hounding and humiliation. He was coming to understand that competence and commitment would not protect him from becoming a target of this kind of treatment. In fact, Isaiah seemed to recognize that Susan's success at running the business is one of the things that made her vulnerable to discrimination.

I just have to tell you about this, the reason they got rid of my manager was, she made that store make more money than it should have really made. She always got a bonus, so she was running the store in perfect condition. The reason to get rid of her was to have a white male there as manager since it was supposed to be making more money. It was supposed to be a better opportunity. It was racially motivated, racially motivated; they had no reason to get rid of her. I already told you he got rid of the black customers by giving them bad treatment and whatever; he was a racist.

I do not think the intensity of this story comes across on paper as it did in person. I could feel the pain in Isaiah's voice, facial expression, and posture. These are hard lessons for an ambitious and optimistic young person. Isaiah transferred out of his first job at the Hamburger Emporium to find better work with more promise of promotion. By the time he left his second job at the Pizza Palace, he was moving on to avoid bad treatment, social isolation, and racism.

Isaiah quickly transferred to the store where his old supervisor was assigned, although it was a much longer drive. In fact, he could not have gone there without a car. Isaiah continues talking about racial discrimination of another type when he recounts working at the new pizza store with his old manager:

> I went to work at the Pizza Palace in [a distant suburb]. I got out there a week or two after my manager, Susan, did. She had brought only one other person out there. Working under Susan again, it was pretty much an all-white staff. The last thing they wanted to see was a black manager. It was Susan, Rose, and me out there working. Like I said, they couldn't stand it, the crew that was already there. They couldn't stand taking orders or anything from Susan. They didn't get along with her. The assistant manager just quit. They couldn't stand us.

Isaiah realized that the mistreatment of his boss, a woman whose skills and ambition he admired, was based on race, not competence. He continues:

> Susan was able to bring some more people in. She brought some white people in who had lived around black folks their whole life. They didn't have any problems with blacks. They came in; we were like a family. A couple of the people who were there when we started stayed there. Working there was a little bit different because you were working way out there where all white customers came in. Practically all white people never had any problem with you waiting on them; they never had any problem with black people waiting on them.

Encouraged by this experience, Isaiah decided to find a job in a larger, national corporation that he believed would have greater opportunity for promotion:

> I was thinking that if you could get a job at a big retail store you could, as long as you did your work, you could get a little promotion or something. I figured it would be like that because it was a retail place, it was a big corporation. That wasn't the way I found it out to be after working there for a while.

His expectations were dashed. At the retail store, he encountered "blunt racism," as he calls it. He remembers it with anger:

Working there was probably one of the worst jobs I have had. . . . The management was just terrible. Working there, that's where I first I experienced racism like at a workplace. Before that was minor racism, but the big retail store was blunt racism. . . . It was an almost all-black staff and practically an all-white management staff except for one black lady, one black manager. And even the people who were working there who had my status like crew chief there, they were white also.

Here he learned about the inequality of job opportunities for African-Americans and blatant favoritism shown to white employees. Only one black had a management position. Isaiah deeply resented that he himself was treated without respect. When asked whether he thought that the experience at the big retail store had altered his attitude about work, he answered:

No, it didn't, that was just an experience. I knew how white people could be, especially when they are completely in control. Well, they just felt they were so much better than you. The things they did, they would talk to you like you were crazy, like you didn't have a bit of sense, explain directions to you like you couldn't comprehend what they were telling you.

Perhaps the most disturbing impact of his experience at the big retail store was Isaiah's loss of conviction that hard work would advance his employment opportunities. While he acknowledges that the experience was constructive, because it opened his eyes to certain realities of the workplace, particularly for African-Americans, Isaiah lost his enthusiasm for learning new skills and he quickly came to understand the futility of seeking promotion.

They fired people constantly, it was like a rotating door; they hired people in and they fired them. They fired people; it was just a matter of time before you got fired there. I guess, because they knew that after so long people would not be any good to them after taking that treatment from them. . . . When I got fired from there, it was no surprise. I can tell you some more examples. The older people working there, thirty or so with families, the bosses would really bicker with them because they knew they were depending on that job. They would have people scared and crying because they were afraid they would lose their little job. I didn't care, I knew what the game was whether you kissed their butt or not, it was going to be the same outcome. So I just played the game and did my job because I knew I was eventually going to get fired. You came in and worked for a year or less and knew they were going to fire you. . . . I saw countless people get fired, always for low productivity or something like that. They would always fire people to bring in people with new energy. That's all I can remember about that job. It did give me the best experience; you can't get any more blunt racism than that in the workforce. You didn't have a union to protect you; management did what they wanted to. You got your raise after a year I guess that's why they got rid of people before a year.

I did my job and made sure I didn't do any extra things. . . . In my mind was to give them what they wanted because I knew there was no outcome; there were no promotions. As far as promotion went, the black people didn't get any promotion; you came in there at a position or you didn't. I saw the white people come in. This particular instance, one guy, he was a Russian or something, he didn't even start in stock or maintenance, he started right in the department. It didn't surprise me; I knew how they were running things in there.

Isaiah left the big retail store and found work at a suburban bank. I expected that after he had been splattered by hot hamburger grease, cleaned rest rooms, and stocked shelves, Isaiah would be happy to work in a white-collar job earning $7.33/hour, much more than he had earned at the other places. Not so. He tells a story of being both a racial and a gender minority, of feeling isolated and uncomfortable:

The bank was at a suburb. It was a community of white folks who didn't have any more money than black folks. They wanted to act like it. They didn't want to see you out there in their community. They were afraid you would pollute their old precious community or something. Rednecks, really poor white trash. They weren't too poor, but they lived in the same houses we lived in the city, but they cost twice as much. They had a lot of old people who lived there. Racist, I'll just say it, racist all of them were racist, young and old. The customers there, they didn't come out and say they hated you, but it was more like a subtle racism. You knew they couldn't stand you. They would smile in your face and try to crack jokes with you; be a buddy, but if you had any sense you saw through it. The job was pretty much hectic because the people took their money seriously; they would fly off the handle about every little thing, like having a hold placed on their checks. You have to be like a sponge, you have to sit there and take it all. Most of the staff were white. If you work around a lot of white people and you are the minority working there—I don't want to say it, but they are pretty much racist to you and they try to deal with you the best way whatever. You made yourself get along, everybody got along OK. I worked there two years. I hated it. After that experience I said I'd never go back to a bank again. Banking is just not for me; I wasn't the only person who felt that way. I don't want to sound sexist, but banking may be better for women. They can put up with that type of stress better. Two other guys worked there. Jerry was another black guy who worked there. He came home and worked there for the summer. When Jerry did come back, and this other white guy, Paul, when they were there it wasn't too bad, it was like a stress relief. There were some black women there. It was still a stress being around all women and I was the only guy there. So it was OK when I had somebody to talk to; when they were there, it was more comfortable. No, it was not more comfortable. I had somebody to associate with. Paul worked there part-time; we were able to trip out.

Isaiah's banking experience shows the importance of social support on the job. When he was a double minority—male and African-American—work was almost intolerable. When he had two male co-workers, one of them African-American, working at the bank was much easier. It became more difficult when his male African-American friend left, and actually miserable when the other male left the bank.

The job got so stressful I couldn't stand working there any more. I couldn't stand it after I had been there about a year; but I just stayed. I said, why get another job when I can sit here and not do anything? I could go to school while working there, the job allowed me to go to school. I just stayed there for a while longer. It just got to the point, it got so stressful that I couldn't stand the people anymore. After Jerry had left for the summer, I was there in the same situation. Paul had even left, he had quit. . . . I was around all these women and white folks. It got so bad I just couldn't stand the job anymore. Finally I left that job. I was making 7.33/hour, maybe thirty hours a week.

In the job at the bank, Isaiah experienced acute social isolation, boredom, and a lack of incentive to seek promotion. However, he was able to put his energy into school for a period of time and did not feel harassed by co-workers or supervisors, just annoyed by them. In his current job, however, Isaiah has encountered yet another set of obstacles that further encourage him to "lay low" and expect little. In the beginning, he tried to meet job expectations, just to see if he could do it:

The next job I got was working for the grocery warehouse. Production was 100 percent; when you first start working there you have trouble getting 50 percent. A couple of guys quit before they hit production.

Me and this other guy were there for three months before we hit production. I guess they want you to hit production right off the bat. So management was on me about hitting production. I heard so many—"So next week hit production or you are going to get fired, so next week hit production or you are going to get fired." It got to a point that I heard that so much that it didn't really faze me. Finally, I said that they are going to fire me anyway because I didn't think I was going to hit this, as much as I was trying. I think the week I was about to say forget it, I hit production. I said, well, it is possible to hit it. I started working through my breaks to hit it.

Isaiah seemed to realize, at this point, that he was exerting himself only to test his own capacities, not to achieve recognition or promotion on the job. He no longer expects to find a mentor in a supervisor or manager, or to find African-Americans in supervisory positions.

The supervisors there, they some prejudiced cats too. It's racism there. It's the same racism I experienced at other jobs. People get along with other people to the point of where you have to work around them. . . . They try to keep hush-hush the things they do for the white dudes. But the supervisors, they don't particularly care for you, they're some rednecks. I'm not saying the white cats have it made; they get into it with the supervisors like the black cats do. Like I said, the union is there. Without the union, it would be a wild place. So it's not that bad, but it's still hard work. . . . I get along with some people I work with. It's not a bad job. I try not to come into too much contact with the managers. . . . I don't have any interaction with the supervisors. I just work there three days a week. I just come there and do my work and leave.

Isaiah's demeanor disturbed me. His attitude was not what one would hope for in a twenty-two-year-old: he lacked enthusiasm and optimism about a successful future waiting to unfold. Instead, he and many of the other young African-American men I interviewed seemed resigned, depressed, and already beaten down.

Isaiah's story is one of destroyed motivation and wasted human capital. At fifteen years old he began working at a fast-food restaurant and was enthusiastic and competent enough to be promoted to crew chief within eight months. He recognized his ability, as well as the limited opportunity in the fast-food restaurant. He made logical choices, moving to more promising employment opportunities, thinking that if he worked hard and smart, as he did at the fast-food restaurant, he would be promoted and move on to greater heights. In a very short time, his youthful aspirations were dashed.

Isaiah has developed coping skills along the way. He is a bright young man who has already absorbed a lot of tough lessons. He has found ways to adapt to each set of conditions and to avoid serious confrontations, but the impact of all these hard realities on his aspirations has been significant and damaging. While young white workers try to stay as close to their supervisors as possible to get promotions, young, unskilled black workers stay as far as possible from their white supervisors in an attempt to avoid being fired. This process helps young blacks to maintain their jobs; however, it limits the number of blacks in the managerial ranks. Conditions are very different when African-American workers have African-American supervisors. Collegial relations often exist; the workers feel secure and can look forward to chances for promotions when they become available.

As a result of these deeply personal interviews, the men have come to mean a great deal to me. I think about Isaiah often, about his future. I have little doubt that he will finish college, but I wonder how will he fare in a highly technical job, in an industry dominated by whites. As a computer scientist or programmer, he will not be able to hide in a corner, isolating himself from supervisors and co-workers. His job and future promotions will require making a favorable impression on his superiors. The question haunts me, "Have those unfortunate and insidious early occupational experiences established a pattern of behavior that will limit his career?"

Isaiah's story is remarkable both for its detail and for the insight he provides into a workplace marked by overt and aversive racism. But he is not alone in recounting such stories. The other men in this study, both young and old, told of similar harassment and discrimination by supervisors, unequal treatment and pay, and their reluctance to leave a job if a few co-workers make the workplace bearable. Eventually, these processes of racial discrimination discourage or extinguish the desire to seek even the few promotions available.

Other Young Men's Stories of Racial Discrimination

Harold, a twenty-one-year-old oil changer at a quick oil change service, dropped out of high school one semester before graduation and lives at home with his mother; he has a one-year-old daughter. Harold was a cook at a major steak house chain restaurant. He enjoyed cooking and says he did not mind going to work because many of his friends worked there. Things went well until he got a new young white supervisor, with whom he did not get along. Harold describes the experience:

The manager and I, we had a, we had three managers there, then they recruited a young guy about my age. And me and him didn't get along from jump. I guess when he first came in he'd tell me to do something, I'd look at him like you just got here, too. When he first got there, he started switching everything around. Like you know, making me do dishes again when I told him I'm not on that position no more. I guess we just didn't get along. So one day I came in there to pick up my paycheck. And he said I was getting my friend free food. So he came out to hand out the checks, so he came to me and said if I catch you giving out free food I'm going to fire your ass. I said I wasn't giving out free food. We got into a big argument. So the police were called, and they fired me . . . otherwise I'd still be working there today.

Harold's experience illustrates that having friends at work makes work enjoyable, and it shows how tenuous job security is for African-Americans; a change in supervisors can have devastating consequences.

Quincy is a nineteen-year-old high school dropout who works sporadically. Quincy told me of an incident that occurred while he was working as a waiter in a restaurant. One night he received a call informing him that his best friend had been shot and was dying. He called work to tell them what happened and to explain why he would be absent from work. His supervisor accused him of lying and told him he would be fired if he did not report for work. He was fired. After making a number of appeals he was rehired, but he decided not to return to work there. Quincy never mentioned that his treatment could have been racially motivated.

Quincy's mother and I are good friends. She is able to relate to blacks and whites with equal ease and, when necessary, to bridge the gap between the two cultures. They live in a small town where she worked in city government for many years until her employment and her supervisor's were terminated. She says her department was a stellar performer that received national awards. They performed so well that other government officials felt jealous and threatened; blacks in their town were not supposed to have more than a limited amount of power. Even with experiences like this one, she has raised her children to be color-blind. Evidence of this is that all three of her adult children have white mates.

Quincy and his white girlfriend had a dispute. She and her father, who never approved of Quincy, had him prosecuted for rape. He was recently released from a six-month prison sentence. His mother says, "He'll learn. After his stay in prison, he seems to be much more in touch with reality." But Quincy has yet to accomplish the developmental task of acknowledging that racial discrimination affects his life.

Keith was a porter at the auto dealership where my car was being serviced. As Keith drove me to the university, he told me of his experiences at a southern university where he completed only his freshman year. His roommate played music very loud, which angered the resident adviser who had admonished the students to be quiet. The white students played music even louder, but when the sheriff was called in to solve the problem, Keith was arrested for his roommate's infraction. His mother convinced him to finish the year. Keith vowed never to return to the South, nor has he returned to school. This is yet another story of motivation being destroyed by racial discrimination.

I interviewed Paul at a community center where he was working as a youth counselor for the summer. During the school year, Paul is a premedical student at a major university. When asked about racial discrimination, Paul acknowledges that it is ubiquitous and that one has to live with it and deal with it. He is dealing with it by making the most of his life.

When I interviewed Odell, he had just graduated from high school. He lives in the same public housing project as Lucas, whose success story will be covered later. Lucas is his role model. Odell was a member of an African-American gang at his high school that frequently fought with white students. School officials thought he was the leader of the gang and suspended him from school. He eventually graduated from night school, with his mother's constant encouragement. Odell was scheduled to begin working at the community center where both Lucas and Paul were employed, and he had been admitted to the college where Lucas attended his first two years. Odell's story illustrates the benefit of having role models who can provide examples of successful strategies and paths to success. Middle-class youths are often surrounded by role models; unfortunately, positive role models are scarce in inner cities.

The younger men who have the brightest futures are those who are pursuing higher education, followed by those who are working at unskilled occupations. Those whose outcomes are bleakest have not dealt with racial discrimination and are not seeking higher education.

Older Men and Racial Discrimination

The older men told similar stories of racial discrimination. African-American workers are victimized by excessive threats of dismissal; many supervisors are not at all hesitant to use the threat of firing their black workers. Promotion is rarely an option for blacks, and African-Americans are often reluctant to accept promotion when it is available.

Gordon is thirty-seven years old, grew up in a poor single-female-headed household, began abusing substances at age nine, and is dyslexic. He currently works as a laborer at a recycling center and as a part-time janitor. He works two jobs because neither job pays enough for him to live on. Gordon recounted experiences of blatant and overt racial discrimination on the job. He was hired as a porter at an automobile dealership and got along very well with the white supervisor who hired him. However, things changed when he got a new white supervisor; the supervisor did everything possible to get him in trouble, including telling him, "Now I'm the boss on this plantation." Gordon was eventually fired. Gordon's story illustrates how tenuous African-American job security can be. Merely getting a new supervisor who is an overt or an aversive racist can result in arbitrary and devastating dismissal.

Anthony is a forty-eight-year-old social science doctoral candidate at a major university. In his pursuit of occupational success he had to deal with growing up in a single-female-headed household in a notoriously tough inner-city neighborhood, incarceration, substance abuse, and subsequent homelessness. Anthony is a very large and dark man who can be intimidating. Earlier in his life, he worked at a telephone company for six years. On three occasions he was harassed and suspended by white supervisors who were not his regular supervisors. At the phone company, any supervisor could supervise an employee. He worked on the switching panels, but field supervisors would come in and arbitrarily exercise authority over him. Anthony fought the first two suspensions, was acquitted, and received his pay for the periods of suspension. He got tired of the harassment and quit after the third suspension.

Edward is a forty-nine-year-old social scientist who earned his doctoral degree later in life. His father died at an early age and he spent some of his youth in a female-headed household. About 25 percent of the boys who grew up in his neighborhood died of homicide or suicide, and many of the survivors are alcoholics or drug addicts. At his first full-time job as an eighteen-year-old unskilled laborer in an auto plant, Edward remembered being in a group of young men who were temporarily transferred to a different department of the auto plant. There were five men: four black and one white. Two foremen met them to assign them work; one said, "You take the colored boys, and I'll take the white boy." Edward and the other blacks were assigned extremely difficult jobs and had to work at a feverish pace. On their break, they passed the white fellow who was working at a leisurely pace. This was Edward's repeated experience at the plant. He recalled his orientation there:

> At the time, I didn't think it was strange that at the orientation there were only black new hires. Now, I realize that there must have been two orientations, one for the whites and a separate one for the blacks. The black new hires were told, "You will do what we tell you, how we tell you to do it, and you will not ask any questions. If you can't do that, there is someone on the street waiting for your job."

He said that even thirty years later, those words continue to resonate in his thoughts. Edward worked at the auto plant for three years before leaving for employment that offered more opportunity for advancement.

Unequal Pay

Often, African-American workers do not earn as much as their white counterparts. John is a thirty-seven-year-old auto plant worker who has a wife, six children, and two dogs. After high school, John worked for his father who he says did not pay enough. Then he entered the military. After leaving the military he moved north and worked at a small paint factory for about nine years. At the paint factory, conditions were not good for blacks under the supervision of the old owner, but when the son took over the business, it became unbearable. Racial discrimination became unabashedly overt. Blacks were hired at $5.00/hour while whites were hired for the same job at $7.50/hour. John drove trucks at the company for three years, earning $9.00/hour; a new white driver was hired at $10.00/hour. Eventually John quit, as did all the other blacks with one exception. He took a better job as a garbage collector for a few years before taking his current job in an automobile plant.

Edward also recalled his experience of working at a small machine shop many years ago. He was the best of the young machinists in the shop and was paid $2.50/hour. A white fellow who was not nearly as good was later hired in at 4.50/hour. He would make mistakes that Edward would work overtime to correct. Edward says it is much more difficult to correct mistakes than to make the parts correctly in the first place. He quit when the company would not give him a raise to $3.50/hour.

Avoiding Promotions

Many of the African-American men I interviewed prefer not to seek promotion because of discrimination on the job. Racial discrimination creates such an adversarial environment that many African-American men will not accept promotions when they are offered to them for fear of defecting from their group. They fear social isolation and feel that they would be selling out to the enemy if they become supervisors. They also fear losing the safety of union protection.

While in a restaurant, I talked with an articulate twenty-six-year-old auto plant worker who resists moving into a management position. He has seen black supervisors mistreated by higher management while their white counterparts are treated well. He fears what will happen to him if he loses union protection. Like so many other African-American men, he cannot stand the thought of selling out to the company.

Men were willing to talk with me because they correctly perceived that I empathized with them. Some of the conversations were cryptic because we were able to talk in the "code" of shared experiences of undereducated blue-collar black men. The code of the auto plant provides an example. I spent a few years in the plants; and I hated nearly every minute of it. The lines were run at breathtaking speeds. To blow your nose you had to work your way up the line, which is no small feat, then catch up after blowing. The whole thing could take five to ten minutes. One plant did not allow anyone to sit down, even in the restroom, while on break. There were stories of management raiding the restrooms and suspending anyone who was sitting on a toilet that did not contain feces. The management of the plant mistreated most workers; however, the whites could look forward to both horizontal and vertical advancement, something that was difficult or impossible for most blacks. It is understandable why African-American workers would be reluctant to become supervisors, to become the enemy.

Many of the younger workers, both blacks and whites, vowed not to stay in the plant. We referred to the older workers as "lifers" because the plant made people dull; it seemed to take away some of their humanity. Often, the lifers' most important job expectation was retirement. Richard, one of my oldest and dearest friends, entered the auto plant immediately after high school and eventually became a lifer. We grew up together; I am a few years older than he. We share a fictive kin relationship—in fact, we call each other Cuz. Years ago I worked at the Big Auto Plant where Cuz works. One day when Cuz and I were talking, I became excited about his being offered a foreman's position. I was equally dismayed when he told me of his decision to refuse the promotion. I tried my best to convince him to change his mind by listing all of the benefits: he would not have to do the hard physical work, get greasy every day (years ago people used to refer to us as "greasy Big Auto Plant niggers"), earn more money, have the additional benefits of a salaried worker, and so on. My pleading and cajoling had no effect. He said:

> Na Cuz, I just can't do it. It's not as bad as when you were in there, but you know how it is. Those guys are my friends; I couldn't treat them the way I would have to.

I did not respond because I understood; my understanding was more emotional than factual, but I understood nevertheless. Cuz is OK; he is looking forward to early retirement in a few years at the age of forty-eight. The "30 and out" retirement program gives autoworkers hope.

With the support of supervisors and co-workers, some African-American men can achieve their potential. John, who now works at a large auto plant after his painful experience at the paint factory, has always been comfortable staying on the assembly line. He told me there was a team leader position available in his work group and that both management and his co-workers were encouraging him to take it. When I talked with him about becoming a supervisor, he replied that he could not "sell out." Becoming a supervisor would mean joining the enemy. Eventually, and reluctantly, he did accept the position; the new job has been going well.

These stories reinforce Isaiah's account of overt and aversive discrimination in the workplace. They show that mistreatment on the job limits both opportunities and the ambition to strive for them. Supportive co-workers and supervisors are not just luxuries, but necessities. Fighting back against racism exacts a high price—workers quit when their successful appeals are followed by another round of suspensions; they move from job to job looking for fair treatment. Formal remedies for discrimination, such as antidiscrimination laws and investigations, are certainly important. But while they may provide some relief, they do not address job records checkered by frequent job changes, the inability to ask for recommendations from racist employers, or the self-limiting of ambition. To address these problems, aversive racism in the work environment must end.

Yet the success that some of these men have achieved should not be overlooked. Their ability to recognize racial discrimination and to accept the limits it places on their ambition can, paradoxically, better prepare them to overcome its ill effects. In addition, the presence of people who can provide support and encouragement, who go out of their way to honor these men's equality and worth, can also serve as a psychic buffer to distress.

Preparing for Discrimination and Finding Social Support

In the interviews, both older and younger men report having been victimized by occupational racial discrimination, but the younger men's response to it is quite different. The older men have become tougher and accustomed to racist treatment; talking about racial discrimination seems more painful for the younger men. Upon entering the labor market, young African-American workers have to internalize the realities of racial oppression and learn strategies for coping with discrimination, the first of which is to recognize and anticipate it. Some of the occupationally unsuccessful young African-Americans in this study have not yet come to terms with the stark reality of racial oppression in the occupational domain. Learning that opportunities are limited and that they will receive unfair treatment in the workplace is often a traumatic but necessary experience.

It appears that a developmental task for African-American men is to internalize their second-class citizenship. Younger men in this study who do not acknowledge racial discrimination's effect on their occupational status or occupational conditions are not consistently employed. The younger men who understand their position in a racist system are the ones who are consistently employed. The men who are thriving acknowledge and recognize racial discrimination in their lives and are actively dealing with it. This recognition may, at times, have a negative impact on aspiration. However it is nonetheless crucial to psychological stability and balance, to the ability to determine a realistic path in society and pursue it, to establishing a strong sense of identity, an armor, a way to deal with and deflect rage.

When the effects of racial discrimination are ignored, efforts to succeed may be misdirected. African-Americans use a myriad of strategies to deal with racism. Naive African-American workers may not steer clear of supervisors who are aversive racists. They may not know that changes of employment to find a more egalitarian employer may be necessary to achieve success. When racism is not acknowledged, necessary survival strategies may not be used and success may become more elusive.

Life is a battle for African-Americans; thank God, most do not quit. Some people are able to acknowledge racism's devastating effect in their lives. When it knocks them down, they make the appropriate attributions, get back on their feet, and fight another round. Isaiah is an example of a successful young warrior. At twenty-two years of age, he has been in a seven-year occupational battle. He is aware of his abilities and of occupational racial discrimination. When he encounters difficulties, he makes a situational attribution and keeps striving forward. The effects of racial discrimination have psychologically scarred most of the men in this study, but they keep on going.

Substance Abuse

Substance abuse plagues American society. It is most devastating in the African-American community where resources are limited. Substance abuse is a major obstacle to occupational self-sufficiency. Seven of the ten older men I interviewed had to overcome substance abuse in their quest for occupational success. At least two of them are still struggling with crack cocaine addiction. They reported that the periods of substance abuse were the worst times in their lives. It is important to note that both of the unemployed men have current substance abuse problems that affect their employment status.

Recovery from substance abuse often marked a transition point in these men's lives. Barry's was one of those stories of positive transition. Barry spoke of using substances since elementary school. His mother, who headed their household, had parties at their house to supplement her income. Barry would sample leftover alcohol, marijuana, and heroin. He did well academically but was often at odds with teachers because of his behavior. He described himself as having been a full-blown drug addict by high school. After graduating from high school, he took a job at an auto factory, which he lost because of drug addiction. In any case, working in the plant as un-skilled labor is not suitable employment for people of above-average intel-ligence, and Barry is smart. As a consequence of drug addiction, Barry was incarcerated a number of times and also became homeless. He said that dur-ing his periods of homelessness he could always depend on his grandmother for a place to take a bath and get a good meal. Some very special people in drug treatment centers and human service agencies went above and beyond the call of duty to facilitate his rehabilitation.

When I met Barry, he worked as a counselor in a community-based youth program. I was impressed by his dynamic approach to his work and his dedication to the children. Barry was within six credit hours of gradu-ation from a local university and was looking forward to attending gradu-ate school. Then things began to fall apart: the relationship with his daugh-ter's mother, who had been very supportive of him, soured. He was denied visitation with his daughter, and he began having trouble at work. Soon he was back on the crack pipe. He lost his job and his apartment. The last thing I heard about him was that he had been seen on the street without a jacket or shoes in the middle of winter. Barry's story illustrates how tenuous oc-cupational success is for men who have substance abuse problems.

Nathaniel's history of substance abuse has also caused him some losses. He most regrets losing his supervisory position at a chemical plant. He says that he was totally at fault in that loss, as well as in others. He denies that racism could be a factor in his difficulties; instead, he attributes all of his problems to substance abuse. He gets social support from his family, but his girlfriend encourages his participation in her world of illegal substances. I was told that he had been clean for a while before my interview with him. However, he immediately took my interview payment to the crack house. I have heard that he is completely back into his world of substance abuse.

David was working in an auto plant when I met him. He quit the plant and began working for a small construction company. In our first short in-terview he told me that he had almost always been in trouble. His troubles included substance abuse. Soon after being released from prison, he began seeing the woman who is now his wife. He says that she is the person who turned his life around, giving him support and direction. Although our first interview was short, he was eager to tell his story of reform and his wife's role in his recovery. I wanted to learn more about this man who had made a positive transition and impressed me as having a great amount of potential. He was busy and hard to pin down for an interview. Once when I called his house, his wife told me, with great sadness in her voice, that he had been working out of the state and would be gone for a few more months.

I remembered one of my good friends having told me that after long absences from his North Carolina hometown, men would often tell of being in New York when they had actually been incarcerated. When David returned I was eager to reinterview him, but he was evasive and did not want to talk about himself. I think he had been back to "New York."

Frank is a forty-one-year-old auto plant worker. He told me of a childhood of abuse and many years of substance abuse from which he is now clean. He is a divorced father of several children by different mothers. He has been on his job for about four months, his first regular job in nine years. Many years ago, I had briefly worked at the same plant. My last week there was the week of Thanksgiving. Those four consecutive days off felt so good that I did not return; I never regretted it. During many of our interviews, Frank and I would have to wipe away tears. Frank's interview was so distressing that I could neither revisit it in another interview nor in this paper. I hope Frank is able to do well, but I doubt it.

Charles is a very adaptable forty-one-year-old man who described himself as having been an abused child and a drug addict. He had been committed to a mental institution, incarcerated, and homeless. Miraculously, with all his previous problems, he is doing well. His pastor has been a source of strength and refuge for him. At a time in life when things were not going well, the pastor gently gave him much needed support and encouragement. Charles currently supplements his Social Security disability income with part-time jobs. He has found a supportive girlfriend, established good relations with an adult son who lives in a distant state, and stayed active in the church. Charles helps many elderly people who, I believe, are another source of social support for him. Charles only completed third grade; what he lacks in formal education, he compensates for with common sense.

Gordon, mentioned earlier in this chapter, is thirty-seven years old and one of nine siblings who grew up in a poor female headed household. He began using substances at about age nine and used them almost continuously until about two years ago. He lost an unskilled factory job as a result of downsizing in the auto industry. He never did well in school and could not understand his difficulties until he was diagnosed in adult night school as having dyslexia. He says that he was given a new lease on life in a long-term substance abuse treatment center. The center's staff placed him in positions where he was forced to read and to accept responsibility for his life. He can now hold jobs that require limited literacy. Gordon has held a succession of unskilled jobs, often working two jobs to afford a car, which increases his employment opportunities. In addition to regular employment, he and his live-in girlfriend have started a small janitorial service. Gordon is doing well and will probably continue to do so unless the substance abuse problems resurface.

As did many men of my age cohort, Anthony began using drugs in Vietnam. As a consequence of substance abuse and drug dealing, he lost many jobs, and the confidence and support of his family. He was incarcerated and ultimately became homeless. When he hit, as he calls it, "rock bottom," a very special person appeared in his life. A community college professor noticed him sleeping in a drive-in theater across the street from the college. The professor gave Anthony some words of encouragement and told him that once he got himself straightened out, he should attend the college. He checked himself into a Veterans Administration substance abuse treatment center. Other special people recognized that he needed more than the allowed three months of treatment and argued his case. He was admitted to an eighteen-month program. After the treatment program, he enrolled in the community college. We met while we were both graduate students. Anthony is now a doctoral candidate, looking forward to a collegiate teaching career. We each recognize and acknowledge the effects of racial discrimination in our lives. We understand that it affects us educationally, occupationally, in our business dealings, and even in our personal relationships.

Crack is epidemic in the African-American community. It destroys individuals and removes financial resources from the community. Both of these effects make it more difficult for African-Americans to achieve occupational success.

Social Support and Structural Support

Social support from families, friends, co-workers, teachers, and supervisors is critical, often pivotal. The respondents in these interviews consistently referred to the importance of supportive people who went above and beyond the call of duty to assist them. Lucas's story illustrates how effective social support can be in facilitating positive educational and life outcomes.

Lucas is a twenty-year-old elementary education major, a junior at a local university. He grew up and still lives in a tough housing project. Lucas had been in trouble early in his high school career, expelled and sent to a youth home three times. In his freshman year, he brought a gun to school, got caught, and was transferred to another school where he met Mrs. H., a teacher:

> I had a teacher at the new school that came into my life and really turned me around. She had kids my age. I had actually met her sons

the summer before at basketball camp. Then I came to class one day, and I had my camp T-shirt on. She said, "Oh, I remember that." I wore the shirt the first day, you know, and we just started talking. I didn't, I wasn't picking up on it then. But now I look back. She was probably showing me the attention I needed. Probably, you know, just little things like, you know, giving me a ride home from school every day, taking me out to eat. She had twins my age too, so I had, sometimes I used to just spend the night at her house and come to school with her. Spent the night. Slept in the bed. Whenever I went to her house or something with her and her kids, they drove. We always went out to eat and places.

When I first went there I was, I don't know, trying to be tough. She used to call me a punk, that's what she called me. She called me a punk. Let's see, I don't know, I just can't really explain it. When I first started the new school. I was still getting into trouble. To everybody else it was, Oh you still doing that, well don't come around me. But Mrs. H. kind of like played around with it, OK you don't need to do that. . . . I can't really find words for it. I haven't really told you all that I should have told you about like my teacher. How she turned me around and stuff like that. I don't really have words for it; it's a lot deeper than what I was saying. Like just the time she spent. I mean that was just the one person that I knew I wasn't just a paycheck to.

Lucas talked about his four best friends from his neighborhood:

One of them is paralyzed; he got shot in the back. Two are dead. One, he finished school, but he just got married after that. Better than me in basketball, just let it go. He got a scholarship and let it go.

Without the intervention of Mrs. H., Lucas may have ended up like his friends. Mrs. H. went far beyond the call of duty to save Lucas from his environment. And this, it appears, is what it takes.

Structural support offers as much as social support. Men who had the best occupational prospects achieved them through higher education. Without government support in the form of scholarships or fellowships, obtaining higher education would have been much more difficult, if not impossible.

All of the interviewees came from poor or working-class backgrounds. The young men who are currently undergraduates receive state and federal educational support; they could not attend school without it. While in high school, some of the men participated in work-study programs that encouraged them to stay in school. John's company is training him to become an electrician, and he is looking forward to earning a college degree. Some of the men received education as part of prison rehabilitation programs. Many of them received structural support in substance abuse treatment programs where they often were able to turn their lives around.

Edward, Anthony, and I have earned or are earning doctoral degrees late in our development, in our forties or fifties. Like Anthony and myself, Edward came from a working-class background, held a number of other jobs, and overcame numerous obstacles before achieving success that is commensurate with his abilities. Each of us has quit "good unskilled and semi-skilled jobs" in factories, construction, or communications before achieving our current status as social scientists. I believe that had we been white, our abilities would have been recognized and developed earlier in our lives and we would have achieved our current positions some twenty years earlier.

I have received educational support from universities, government agencies, and foundations. After obtaining my baccalaureate degree, in addition to educational loans and graduate student employment, I received over a quarter of a million dollars in the form of tuition waivers, health insurance, and stipends. Although barely enough to support my family, this financial aid allowed me to earn a doctoral degree, conduct research in a postdoctoral fellowship, and to obtain my current position as an assistant professor.

Conclusion

The interviews with men in this project reveal that racial discrimination and substance abuse are two major barriers to achieving occupational self-sufficiency for African-American men. The study also shows that a combination of social support and structural support facilitates their success in the labor force.

Finding ways to address the structural barriers that block the advancement of young, poor, African-American men is clearly important. To be most effective, these structural remedies should be provided within a supportive social context that also acknowledges the blunt fact of racism in our society. Barriers to occupational success are social and psychological as well as structural; so too must be the solutions. Research in this area must explore ways to encourage the provision of social support and to help African-American men develop the coping skills to confront racism. The lessons that have come from this study are that African-American men must surmount numerous and formidable barriers to achieve occupational success, and that surmounting the barriers is a group rather than an individual process.

REFERENCES

Anderson, E. 1990. *Streetwise.* Chicago: University of Chicago Press.
Dovidio, J. F. 1993. "The Subtlety of Racism." *Training and Development* 47 (April): 50–57.
Dovidio, J. F., and S. F. Gaertner. 1986. *Prejudice, Discrimination, and Racism.* Orlando: Academic Press.
Kirschenman, J., and K. M. Neckerman. 1991. "'We'd Love to Hire Them, But . . .': The Meaning of Race for Employers." In *The Urban Underclass,* ed. C. Jencks and P. E. Peterson, 203–32. Washington, DC: The Brookings Institution.
Massaquoi, H. J. 1996. "The New Racism." *Ebony* 51 (August, no. 10): 56–60.
Sternberg, S. 1991. "Occupational Apartheid." *The Nation* 253:744–46.
Wilson, W. J. 1987. *The Truly Disadvantaged.* Chicago: University of Chicago Press.

PART 3
Parenting: From Enforcing Responsibility to Enabling Care

CHAPTER 8

Mother, Worker, Welfare Recipient: Welfare Reform and the Multiple Roles of Low-Income Women

Ariel Kalil, Heidi Schweingruber,
Marijata Daniel-Echols, and Ashli Breen

The Personal Responsibility and Work Opportunity Reconciliation Act (PRWORA) of 1996 ended the federal guarantee of cash assistance and re-placed the Aid to Families with Dependent Children (AFDC) program with the Temporary Assistance for Needy Families (TANF) program. PRWORA gives states a block grant of fixed size, places a five-year lifetime limit on the receipt of welfare benefits, and requires most welfare mothers to go to work no later than two years after entering the program. For the framers of this legislation, the policy will "succeed" if the new programs are efficient in moving recipients from welfare to work. Notably, success is not defined in terms of women's economic well-being or whether they can successfully manage the responsibilities of full-time work and caring for children.

In previous research, low-income women's perceptions of the risks and opportunities associated with leaving welfare for work have been cast as a human capital problem—a "mismatch" between the labor market oppor-tunities for self-supporting employment and the credentials possessed by low-income single mothers (Burtless 1995; Harris 1996; Holzer 1995). Wel-fare recipients, with their limited education, training, and work experience, find themselves on a "carousel" of low-wage, temporary, and unstable jobs, with little chance of promotion to self-supporting employment (Blank 1996; Edin and Lein 1996; Spalter-Roth et al. 1995; Wilson 1996). Moreover, as Edin and Lein (1996) describe, transitions from welfare to low-wage work often increase women's economic vulnerability due to the hidden expenses of work, such as increased costs in child care, medical care, transportation, housing, and suitable work clothing. Having cycled between welfare and low-wage work, the welfare-reliant women in Edin and Lein's study recognized their labor market prospects, human capital shortcomings, and economic vulnerabilities. They firmly believed that gaining skills and education would be the only route to self-sufficiency. Thus, faced with a choice between welfare versus work at a low-wage job, many of the women in this study (conducted prior to the 1996 Welfare Reform Act) chose the former, hoping to combine limited welfare use with continuing education or skills training.

Edin and Lein's (1996) analysis suggests, however, that women's perceptions of the vicissitudes of leaving welfare are also shaped by another important, albeit less-discussed, consideration—their maternal responsibilities. Specifically, women discussed the noneconomic "costs" of working, including whether full-time work accommodated purposeful and competent parenting, or whether work schedules would interfere with important family management responsibilities such as the supervision and monitoring needed to ensure children's safety and well-being. As Heymann and Earle (1998) point out, when parents have inflexible work schedules and lack social support or adequate substitute care, they are often forced to choose between work demands and meeting children's needs. In this chapter, we pursue this line of inquiry by exploring ways in which single mothers' attitudes toward their maternal responsibilities and their children's well-being affect their perceptions of the liabilities and rewards of welfare and work.

The analysis we develop provides insight into how women think about their roles as caregivers and how their desire to be good mothers influences their views regarding welfare and work. Our discussion of these issues is based on interviews and focus groups with twenty-three low-income mothers living in two counties near a major metropolitan area in Michigan. All mothers were receiving or had previously received welfare, and all had worked at some point since having children. Through interviews and focus groups, we draw on these women's experiences to develop a framework for understanding how their struggles to fulfill multiple roles influenced their attitudes about work and welfare. We demonstrate that women's perceptions of welfare and the low-wage labor market are as often shaped by their concerns about caregiving as they are by economic considerations.

We recognize that balancing the needs of children against the demands of employment is a challenge faced by all working mothers today. In recent years, changing family structures and increasing numbers of women in the workforce have reshaped the social roles that women are asked to adopt. Recognizing these changes, researchers have explored the stresses placed on women as they struggle to negotiate multiple roles and the demands that accompany them (Goldberg et al. 1992; Greenberger and O'Neil 1993). We argue, as have other researchers, that the tensions between work and parenting can be particularly difficult for low-income, single mothers who have limited resources and experience stressful living conditions (Edin and Lein

1996; Heymann and Earle 1998; Oliker 1996). For example, employed single mothers with preschoolers may experience more role strain if they believe that maternal employment has negative consequences for children (Goldberg et al. 1992). Relatedly, the predictability of sources of income and the extent to which income meets one's needs have been linked to women's mental health and well-being (Pett and Vaughan-Cole 1986).

Although the concerns just outlined are not exclusively relevant to welfare mothers, the choices mothers make in the new world of welfare are likely to carry more serious consequences for themselves and their children. For example, under new regulations, women who fail to successfully balance the multiple roles of mother, worker, and welfare recipient face sanctions that could increase stress and economic hardship. Ultimately, at least in some states, lifetime limits on cash assistance will force some women to find other ways to support their families.

To understand the tensions between work and parenting faced by low-income, single mothers, it is important to consider the multiplicity of social roles women must fill and the importance an individual attaches to each role. For this reason, we suggest that low-income mothers who receive welfare face further complications because they must also negotiate the regulations of welfare agencies in conjunction with making decisions about working and caregiving.

Our analysis is based on conversations with women about the ways that parenting, work, and welfare are interwoven. From our inductive analysis of these conversations, we identified four dimensions of caregiving that together constitute these women's conception of child rearing. These four areas, which we developed from the women's own descriptions of parenting, are not exhaustive in that they do not capture all of the aspects of parenting that women mentioned. They do, however, provide a structure for our analysis that captures the primary aspects of caregiving as described by the women with whom we spoke.

First, women were concerned with the provision of material goods. This included meeting basic needs, such as providing food, clothing, and shelter as well as gifts or other special treats. Second, women talked about the need to provide adequate health care for their children. Third, mothers were concerned about providing quality child care. This included the care that mothers themselves provided as well as that provided by other caregivers. Finally, mothers had concerns about the amount of time they were able to spend with their children. These concerns about time related to both the quantity and quality of the time mothers felt they spent with children. For example, some women were concerned about whether they had the time and energy to provide cognitively enriching activities for their children. Others indicated that after a long day at work they did not feel that they always had the patience to offer sufficient emotional support while simultaneously filling the role of both mother and father.

For the women in our study, successful parenting entailed meeting the needs of children along the four different dimensions at once. In assessing the benefits and liabilities of work and welfare, they considered whether work or welfare would allow them to meet their responsibilities in each domain. For example, a woman may recognize that full-time employment, although it might allow her to better provide material goods for her child, could severely limit the time they can share. Similarly, despite women's desires to work and demonstrate a good work ethic to their children, they worried that a full-time, low-wage job might not provide enough money to pay for day care or provide health insurance. Women's comments indicated that the ways in which they perceived and managed these risks in relation to their assessment of maternal responsibilities played a key role in the opinions they held about welfare and work.

In our analysis, we consider in depth each of the four dimensions of parenting and describe how mothers conceptualized each domain. We also explore the tensions mothers experienced between welfare, work, and parenting within that domain. It is important to emphasize, however, that in these mothers' own discussions of the advantages and disadvantages of welfare and work, they did not focus on one dimension of parenting at a time. Rather, they simultaneously speculated about the consequences of welfare and work across the four domains of caregiving. Therefore, our summary of these descriptions of parenting responsibilities synthesizes the interplay of these domains as they relate to perceptions of work and welfare. This synthesis reveals how concerns about maternal responsibilities in each of the domains, as well as individual differences among mothers, affect perceptions of the risks and opportunities inherent in welfare and work.

Method

Our analysis is based on information gathered during individual interviews and focus groups. The twenty-three women who participated in the study, conducted between June and August of 1996, varied in terms of work experience and history of welfare receipt. We recruited participants from multiple sources. Flyers describing the study and asking for participants were posted at various locations throughout the community, including local welfare offices. We also called child-care facilities that served low-income populations to find out about potential parent groups from which we could recruit focus group participants.

Mothers who responded to the flyers were recruited for individual interviews. The interviews were conducted either in the women's homes or at another convenient location such as a local park or fast-food restaurant. Selected demographic characteristics of the ten women who participated in individual interviews are illustrated in table 1.

Participants in the focus groups were recruited from local programs designed to support low-income mothers. Our goal in recruiting these groups was to observe a range of women's experiences. In all, thirteen women participated in three focus groups. The first focus group consisted of four teenage mothers who lived in a private group home with their children. The criteria for residing in this home included attendance at high school and participation in parenting education and support activities. The second focus group was conducted at a neighborhood community center and included four women who were participating in a short-term work-readiness program of the type that most resembles those offered under new welfare rules. The third focus group consisted of five women who were attending a local community college as part of a program that focused primarily on placing welfare recipients into education and training programs (programs of this type have been phased out under new welfare rules). Selected demographic characteristics of these thirteen women are illustrated in table 2.

The diversity of the sample allowed us to explore issues of parenting, work, and welfare among women in different situations and at various points in the life span. This enabled us to identify aspects of parenting that differed depending on a woman's background and experiences, as well as

TABLE 1. Selected Demographic Characteristics of Individual Interview Participants

	Race	Age	Marital Status	Number of Children	Currently Working	On AFDC
Individual 1	Black	23	Never Married	2	No	Yes
Individual 2	Black	23	Never Married	1	No	Yes
Individual 3	White	42	Divorced	3	No	No
Individual 4	White	40	Never Married	1	No	No
Individual 5	White	22	Never Married	1	Yes	Yes
Individual 6	White	22	Never Married	1	Yes	No
Individual 7	White	36	Divorced twice	3	No	Yes
Individual 8	White	23	Never Married	1	No	Yes
Individual 9	Black	29	Married	1	Yes	No
Individual 10	White	35	Divorced	1	Yes	No

those that were common to all the mothers. We were initially concerned that the teen parent group might differ too much from the other women who participated; however, due to the housework participation and school requirements of the group home in which they lived, they expressed many of the same tensions that other mothers expressed over role strain in caregiving. For example, in addition to completing their high school education, these young women were responsible for their own cooking, cleaning, and shopping and were required to participate in a series of independent living skills and parenting education classes at the residence.

The interviews and focus groups were broadly conceived as an exploration of the impact of the transition from welfare to work on family functioning.[1] Four main topic areas were of central interest: parenting behaviors, attitudes toward parenting, mental health and coping, and welfare and work. Both an interview guide and a focus group protocol were developed to ensure that the issues central to our research questions were discussed. The guide and the protocol were similar since we wanted to be able to summarize the information gathered from both sources together.

The guide and the protocol were used differently during the interviews and focus groups. During interviews the conversations were unstructured and the guide was used mainly to remind the interviewer about topics to cover. During the focus groups a member of the research team acted as mediator and used the protocol to structure the discussions. The mediator set ground rules for discussion and led the participants through discussion of the chosen topics in the order designated in the protocol (Morgan 1997). A second member of the research team also attended each focus group to observe and take notes.

In the remaining sections of this chapter, we draw on this information to explore the ways that women formulate attitudes about the liabilities and

TABLE 2. Selected Demographic Characteristics of Focus Group Participants

	Teen Parent Program (N = 4)	Training Program (N = 4)	Community College (N = 5)
Race	3 Black, 1 White	3 Black, 1 White	3 Black, 1 Native American, 1 Asian
Work	No (all students)	No	No (all students)
AFDC	Yes (all)	Yes (all)	Yes (all)
Number of Children	1 (all)	2 (N = 2); 4, (N = 1); 8 (N = 1)	1 (N = 3); 1 grandchild (N = 1); 3 (N = 1)
Age Range of Mothers	17–18	33–35	30–42

benefits of welfare and work within the context of parenting. As noted, our concept of parenting was developed from women's own descriptions of their role as mothers and what this role entails. We begin by considering women's beliefs about how work relates to parenting with an emphasis on their dual commitment to working and parenting. This discussion sets the stage for our analysis of work and welfare in the context of caregiving responsibilities.

Commitment to Work and Parenting

All the mothers in this study were heavily invested in their roles as care-givers. At the same time, they were committed to working for what they perceived to be its economic and personal rewards. Their commitment to work is evidenced by the fact that all had worked at some time in the past. Of the twelve women who were not full-time students at the time of the study, four were working full- or part-time, and eight were actively looking for work. In addition, most of the mothers discussed working in a positive light, emphasizing the satisfaction of providing for their families economically and the opportunities for personal growth. At the same time, since they had experienced firsthand the vagaries of the low-wage labor market, they recognized that employment would have to offer a certain minimum wage to promote exits from welfare and eventual economic self-sufficiency.

Mothers in our study mentioned a variety of positive effects of employment, both for themselves and for their children. They commented on the improvement of their own self-image and mental status when they were working. For example, they discussed feeling more confident and having higher self-esteem when they obtained employment. As one mother stated, "I enjoy working and getting out and meeting new people and growing. I feel like there was something that I could do for myself one day, and live better."

Some mothers also saw working as a way to relieve the stress of caring for children twenty-four hours a day. Since these mothers often spent much of their time at home while they were on welfare, they described work in terms of an outlet and a place to have adult conversations. This time away, in turn, enabled them to return home better able to deal with their children. A young mother of two children under age four expressed the difficulty of being around her children all day without any other types of stimulation:

> . . . if you don't have a job, it kinda sometimes gets kind of sad, so you just try to find other things to do. Because I'd rather be working, honestly, and then you know, have some time with the children. Because being around kids all day, or anybody all day constantly, every day, it

could just make you sit there like, "I really don't want to be here right now, I'd rather be somewhere else for a couple hours or something."

Mothers also described the positive effects of employment on their children. For instance, although some mothers expressed a preference to stay home and raise their children, many described the potential advantages of day care, such as the social and cognitive skills that children develop as a result of being around other children.

Last, mothers talked about their desire to work because it reflected their own ethic and the example they wanted to set for their children. One unemployed mother said: "I just think that I should be doing it myself. I think I should be paying for my own living, I should be paying for my own house, and everything, where I'm not." Another mother said it made her feel better to know that she would be getting a paycheck every week, rather than waiting at home for the welfare check to arrive.

Given this positive orientation toward working, the question of how women's commitment to parenting contributes to their perceptions about welfare and work becomes even more compelling. From their comments, a key factor seems to be the belief that good parenting is multifaceted. In the next sections, we describe women's perceptions of the multiple domains of successful parenting. We illustrate how these beliefs shape women's attitudes and actions as economic providers and as caretakers and also highlight the potential conflict between these two important and sometimes competing goals.

Material Goods

A fundamental dimension of caregiving that concerned all of the mothers with whom we spoke was the ability to provide the material goods that would help them meet children's basic needs. These responsibilities constituted caregiving at its most basic level; if mothers could not take care of these needs, it represented for them their most serious failure as a parent. In our sample, the specific material goods discussed varied as a function of the child's age. For example, mothers of school-age children were particularly concerned about school clothes. In describing her family's routine at the start of the new school year, one mother remarked:

Well, I'd like to provide more than just their basic needs for survival. I'd like [my daughter] to get the new sandals—look at them sandals. I'd like to be able to get her a new pair. And at school time it's really hard. I don't want to send my kids to school in the same clothes they wore last year. . . . That first few days of school, I don't want to go fishing through a clothing closet looking for school clothes for the kids. Sometimes [my daughter] is like "cool, I get that dress," but other times it's like, "Mom, these are raggedy." I'd like to go to the store and have a coupla hundred bucks and then some—I want them to smell new like every other kid in school does. That first day of school every kid smells like Kmart. I want them to have those things, but I just can't give them to them. I just can't do it. Not right now.

Although provision of these basic necessities was not an aspect of caregiving that mothers discussed at length, concern with meeting such needs was an integral part of their perceptions of the costs and benefits of welfare and work.

In addition to ensuring that children's basic needs were met, mothers were also concerned with providing special treats for their children, such as birthday and holiday gifts, special outings, or grocery store "goodies" that food stamps did not pay for. Although many of the mothers we spoke with had enough money to provide basic necessities, few had enough for treats. One mother described the situation she faces during the holidays when she wants to give gifts to her children but cannot.

My biggest problem is when Christmas comes around, you can't really buy them what you want them to have. And then a birthday might come around at the time when you don't really even have $1.00 in your pocket, and they're looking like, "I'm not important, my birthday passed." School clothes are coming around [sounds of agreement by others]. I'm worried about that already, and I still got two more months. I'm like, how am I going to stretch out the money when the bills are constantly coming in? What do you tell AT&T or Ameritech— "I can't pay you, I want to buy my kid something?" They don't want to hear it so . . . [you] just try to do the best that you can.

In describing how a lack of money made them feel as parents, mothers were often most frustrated when unable to purchase these extra things for their children. This frustration seemed rooted in their belief that their children would feel neglected or unimportant. Moreover, these mothers constantly negotiated the social pressure created by a consumer society in which self-worth is derived from a continuous supply of material goods. The tensions produced by living in this kind of society without resources is illustrated in this mother's comment:

. . . I guess the hard part is being on ADC you don't have a lot of money and a lot of things that they want, they'll say, "Well, so and so has this, why can't we?" I'll be glad when I finish school so I can make more money. Not give them everything they want, but be able to give them some of the things that they want because on ADC you can't do that. You barely can pay your rent. So it's hard. And, having them compare themselves to other children, about "well, they got this and they got that."

Almost uniformly, this financial insecurity diminished mothers' self-esteem and fostered self-doubts regarding their adequacy as mothers and providers relative to their more affluent counterparts. These feelings of fiscal and parental inadequacy were closely related to feelings of embarrassment and shame felt by mothers (and sometimes children as well) when their lack of money was made public, as in receiving free lunch at school or using food stamps at the grocery store. One woman remarked:

[In the grocery store] everybody sees where we get our money. Even his playmates, he goes to a nice school. You have all these professor children going there, and all this stuff. When I run into his friends with their parents [in the store], I get totally embarrassed. I don't even want to show them the stamps. And I have, at a point—I didn't buy the food [at that store]. That's how embarrassed I can get.

The temporary strategies mothers developed for negotiating their economic limitations were varied. Sometimes mothers simply skipped payments on bills that were due in order to provide something for their children. In other instances, mothers borrowed or were given money from family members to get special things for their children. Admittedly, such practices do not represent effective long-term money management strategies; however, they did allow women to alleviate the short-term stresses associated with their limited finances. Interestingly, some of the mothers adopted the philosophy that children should realize and understand their families' economic situations. This strategy was used by two mothers who participated in one of the focus groups:

I let the children know exactly where the money goes in our family. I give them a reason and I let them know that I have to take care of business first.

. . . yesterday [my son] was getting ready to ask me something and I said "what" and he said, "Ahh, that's right, I forgot, we don't have any money." And I said, "What is it?" "Never mind, Mom, we don't have any money."

The women we interviewed clearly wished to provide financially for their families and believed that work could improve their own emotional well-being as well as that of their children. Some would have preferred to avoid the stigma of relying on public assistance. However, they also recognized that the low-wage jobs they could realistically consider did not offer much economic potential. For example, in 1996, a single woman with two children in Michigan could work nearly full-time at a minimum-wage job and still qualify for cash assistance. Since 1992 Michigan has had a fairly generous earnings disregard policy—the first $200 plus 20 percent of remaining monthly earnings are not counted in determining eligibility for cash assistance. Although we did not specifically ask women if they were aware of this policy, it is noteworthy that none mentioned it in any of our discussions about economic trade-offs between welfare and work. This confluence of economic realities, knowledge (or lack thereof) of welfare rules, mothers' commitment to providing for their children, and their values regarding the role of welfare and employment in family life were interconnected in shaping perceptions of welfare and work.

Health Insurance and Work

A key point in policy discussions regarding "making work pay" for welfare mothers is the disincentive that exists for families who risk losing health insurance upon leaving welfare (Ellwood 1988). The mothers we interviewed confirmed that this factor shaped their perceptions of the risks and advantages of welfare and work. Most of the mothers we interviewed could see no utility in working at a low-wage job that, although making them marginally better off financially, would leave them and their children without health insurance. For example, one mother explained that the loss of Medicaid when she began working full-time created such anxiety for her about how she would cope financially if her child needed medical attention that she "ended up going right back (to welfare) and trying ever since to get off." At the time we conducted our interviews, Michigan allowed families to receive transitional Medicaid for one year after leaving welfare, and shortly thereafter it approved a small-scale "Medicaid buy-in" pilot project that allows families to continue the coverage by paying premiums of about $100 per month for one parent with any number of children. Nearly two years later, however, the buy-in program had yet to be expanded beyond the six pilot sites (Lipson et al. 1997).

For the most part, mothers in our study placed their children's health interests first and were often willing to forgo health insurance themselves in their efforts to leave welfare. For example, one mother we interviewed became ineligible for Medicaid upon accepting a part-time job at the city health department. While she was able to enroll her three-and-a-half-year-old daughter in a state-sponsored insurance program for low-income children who are ineligible for Medicaid, she herself went without health insurance for nearly a year until her position increased to full-time and she was offered health benefits. Another mother we interviewed had left welfare but had lost Medicaid benefits as a result. Although she was not comfortable being uninsured, she also had strong views about having left welfare. As she said, "I know women who won't work as much because they don't want to lose their benefits. I'm just not that kind of person." This woman's daughter was also insured in the state-sponsored program for low-income children described in the last paragraph.

Other mothers described complicated personal situations that they entered into to secure medical insurance for their children. Sara,[2] a young mother in the study, had recently completed radiation treatments for cancer. At the time we interviewed her, she was excited about the full-time job she had just accepted, as it would offer her health benefits after a short trial period. Unfortunately, her transitional Medicaid was about to expire and she was facing two months without insurance. For herself, she was simply hoping to not need medical attention during that two-month period. She refused to leave her daughter uninsured, however, and so had asked the child's biological father to insure their daughter through his program. Sara described her dealings with him as emotionally stressful, but she believed strongly in her opportunity to leave the welfare system and independently support herself and her daughter.

Similar concerns were expressed by a thirty-nine-year-old mother regarding health coverage for herself and her daughter:

> She's—she's on her father's insurance, she's supposed to be. But they keep on saying they have no record of it, and he won't take care of it. But he'll have to do something. Because she'll be insured no matter what [even if I am not].

This mother described her apprehensions about getting into disputes with her daughter's father as he had previously been physically violent toward her.

Although these mothers described having to negotiate on their own with their children's biological fathers, provisions in the Welfare Reform Act aim to strengthen this part of child support. Since 1985 state child support programs are required to take steps to ensure that children receive any health-care coverage available to the noncustodial parent. This medical support is supposed to be established as part of a child support order and is generally enforced by directing employers to enroll noncustodial parents' children in their group health plans and make appropriate premium deductions from parents' wages. However, according to 1991 Census Bureau data, only 40 percent of child support orders also provided for medical support (Yates 1997).

Overall, the mothers we spoke to expressed a willingness to work, but concerns about health insurance affected their perceptions of the risks that leaving welfare might entail. In particular, these women viewed their children's lack of health insurance as a barrier to leaving welfare. The priority they placed on insuring their children's health illustrates the interconnections of parenting concerns and perceptions of work and welfare among low-income mothers.

Child Care

The third dimension of parenting that affects mothers' perceptions of work and welfare is child care. Concerns about costly child care of indeterminate quality were relevant to all of the mothers we interviewed. A wide number of empirical studies have documented the lack of affordable, quality child care for low-income working mothers (Myers 1993). A central conflict expressed by the women in our study was that by working to provide economically for their families, they were required to spend long hours away from their children. At the same time, mothers believed that most of their earnings were going to the child-care provider. They also recognized that higher-quality care usually demands a higher price.

Mothers expressed a reluctance to place their children in the care of people they did not know, particularly if they had no systematic way to assess the background and qualifications of the day-care providers. One mother described having sought out inexpensive day care by contacting in-home providers. What she learned about the quality of the facilities and the daily activities alarmed her, prompting her comment, "Oh, my God, they might be cheap but I'm not sending my kid there."

Another mother, Karen, who was attending classes twenty hours a week to comply with Michigan's work-readiness program, related her conversation with a caseworker:

> —there's a whole situation where if you go to the classes and you don't know who's going to watch your kids, they expect you to find just anybody to watch your children. And you can't do that. I can't just be like, "Do you want to watch my child?" Especially if you don't know who that is. The job training director said, "Well, can't you just find anybody to watch your children?" I said, "I can't do that. Do you have chil-

dren?" He said, "Yeah." I said, "Well, would you just let somebody watch your children and you don't know who they are?" Because he was like, "Well, look in the newspaper." "Let me get this straight. You have children, right?" He said, "Yeah." I was like, "You look in the newspaper, you need somebody to watch your children and you don't know who they are, you don't know how your children will feel comfortable around them, and you don't know what they could do to them, would you leave your child with them?" "No." "Well, why are you telling me to?" It doesn't make sense. Like, if I knew somebody, I wouldn't mind getting off ADC and then having somebody to watch them.

Karen's comments allude to feelings that the caseworker was not sensitive to her concerns about her child-care options. Such interactions with the welfare system played an additional role in shaping women's perceptions of the trade-offs between work and welfare as they relate to parenting responsibilities. Under current rules, the state can sanction a mother for not working unless it is determined that child care is unavailable. However, the state is under no obligation to assist mothers in locating child-care programs that accept payments from the welfare agency and it does not afford them the luxury of comparing different arrangements to find the one best suited to their needs. In all likelihood, if Karen had persisted in being resistant to her case manager's suggestions, she would have been sanctioned for noncompliance.

Prior to the Welfare Reform Act, employed welfare recipients in Michigan primarily received child-care assistance through the AFDC child-care disregard. Recipients paid for child care on their own and were reimbursed for their expenses in the form of a higher AFDC grant. Several of the women we interviewed said that this system had failed. One mother described how she had been forced to quit her job as a result:

And I hated I had to quit, because social services would not pay for my daycare. . . . I had to quit my job because I couldn't pay the child care, and social services wouldn't pay. Then Work First [Michigan's welfare-to-work program] started harassing me saying I wasn't in compliance. And I'm like, "Well I had a job . . . my baby was two months old, and I had a job." And so now they getting ready to sweat me about noncompliance. And I'm trying to tell them, "I had a job." And they're crazy. So whenever I get my focus back on, we're going through the hearing. We're going to have a hearing, and I'll bring my boss and all my paperwork that I had, and all my receipts for day care. Because no one's going to watch those children for free.

Women perceived that the welfare system operated at odds with them as they made decisions regarding welfare, work, and child care. There was a feeling that bureaucratic red tape made working difficult, particularly with regard to child care. For example, a self-employed mother who had recently worked her way off welfare expressed frustration with a system that did not appreciate the fact that her income and hours, and therefore her need for help with child-care expenses, varied seasonally. A newly unified system of child-care assistance in Michigan should improve the situation for low-income working mothers. Payments for child care now take the form of direct payments to providers based on an hourly rate that accounts for the geographic area, child's age, and day-care setting. There will be little change in how families access the system as they transition from welfare to work (Michigan Family Independence Agency 1996).

One option that sometimes minimized cost and quality concerns was to have friends and family provide child care. While fathers and friends sometimes helped with child care, grandparents often served as secondary caregivers. They helped mothers juggle tight work and school schedules by providing flexible assistance in the off hours not covered by day-care centers. Importantly, among many low-income families under TANF, these substitute caregivers will now have to meet work requirements of their own and may have even less time to assist mothers like the ones we interviewed.

Other mothers described clashes over parenting styles and the interpersonal jealousies that were created when kin provided child-care assistance. One described the lack of control she had in disciplining her daughter, who spent the majority of the week with her maternal grandmother. She said, "My mom ended up with a lot of control over my daughter and this was a problem because my mom would let her get away with anything and everything, and I wouldn't." When the weekend came and this mother finally had time to spend with her daughter, their interactions were difficult. She recalls, "My daughter didn't want to be with me because I wanted her to listen and Grandma would let her do anything she wanted." This illustrates a difficult choice faced by mothers who relied on and were grateful for the care provided by relatives. They felt that they could not dictate how these relatives interacted with their children, and that they were potentially sacrificing their own authority as mothers. Women were continually making choices about whether work that required such extensive kin assistance was worth straining these family relationships and using the precious energy it took to reconstruct parenting practices that kin had undermined.

Mothers also felt uncomfortable having to consistently call on the help of friends and family when these support persons had their own responsibilities to tend to. Here is how one mother, a figure-skating instructor with variable work hours, described feeling:

. . . my family helps with baby-sitting. But I never like to ask too much because a lot of times the help I get is because I'm still teaching skating and the day care closes at 6:00 and I have to rely on grandparents to pick her up from day care. And like tonight, I have to go back and teach a class from 6:00 to 8:30 and my mom will pick her up from day care and bring her back until I get home. And so then I'm asking for like—I absolutely need family help for that. So then it's really hard for me to ask "Well, I just want to go out on a Saturday night." They'll do it, but I never like to ask a whole lot.

These examples demonstrate how child-care considerations were intertwined with women's roles as parents and workers and recipients of welfare system. While not working for a period of time was perhaps seen as a way to reduce child-care costs, guarantee quality, and increase the time spent with their children, most of the women we interviewed had previously worked and were actively trying to leave welfare and comply with work or school requirements. Some had confronted system-level barriers in their efforts to coordinate child care, such as seemingly indifferent caseworkers who pressed them to choose a provider quickly and at random. Ironically, women's reluctance to choose a provider based on concerns about quality or safety could result in economic sanctions that could threaten children in other ways. Other mothers, while grateful to relatives for helping fill gaps in child-care schedules, were concerned that these arrangements could negatively affect mothers' own relationships with their children. These various considerations interacted in shaping women's views of the benefits and drawbacks of welfare and work.

Time with Children

The fourth dimension of caregiving that concerned mothers was their ability to spend time with their children, building a strong emotional bond by providing emotional and cognitive support. Among mothers of young children in particular (about three-quarters of our sample), employment was sometimes seen as interfering with women's responsibilities for their children's developmental needs. This issue was also related to the work and child-care issues already discussed; that is, some mothers viewed the time that children spent in the care of others as a missed opportunity for strengthening the mother-child relationship. The mothers we interviewed felt that time with children was particularly important because, as single parents, they had to fulfill multiple parental roles, an issue noted in work with other low-income single mothers (Jarrett 1994). As one mother reflected, "Trying to be both parents at once is the hardest thing. When the dad does not live with you and the dad is not helping to support the family—trying to be the father figure, the disciplinarian, and the nurturing mother is almost impossible."

Concerns about spending time with children are illustrated by mothers of young children during the following exchange at the community college focus group session:

> MOTHER 1: You cry a lot when you've snapped at your child and didn't mean to. When you don't have time to just like sit down and talk to your child when you realize it has been six days since you've read a story to your little one, who just stood there and said, "Hey, I want to hear this book", and you said, "No, I'm busy." You feel guilty a whole lot. And sometimes you cry a whole lot . . .
>
> MOTHER 2: [But] you look at that big picture and say, OK, if she misses this story tonight, in the future we have the opportunity—
>
> MOTHER 1: Except [the] problem with that is that in the future, four, five, six years later when you actually do have the quality time, she's grown. And she doesn't need for you to read it to her any more, she can read it herself. So this is the—the real guilt comes in when this is the quality time they need. You don't have time to waste and say, "Hold up." So you have to, there's no room for you to say, "I'm sorry," because they need it now, not later.

Thus, women's hesitancy to leave welfare for work was often twofold—not only did they recognize that working at a low-wage job was often pointless in terms of actual economic advancement, but also that such work represented lost time with their children. One thirty-nine-year-old mother said:

> . . . at my age, I didn't have a child so I could have someone else raise it. Obviously, she's going to have to go to day care now anyway. But I was with her—she's fourteen and a half months and I've been with her, and I think that is very important. I don't regret it at all. It was hard for me to accept handouts, to accept welfare.

Although these concerns might suggest a motivation to avoid work, many mothers described the ways that working actually helped to foster better relationships with their children. As we noted previously, many women we spoke with believed that working improved their feelings of self-worth and gave them opportunities for personal growth. Thus, working often fostered a more positive outlook and left them better able to cope with the stresses of parenting. Mothers remarked that getting some time away from children and interacting with other adults often gave them more patience and allowed them to deal more constructively with conflicts and discipline. These competing views of the costs and benefits of welfare and work, combined with women's commitment to investing time in their maternal responsibilities, sometimes caused mothers to question the choices they had made:

> [I was] working forty hours a week, and I was feeling like I never spent time with my baby, and everything. I still feel like that though. It's like when you work you feel guilty like dang, I'm doing this and I can't spend enough time with [my child]. Your child may be looking nice but you feeling guilty . . . am I neglecting my baby?

Under current welfare rules, however, low-income single mothers will have little choice about staying home with their children; with few exceptions, the law requires mothers to participate in work or training for twenty hours per week as soon as their children are twelve weeks old.

The Interplay of Parenting, Work, and Welfare

Clearly, each domain of parenting we have described exerted unique pressures on mothers in their efforts to reconcile their desire to leave welfare for work with their commitment to fulfilling their role as mothers. Within each domain of parenting, we have illustrated that both work and welfare were perceived by mothers to have potentially negative as well as positive consequences. A mother's assessment of the consequences was shaped by her sense of the range of options available to her as well as by the constraints of her situation. For example, low educational attainment limited the kinds of jobs women could find and made it unlikely that work alone would allow them to meet all of their children's material needs. Similarly, women who felt constrained in their choice of child-care arrangements expressed doubts about work outside the home.

The relative importance of each domain also varied depending on mothers' unique situations. For example, if a mother had ready access to kin who could care for her children, child-care costs and quality became less of a concern. However, as discussed earlier, kin-based care could also interfere with mothers' parenting abilities, often because of competing parenting styles between mothers and other family members. Age of children mattered as well; if a woman had very young children, spending time teaching developmental tasks was a greater concern than being able to provide the right sneakers to wear to school. Mothers with older children became concerned about how best to communicate with their children about issues of poverty and welfare receipt. As we have described, some mothers adopted an avoidance strategy by, for example, hiding their food stamps from their children's friends, while other mothers engaged their children in frank conversations about the family's limited economic resources. These activities represent an additional layer of the parenting roles of low-income mothers.

Thus far, we have focused on each domain of parenting separately to illustrate the unique set of trade-offs that constitute the domain in question. In reality, mothers struggled with balancing multiple aspects of parenting simultaneously. As a result, in the attitudes they developed about welfare and work, mothers considered the trade-offs within each domain of parenting as well as the trade-offs across domains. The experience of one young mother, Anna, illustrates this point.

At the time we spoke with her, Anna was twenty-two years old and living alone with her five-year-old daughter. Anna had lived with her family for several years after her daughter's birth to complete high school and save some money. She realized she would need postsecondary education to be able to earn enough to move to her own apartment with her daughter. Therefore, she enrolled in a local community college full-time, hoping to complete an associate's degree in two years. To support herself during this time, she applied for welfare, a choice she viewed as a short-term strategy that would allow her to complete school and become self-supporting.

Due to recent changes in the welfare laws, however, Anna discovered that she was no longer allowed to combine welfare and college. Unwilling to give up on her goal of earning a college degree, Anna tried to work and remain in school. Between her job and her classwork, she was soon working fifty hours a week but found herself sleeping only a few hours per night and rarely spending time with her daughter, who was often in the care of her paternal grandparents.

Unable to juggle full-time work as well as school, Anna quit school after one year, at which point she began working full-time. Her new job, which eventually provided health insurance, paid enough so that she was able to leave welfare. Anna was also able to move out of her parent's home. While she still depended on her family and the paternal grandparents for baby-sitting, she said she noticed a positive difference in her relationship with her daughter once she moved to her own apartment.

Anna said of her job, "[It] makes me feel better about myself, but I would really much rather stay home with my daughter until she was in kindergarten, or until she was in full-time school." Anna recalled that her favorite times were when she was not working and she could just stay home with her daughter. She felt it was important that mothers be allowed to stay home and raise their kids and "not just ship them off to day care."

Anna's situation illustrates the complicated decisions facing mothers who are committed to following through on a long-term plan for economic independence for themselves and their children, but are also dedicated to spending time with their children. These competing responsibilities can often dramatically constrain the time mothers have to meet their own basic needs. From the standpoint of the welfare system, Anna is a clear welfare success story. Unfortunately, leaving welfare required Anna to sacrifice her educational goals and settle for less-lucrative and personally fulfilling employment.

Conclusion

In our interviews, we found that women constantly negotiated the competing demands of work, welfare, and parenting. Importantly, most of the women we spoke with expressed a positive view of work; it provided opportunities for personal growth, raised women's self-esteem, and gave women the sense of accomplishment that they were providing for their children without the support of welfare. In addition, many mothers felt that by working they provided a positive role model for their children. Very few women were this positive about receiving welfare. Nearly all of the women we spoke with said that, in retrospect, they would have liked to have avoided welfare. Despite these sentiments, all of the women in our study had at one point in their lives chosen to receive welfare and limit the number of hours they worked. Our descriptions of parenting suggest that this choice is often the result of a strong commitment to children and concerns about meeting their needs. Often this involved using welfare as a short-term strategy to build a bridge to long-term economic stability. Under current welfare rules, women will no longer be able to exercise this choice. These restricted options may affect the success with which women are able to meet their parenting responsibilities.

A common thread woven through these stories is that in negotiating the trade-offs between welfare, work, and parenting, many mothers resorted to sacrificing themselves in order to meet the needs of their children. Mothers told us that they did not buy things for themselves or that they did without health care to try to improve their long-term economic situations. In addition, they seldom had time for themselves and were often forced to forgo an activity that would foster personal growth, such as choosing a particular job or enrolling in continuing education, in order to fulfill obligations to their children.

Our discussions with low-income women highlight three policy-relevant issues: that work does not pay from an economic perspective; that women consider the combination of welfare and education their best long-term strategy for self-sufficiency; and importantly, that women arrive at both of these conclusions in the context of their dual roles as workers and mothers. Much welfare policy research and debate has addressed the first two issues, yet little attention has been paid to women's roles as mothers and the priority they place on their children in making decisions about welfare and work. In this chapter, we have illustrated the various values and goals women hold for themselves as providers for their children.

The women we interviewed had all experienced firsthand the difficulty of leaving welfare for work. As others have documented (e.g., Edin and Lein 1996), women realize that they are often in no better economic position (and may even incur debt) if they work. Many lament the fact that welfare rules disallow savings that would either allow them to cover the costs of going to work or allay some of their fears about the financial risks of leaving welfare, food stamps, and Medicaid. Particularly for women with serious health conditions (their own or their children's), the risk is not worth taking. Although most states allow cash assistance to phase out gradually and many offer transitional medical benefits, the women we interviewed did not generally believe that current policies offered viable economic solutions for successful transitions to work.

The women we interviewed had strong ideas about the best long-term solution for economic self-sufficiency: more education. They recognized what researchers (e.g., Holzer 1995) have already documented—that they lacked the skills and credentials that employers who offer a livable wage are looking for. Several of the women we interviewed had tried to juggle school, work, and parenting while others had had their education interrupted in order to participate in job-search activities that were of little long-term value to them. These mothers agreed that they would have been able to leave welfare permanently if they had been able to acquire a vocational or associate's degree. Ironically, most women would have been able to accomplish this within the two-year time limit established by current welfare policy.

The third issue we highlight is that women's decisions regarding work, school, and welfare are made in the context of their roles as mothers. Few current welfare-to-work programs provide support for the energy (physical and psychological) single mothers need to move from welfare to work while attending to family responsibilities and values. Even fewer consider that the trade-offs women make between work and welfare are often based on their opinion of the best thing to do as mothers. A central point in our discussions with mothers about work, welfare, and parenting is that regardless of the choice that each ultimately made (e.g., some combination of work, welfare, and school), each mother faced the reality that her choices regarding the balance between working and parenting were limited, not only because she had little economic power, but also because the welfare system offered her few options.

As Heymann and Earle (1998, 320) argue, "forcing parents to make an untenable choice between the needs of their children and work is as costly for society as it is for individual families." We have shown that providing quality care for and fostering positive relationships with their children is a top priority for many women. We do not believe that helping women overcome their commitment to parenting is the correct way to support their transition from welfare to work in the new system. Since economic considerations alone do not account for women's decisions about labor force participation, we argue that successful transitions from welfare to work can occur only when policies respect and support women's need to balance a multiplicity of demands.

NOTES

1. These interviews were part of a pilot study in preparation for a larger, structured study of welfare-to-work transitions among single mothers.
2. All names have been changed.

REFERENCES

Blank, R. 1996. *It Takes a Nation: A New Agenda for Fighting Poverty.* New York: Russell Sage Foundation.

Burtless, G. 1995. "The Employment Prospects of Welfare Recipients." In *The Work Alternative,* ed. D. Nightingale and R. Haveman, 71–106. Washington, DC: The Urban Institute Press.

Edin, K., and L. Lein. 1996. *Making Ends Meet: How Single Mothers Survive Welfare and Low-Wage Work.* New York: Russell Sage Foundation.

Ellwood, D. T. 1988. *Poor Support: Poverty in the American Family.* New York: Basic Books.

Goldberg, W. A., E. Greenberger, S. Hamill, and R. O'Neil. 1992. "Role Demands in the Lives of Employed Single Mothers with Children." *Journal of Family Issues* 13:312–33.

Greenberger, E., and R. O'Neil. 1993. "Spouse, Parent, Worker: Role Commitments and Role-Related Experiences in the Construction of Adults' Well-Being." *Developmental Psychology* 29:181–97.

Harris, K. M. 1996. "Life after Welfare: Women, Work, and Repeat Dependency." *American Sociological Review* 61:407–26.

Heymann, S. J., and A. Earle. 1998. "The Work-Family Balance: What Hurdles Are Parents Leaving Welfare Likely to Confront?" *Journal of Policy Analysis and Management* 17:313–21.

Holzer, H. 1995. *What Employers Want.* New York: Russell Sage Foundation.

Jarrett, R. L. 1994. "Living Poor: Family Life among Single Parent, African American Women." *Social Problems* 41:30–49.

Lipson, D. J., M. Birnbaum, S. Wall, M. Moon, and S. Norton. 1997. *Health Policy for Low-Income People in Michigan.* Washington, DC: The Urban Institute.

Michigan Family Independence Agency. 1996. *To Strengthen Michigan Families 1992–1994–1996 Block Grant Reform.* Lansing: Michigan Family Independence Agency.

Morgan, D. L. 1997. *Focus Groups as Qualitative Research.* Thousand Oaks, CA: Sage.

Myers, M. K. 1993. "Child Care in JOBS Employment and Training Program: What Difference Does Quality Make?" *Journal of Marriage and the Family* 55:767–83.

Oliker, S. J. 1996. "The Proximate Contexts of Workfare and Work: A Framework for Studying Poor Women's Economic Choices." *Sociological Quarterly* 36:251–72.

Pett, M. A., and B. Vaughan-Cole. 1986. "The Impact of Income Issues and Social Status on Post-divorce Adjustment of Custodial Parents." *Family Relations* 35:103–11.

Spalter-Roth, R., B. Burr, H. Hartmann, and L. Shaw. 1995. *Welfare That Works: The Working Lives of AFDC Recipients.* Washington, DC: Institute for Women's Policy Research.

Wilson, W. J. 1996. *When Work Disappears.* Chicago: University of Chicago Press.

Yates, J. 1997. "Obtaining Health Care Coverage through Child Support." <http://www.welfareinfo.org>.

CHAPTER 9

Work Preparation and Labor Market Experiences among Urban, Poor, Nonresident Fathers

Waldo E. Johnson Jr.

Introduction

Dramatic changes, such as the diminishing number of blue-collar jobs, their increasing relocation out of the cities into suburban communities, and the accelerated shift to a service economy that requires more specialized training for entry, suggest the need for a reexamination of current urban policies. Urban residents, especially young African-American males, have been the biggest losers in terms of lost employment opportunities on quality of life (Wilson 1996). As fathers, these young African-American males are severely affected by the relocation of employment opportunities out of the inner city and into suburban communities and foreign countries, not only because their capacity to achieve and maintain self-sufficiency is threatened, but also because their ability to provide paternal support to their children is weakened.

Some older workers have been buffered by their longer work histories and willingness to accept minimum wage and lower pay (Forman 1995; W. Johnson 1998). But young men often lack developmental work histories through which they can acquire job readiness skills that prepare them for sustained entry into the labor market (Grubb 1989; Moss and Tilly 1991). This weak labor force attachment is partially responsible for their failure to make the adolescent-to-adult transition that includes emancipation from the family of origin and the assumption of adult roles such as husband and father. This chapter provides a contextual framework for examining out-of-wedlock fatherhood among poor, urban nonresident fathers.

The labor force attachment of these young men has strong implications for their subsequent functioning as partners and parents. Their general reluctance to form traditional family structures often leads people to see them as "deadbeat dads," fathers who shun their paternal responsibility. But interviews with these low-income, nonresident fathers clearly show that not all are trying to avoid the identification or the responsibilities of fatherhood (W. Johnson 1998, 1993; Marsiglio 1989, 1988; Sullivan 1985). Instead, these young fathers are limited in their ability to assume the responsibility of parenting because their partners', their communities', and even their own understanding of fatherhood emphasizes the provision of income as a prerequisite to all other roles. Their detachment from the workforce and uncertain prospects for future income diminish their ability to be consistent providers, which in turn prevents these fathers from fulfilling noneconomic parenting functions such as teaching and nurturing. The mothers of their children, and the community at large, exacerbate this problem by conditioning their acceptance of the father's role upon his consistent ability to contribute financially to his children's care.

Collectively, these factors point to important issues concerning self-sufficiency, which is generally assessed in terms of an individual's sole reliance upon him- or herself in the provision of food, clothing, shelter, and other basic needs. In American society, fathers are expected to be the principal breadwinners for their families. Their success as fathers is generally assessed in terms of their ability to earn a living for their families. This chapter examines self-sufficiency and readiness for the assumption of paternal roles among low-income, urban, nonresident fathers.

The Context of Paternity

After World War II and throughout the 1950s, marriage (as a precursor to family formation) frequently occurred during adolescence for both males and females. In sharp contrast to the current labor market, blue-collar jobs during this period were more available and required less formal education and/or specialized training for sustained entry (Wilson 1987, 1996). Relatively unskilled male laborers could find and secure jobs that enabled them to assume provider and other paternal responsibilities. This context implicitly encouraged marriage and family formation because the labor market offered opportunities for men to assume expected economic roles.

Differences in expectations for sustained entry into the current labor market make it increasingly difficult for early sexual experiences and family formation to be followed by marriage and resident parenthood (W. Johnson 1998; Salter 1997). Lack of formal education, work unreadiness, and poor occupational preparation, often combined with criminal records, are significant barriers to these young men's ability to assume a provider role in the changing American labor force. Contemporary concerns regarding young parenthood in general and young fatherhood specifically focus on the disproportionate number of males and females who become parents before completing high school, prior to acquiring job readiness skills, and their subsequent failure to form family units via marriage (Blankenhorn 1995; Marsiglio 1989).

Many poor young fathers lack the maturity to become serious, committed partners in cohabiting and marital relationships. Age is a prime consideration that minimizes the chances that sexual unions among younger adolescent males (less than age 18) will immediately evolve into marriage. In two earlier research studies, a number of young males identified age twenty-five as appropriate for "settling down [in marriage] and starting a family" (W. Johnson 1993, 1995). Like their peers in these earlier studies, several young men in the current study shared this conviction, but they were already fathers. Their commitment to their present children, in comparison to those children they proposed to father at around age twenty-five, is unclear. They did, however, identify desirable qualities for future marriage partners and coparents with whom they would ideally share their future children. They also broadly discussed factors that contribute to their readiness for assuming the responsibilities of marriage and fatherhood (W. Johnson 1993), and several young fathers stated that the mothers of their present children were undesirable as marriage partners.

Given this context, it is understandable why so many of these fathers, young as well as older adolescents, are nonresident fathers. Although many nonresident fathers are chronologically adults, they have not achieved independence from their own parents and families of origin. They often reside with their parents or other members of their extended families and depend on household and family income to support themselves. As a result, their financial contributions to their children are generally minimal and sporadic, often originating from their families of origin.

There are, of course, young fathers who provide financial assistance to their children. Many of these young fathers are gainfully employed and give money at the end of each pay period. In some instances, the financial support they provide is substantial, given their meager earnings. Several fathers in this study fit into this category. They took great pride in upholding a financial commitment to their children and felt that providing financial support was the strongest indicator of their paternal role functioning. In each instance, these fathers provided regular financial payments "under the table." They did not provide formal child support via the local child support office but gave the money directly to the custodial parent to augment the minimal public assistance grants. This practice is well documented in previous ethnographic research studies of unmarried, nonresident fathers of color (Sullivan 1985, 1986). In some such "social paternity" arrangements, the financial support provided by the young fathers, given their income and other financial resources, will approximate the allocation determined by a family court judge to the custodial parent.

Clearly, changes in the availability of jobs and in the preparation of young low-income men to perform these jobs must occur if these young men are to assume complex parenting roles. These fathers are not just half of a nuclear family unit but are enmeshed in a web of community ties and responsibilities. The fathers in this study claim paternity according to community customs; they also often feel that they owe support to their own parents and relatives with whom they reside and who depend on them. The young fathers may not be "self-sufficient," but they are part of an interdependent and functional community unit. A revised model of fatherhood that recognizes these realities, to which these young men could be held accountable and which they could actually meet, would be immensely constructive.

Research Approach and Methods

Change and diversity have become distinctive features of contemporary fatherhood. Fathers today are less likely than their earlier counterparts to experience the orderly, traditional sequencing of family-related life course events (marriage, paternity, and serving as primary breadwinners while coresiding with their offspring throughout childhood and adolescence). It is now commonplace to observe various permutations of fatherhood (Bozett and Hanson 1991), including wedlock and out-of-wedlock paternity; coresident and nonresident statuses; biological and stepfatherhood; being a father while married, remarried, or single; begetting unplanned children during adolescence or early adulthood; and fathering both biological and stepchildren with or without the same residency status.

Today, parenting roles continue to evolve due to changing gender role expectations for men and women alike. Women's increased participation in the paid labor force has provided both an impetus for and a means to reinforce this process. The norms associated with being a nonresident father, stepfather, or single father are still ambiguous and the expression of the relevant roles is quite variable and difficult at times (Cherlin 1978; Grief 1985; Marsiglio 1995b, Wallerstein and Corbin 1986). But public perception of paternal involvement and commitment remain largely characterized by the provision of financial support attended by increasing recognition of the nurturing benefits of the father-child dyad.

Although the provision of financial support represents only one of the numerous role functions fathers typically assume, it is often viewed as the most salient by fathers and society alike. For nonresident fathers, the opportunities to provide ongoing nurturance and engage in expressive activities with their children are even more difficult to create because of individual and structural barriers that impede paternal involvement. Many of these fathers are not married to their children's mothers and have not established legal paternity. Access to their children is potentially affected by their relationship with the custodial parent, the maternal or paternal grandparents, and the extended family. The nonresident fathers in this study, when possible, tended to concentrate more heavily on providing financial support to their children to offset their physical absence and the nurturing they often failed to provide. The economic loss a child incurs when nonresident fathers pay little or no child support is exacerbated by potential losses in expressive role functioning.

A field-based study of work preparation and labor market behavior among nonresident fathers offers an innovative approach for examining the potential link between intergenerational socialization and the assumption of parental and family roles. This chapter is based on in-depth interviews and survey field research that examine the work preparation and labor market experiences of young nonresident African-American fathers. The sample data were collected for the 1996 Chicago pilot of the Fragile Families and Child Well-Being Study, a national longitudinal study that examines unwed African-American, white, and Latino fathers' capabilities; their attitudes about fathers' rights and responsibilities; and their relationships with mothers and children. It will also provide important information on how unwed parents respond to the new child support policies and practices that are being implemented in different states.[1]

The 1996 Chicago pilot included eight poor young African-American males (several of whom had children from previous relationships) who became new fathers within a few hours to two days preceding the initial paternal interview in February 1996. The fathers in this study were identified via an in-hospital-based survey sample of mothers within two days of the baby's delivery. The mothers were informed of the study's aims and the intended uses for the data collected. They were subsequently asked to provide the names of their newborns' fathers and requested to assist me in contacting the young fathers. Provident Hospital, where the young mothers delivered, is the Grand Boulevard community satellite of the Cook County Public Health System in which Cook County Hospital is the anchor care facility. Grand Boulevard is one of Chicago's poorest neighborhoods.

The mothers were administered a shorter version of the survey instrument to which the fathers were asked to respond. Each mother was paid $25 at the beginning of her demographic interview. She was queried about the baby's health status, the current nature of the relationship between her and the baby's father, and her expectations regarding the father's obligations to the child. The socioeconomic status of the young mothers was probed via a series of questions regarding household composition, educational status, current and past employment history, and the extent of financial help or any other kind of support received during the pregnancy.

I contacted the eight fathers who composed the study sample immediately following their partner's deliveries.[2] The initial interview averaged about 1.25 hours, and the fathers were also paid $25 at the beginning of the interview. Most of the interviews began rather slowly as both the interviewer and interviewee were "feeling each other out." Clearly, there were trust issues to be resolved in this initial contact. Although most of the fathers were on good terms with their partners, most of the mothers could not assure me that the fathers would grant me an interview, and if they agreed to an interview, the mothers could not guarantee that the fathers would show up. Of the sixteen partners of the mothers in the hospital, I scheduled nine interviews and, surprisingly, only one father was a no-show. Still, I sensed that the fathers were somewhat suspicious about the request for information and my veracity regarding the interview's purpose. The interviews occurred within months of the passage of the Personal Responsibility and Work Opportunities Reconciliation Act (PRWORA), and the climate regarding welfare reform and out-of-wedlock births was quite contentious. I am reasonably certain that some fathers, in spite of their seemingly good relationship with their partners, may have suspected their mates of "selling them out" to child support and other authorities as a means to gain financial support for their newborns. Some of the information acquired in the initial paternal interview did not jive with subsequent information obtained in the follow-up interviews of the next several months. Indeed, relationships had to be built between the interviewer and the interviewees over time.

An average of five follow-up interviews, each lasting approximately one and a half hours, were conducted with these fathers. The second round of interviews took place within a month to six weeks following review of the information gathered in the initial survey interview. The second round of the follow-up interviews provided an opportunity to gain more in-depth information on items included in the survey questionnaire. The rest of the follow-up interviews generally yielded more contextual information beyond the scope of the survey questionnaire. These case interviews were enhanced with extensive field notes containing field observations. The fathers were also paid for the subsequent in-depth interviews. These interviews occurred in the eight months subsequent to the survey questionnaire interview.

Although my race and proximity in age to some of the interviewees may have allayed some suspicions, it was not enough to gain immediate acceptance and full confidence. As an outsider to the circumstances as well as the neighborhood, I was both overtly and subtly challenged in the early interviews by most of the fathers. Even those who seemed to accept me as a researcher challenged me regularly to separate facts from fiction, often in an effort to determine if I was "streetwise." My knowledge about out-of-wedlock parenting among poor couples and about the social welfare system was useful in projecting a streetwise demeanor. In some instances, however, the real deal about some situations encountered by the fathers was not revealed until several months later, after a stable relationship was established. Upon final acceptance, the fathers tended to seek out advice and/or assistance with their plights. As a researcher, I was not always prepared to assist as requested, but I generally provided the fathers with contact persons they could access for assistance or advice. As I reflect on these interviews over the succeeding several months, the detailed information I obtained regarding work preparation and labor market experiences was acquired largely due to the extended time frame in which it was collected.

The fathers were queried about the following areas:

1. human capital including schooling, job training, and employment history;
2. demographic behavior about marriage, cohabitation, fertility, and living arrangement histories and contraceptive practices;
3. social capital including involvement in community institutions, both formal ones such as child support, government organizations and churches, and informal ones such as voluntary associations;
4. deviant behavior including involvement in illegal activity and drug and alcohol use;
5. psychological well-being; and
6. fathering behaviors including time and money provided to their children.

The demographic characteristics of the eight fathers included in this study appear in table 1.

My First . . . A Second Chance . . . :
Initial Reactions to New Paternal Statuses

Of the eight fathers in the study, two had already become fathers in previous relationships. Among the six new fathers, the immediate responses ranged from joy to denial and overwhelming anxiety. John, a fifteen-year-old high school sophomore, gave the following reply, "I was really shocked. I mean, I was surprised." For John, it was not only traumatic but, in his words, "disrespectful in the manner [in]which she brought it to me. She told her friends. They told everybody else. When word got back to me, I was, like, pissed because she did not bring it to me first." In a subsequent interview, John amended this statement by saying:

My girl did tell me about the pregnancy but I was not hearing that. I told her not to bring that to me because it was fucked up. She knew that we were not ready to be parents.

Damon, an eighteen-year-old father, recounted a similar reaction:

I didn't believe that it [the baby] was my child. We had sex just two times. The first time we had sex, we had to stop because my folks [returned] home [unexpectedly]. After we got together the second time, I did not see her again until she was seven months [pregnant]. She called when she was [in her] fourth month, but I did not visit her because I did not believe that the baby was mine. [Besides], I thought that she was pregnant when I met her because we had sex when we first met. But her old man called me after the baby was born and said that I should come by and see the baby. I decided to go and when I saw that the baby looked like me. I was convinced that she [the baby] was my daughter.

Keith is thirty-four, and his newborn daughter is his second child; he has an older son. Although he did not deny paternity, he was overwhelmed by the rapid pace at which his paternal responsibilities were mounting.

TABLE 1. Demographic Characteristics of Fathers in 1996 Chicago Pilot Study

Name	Age	High/School Completion	Work Status[*]	Number of Children	Number of Mothers	Residential Status[**]
John	15	Sophomore	E	1 (B)	1	FOO
Damon	18	Graduate	E	1 (B)	1	C/FOO
Greg	16	Junior	U	1 (G)	1	FOO
Russell	25	Graduate	E	1 (G)	1	C/A
Todd	21	Dropout	U	1 (B)	1	C/FOO
Willie	30	Dropout	U	1 (G)	1	C/FOO
Keith	34	Graduate	U	2 (B/G)	2	A
Hershey	43	Dropout	E	2 (G)	2	C/A

[*]E connotes employed; U connotes unemployed.

[**]FFO resides with family of origin; C/FOO co-habitates with family of procreation but resides primarily with family of origin; C/A co-habitates with family of procreation but primarily resides alone; A resides alone; (B connotes boy, G connotes girl).

Childbirth is a miracle. I can hardly believe that my daughter is finally here. I have been waiting for this [her birth], and I thank God every day. But having a child is a lot of responsibility. When I think about it, I break out in a cold sweat. Because I am older and I want to be a better father to her than I was to my son, it's like nothing I['ve] experienced before. I have to be really on it now.

Keith's answer signaled his need to make some changes in his life and in his irregular work patterns.

The expectations of fatherhood have caused Willie, a thirty-year-old first-time father, to reorder his priorities as well. Willie had maintained a steady job as a corporate messenger for several years. He stated that his job has provided him with "a decent salary" that not only enabled him to live independently but to help out his family of origin in times of need. His new paternal status would probably limit his ability to continue to serve as "safety net" for his mother and siblings.

I have to begin to think about my daughter as my first priority. I have to make sure that her needs are taken care of. I probably won't be able to help out my family as much now. As my mother used to say, "I['ve] got another mouth to feed."

Age Ain't Nothing but a Number, or Is It?: Paternal Readiness among First-Time and Veteran Fathers

The Younger Fathers

The term "younger fathers" connotes first-time fathers while "older fathers" refers to those who have experienced biological fatherhood earlier. As a group, the younger fathers seemed to fear the mechanics of responsibility—that is, the "how to" of fatherhood from "holding a baby so that it doesn't break" to providing financial support. Gregory, a sixteen-year-old father, expressed both of these competing concerns in his response:

I ain't had much experience with holding a baby. My daughter is so tiny [that] I am afraid that I might break her. My mother says that that won't happen, but I am still afraid that I might hurt her. I'm more worried about helping out with some money.

Given the psychological and developmental statuses of these young men, their responses are not atypical (Lee 1994). Although only one young man questioned whether he was indeed the biological father of the child, all of the fathers seemed surprised that their sexual liaisons resulted in pregnancies. Although they failed to assume contraceptive responsibility to minimize the chances of a pregnancy, they somehow felt that other factors would come into play: their partners would assume contraceptive responsibility, their partners' menstrual periods would be off cycle, they might deny paternity, or their partners would choose to abort the pregnancy. The young fathers' feelings of invulnerability, that paternity "will not happen to me," is pervasive in their peer group. A previous study of young nonresident fathers revealed substantial denial among the young men regarding their paternal statuses. Informant disclosures and interviewer observations suggested that among those fathers who accepted their paternal status, signs of clinical depression were evident (W. Johnson 1993).

The initial shock that several of these younger fathers felt upon being told by their partners about the pregnancy, in light of their acknowledged refusal to use contraceptives, and the subsequent signs of clinical depression they experience when they think about their poor preparation for fatherhood, can be viewed on a continuum of resulting behaviors associated with feelings of paternal failure. Bowman (1989) contends that the individual and structural barriers encountered by these fathers to becoming financial providers are devastating, resulting in their potential feelings of unfitness to assume equally important expressive paternal roles. Growing up in poor, inner-city communities, attending impoverished and unchallenging schools, lacking community supports that augment parental and familial efforts to properly socialize young males, and possibly missing the ongoing fellowship of a father or father-figure exacerbates the problems that the transition from adolescence into adulthood presents to virtually all young males, regardless of their racial, gender, ethnic, and socioeconomic status (Bowman 1989; Bowman et al. 1996; Henly 1993).

As "accidental dads," these young fathers are often unprepared to assume expected paternal responsibilities that many of them hope to undertake at a later time. The younger fathers are chronologically minors and remain the legal responsibility of their parents. In many such families, parental caretaking in the form of food, clothing, and shelter often continues beyond their sons' minor legal status into adulthood. Social mores, however, cut both ways. While parents may infantilize their sons in economic terms, they often insist that they acknowledge paternity (at least socially) if they become biological fathers (W. Johnson 1993; Sullivan 1986). Validating physical resemblances such as skin color, facial features, and hair texture between the alleged father and child is a long-established procedure for acknowledging or disavowing paternity in the African-American community. These identifying physical features need not be restricted to the father in question but may extend back one to two paternal generations particularly if the physical trait is considered distinctive and indisputable (Anderson 1990; Sullivan 1985). Damon, an eighteen-year-old first-time dad, relied on such social determinations in accepting his paternity status. According to Damon, his daughter bore a striking resemblance to him, and had "his family nose." This observation was supported and validated by both Damon's mother and maternal grandmother.

This social determination of paternity is important because, for poor young fathers whose children are born out of wedlock, acknowledging paternity is an important antecedent to any form of paternal commitment, financial or expressive, to their children (Salter 1997). Russell is a twenty-five-year-old father who is employed as a corporate messenger. He made a personal commitment to be involved in his daughter's life:

> I have been reading about how a father's presence in his child's early development can make a difference in the child's later development. I don't think that this is anything new. A father can give a lot to his child, not just money but that is important. I hope to always be able to meet my daughter's basic needs, but I also hope to guide her in other ways. I'm not trying to be religious on you, but this is where I'm [at] right now.

Russell wants to become a father who not only meets his daughter's financial needs but also helps her to grow and develop into a responsible individual. To do this, Russell contended that he must become more responsible to himself as an individual and as a father. He began reading current popular literature on fatherhood and child development written from an Afrocentric perspective as a means of self-improvement. Similarly, Todd, a twenty-one-year-old father who dropped out of high school, made the following pledge:

> I'm going to be there for my son. I really mean it. I'm going to be there for him. I know what it means to grow up without a dad around, and I do not want him to live that life. I'm going to make sure he knows who I am and that he can depend on me to be around when he needs me.

Todd's pledge is a noble one but will be difficult to uphold. He readily admitted that a father's primary responsibility is providing for his family. He is currently unemployed, and his prospects of finding sustaining work are dim. Even if he remains physically present in his son's life, he is currently unable to give his son the financial support that even Todd feels a father is minimally expected to provide. Among many young nonresident fathers like

Todd, the fathers' commitments to "be there for their children" often erode over time, due in part to their inability to provide financial support and the subsequent paternal anxiety that is either self-imposed or stimulated by the expectations of the custodial parent, the families of origin, and/or society.

The Older Fathers

The young fathers' emotional shift, from their early paternal anxieties to their later hopeful, if unrealistic, commitments to paternity are particularly striking in contrast with the reactions of the older fathers to their new paternal statuses. Several of the older fathers had participated, to varying degrees, in the rearing of their older children. The veteran fathers were unconditionally joyful about their new children but concerned about their ability to live up to the expectations of fatherhood, as measured by their earlier efforts with their older children. Keith acknowledged that he had not been a "good father" to his older son but believed he is now "a far more mature parent who recognizes his responsibilities." He said fathers today, even teenage fathers, "can't get away with not supporting their kids. The laws have changed." Keith clearly was elated at the birth of his new daughter:

> My daughter's birth is a chance for me to get it right this time. I want to be a good father to her from the beginning. I gonna be a better father to her older brother, too. This is the chance I needed to make things right.

But Keith's elation was tempered by his recognition of the baby's financial needs, his present inability to fulfill those needs, and the widening gap between the former and the latter:

> I know that having a new baby means money, money, money, and I will do what I can to help out with the baby. I am not working right now, but I will find a way to support my new daughter and her older brother.

Even those fathers who felt that their efforts to support their older children had been fairly good expressed concern about their present ability to support the new addition to their families. Like Keith, Hershey became a father for the second time. At the time of his first interview, his older daughter was completing her first year of college.

> My daughter is beautiful and I am proud to be her father, but I worry about being able to take care of her the way I took care of her sister.

Even though I am not married to my [current] girlfriend, we have a good relationship, and I am holding up my part [giving child support.] I was married to my older daughter's mother when she was born, and we split up a few years later. I had a very good job working in the south-side steel mills, so the money was always there. Now I am working a maintenance job, and it is hard to make ends meet. I am still committed to paying for my older daughter's college education. But I don't want to let my baby girl down either. It's really tough on a brother out here today.

These disclosures reflect the conditional joy shared by these veteran fathers whose prior experience as fathers provides a reasonably solid background for assuming the responsibilities of paternity. Both Keith and Hershey realized that while the expectations of fatherhood have not changed since they became first-time fathers in the 1970s, their ability to meet those expectations has. Many older fathers find themselves in the midst of a changing economic order in which their unskilled labor experience inhibits their ability to acquire and sustain a good-paying job in the evolving service economy. For these fathers, the changing economic order and the weakening of their labor force attachment exerted an even more devastating effect on their psychological well-being than it did on the first-time fathers, many of whom have never held a job. The plight of both groups of fathers supports arguments for both public and private efforts to remedy the disproportionate number of African-American men who are unemployed and underemployed, especially those who are expected to shoulder parental financial responsibilities.

High School Education and Work Preparation

Individual preparation to sustain oneself in society remains one of the primary goals of secondary and postsecondary education. The thirst for knowledge and socialization remain legitimate goals of secondary and higher education, but for many poor urban residents, these institutions primarily serve a utilitarian purpose. Although countless research studies conducted by social scientists, government, and the business sectors alike suggest that the methods and approaches undertaken by the public schools increasingly fail to prepare a labor force to meet the needs of the emerging service economy, public education remains the primary source of preparation for entry into the labor force for American citizens. Public education is, for many poor, inner-city residents, the only available option, and it is critically important in preparing them for work.

The fathers in this study cite the numerous failures of the Chicago public schools in preparing them for entry into the labor force. Although their commitment to completing high school varied, these fathers were generally unenthusiastic about the public education available in their respective communities.

Younger Fathers' High School Experiences

When asked about the kind of education and job training necessary to gain entry into the labor force today, the younger fathers in the study identified skill sets that are ideally acquired in high school. John, a fifteen-year-old father, provided the following response:

> You need to be able to communicate with others and to get along with others. So many of the jobs today call for computer skills, so you need this, too.

Gregory, a sixteen-year-old father, added the following:

> You need good math and communication skills. I want to be[come] a[n] accountant.

Damon, an eighteen-year-old father, added:

> At my job, things are changing every day. More and more, things are becoming computerized. I think having computer skills is [becoming] a requirement to get jobs like mine today.

Damon and Russell, a twenty-five-year-old father, were the only high school graduates and employed men among the younger fathers in this study (age twenty-seven and younger). Both John and Gregory were currently enrolled in high school, but their immediate attention was aimed at securing jobs so that they could support their newborn daughters. These fathers recognized that strong communication, math, and computer skills are expected competencies of high school and postsecondary training aimed at preparing one for entry into the evolving labor force. It is unfortunate that they must now assume parenting responsibilities that force them to secure jobs requiring skills that they have yet to develop and master.

Yet these young men's responses also demonstrate that knowledge alone does not change behavior, especially among adolescents. When queried, Damon, a high school graduate who felt that he did not possess the computer skills needed to get a job today at his place of employment, made this remark regarding his job security:

> I already have my job pretty secure. I think knowing how to work on a computer will be required for everyone who is hired from this year on.

Damon's self-assurance is probably unfounded. He believed that because he had already gained employment, the current and future hiring standards of his employer will not affect him. As a result, he has not taken advantage of opportunities to gain the computer skills that are now required for new hires at his place of employment.

According to Bowman (1989), the student role during preadulthood (adolescence) has the most crucial psychosocial implications for African-American males; it is pivotal for healthy identity development during adolescence and for navigating the difficult transition to gainful employment in adulthood. Among adolescents, student achievement increases a sense of competence, purpose, and commitment, which enables individuals to energetically pursue future career and family. The young fathers in the current study generally have not excelled academically, athletically, or vocationally as students. Their failure to succeed as students in high school may have diminished their interest in pursuing postsecondary education and training. They expressed little confidence in their educational preparation. In fact, John devalued the high school education he was currently receiving:

> I don't feel that I will be any better off to get a job when I graduate from high school than I am now. I am staying in school because people say you need a high school diploma to get a job. I know people in my neighborhood with high school diplomas and they can't get jobs.

John expressed a general distrust in the Chicago public school system due to its failure to connect its graduates to the workforce. Descriptions of his time spent in class suggest that experiences of students like John in the Chicago public schools discouraged them and that they were seldom intellectually challenged as high school students. When asked if their poor prospects for finding work to sustain themselves and their families were hampered by their own failure to enhance their formal education, the majority of the younger fathers disagreed. Todd is a twenty-one-year-old high school dropout:

> When I was going to school, we were not learning the skills I needed to get a job. I had a part-time job, and I was learning more in that job about work than I was in school. So I quit school because I had to help

out my parents and younger sisters. My mother wanted me to stay in school, but I could not see how it would help me.

Damon, a high school graduate, is employed as an assembly-line worker in a neighboring Chicago suburb:

> When I applied for my job, the foreman asked me if I was a high school graduate. I think if I was not a high school graduate, I would not have gotten the job, but I do not feel that you need a diploma to do the work. I know people who work on my job who didn't graduate from high school. I talk with one of the "old heads" who work there all the time and he says that they making younger workers have a high school diploma is one more way to control jobs and keep blacks out.

The distinction between having the diploma and having the skills that supposedly accompany it is a common one for these young men. Gregory is a junior in high school who believed that a diploma is necessary to get a job and to move up the ladder in the labor force:

> I want to graduate from high school so that I can get a good job. I don't think you stand a chance of getting a worthwhile job unless you have a high school diploma. It's the first thing employers ask for.

But as Russell, a twenty-five-year-old father who is employed as a corporate messenger, elaborated:

> I am a high school graduate but I understand why so many young fellas don't stay in school even though they know that a high school diploma is needed to get a job. The schools really don't prepare you.

Asked to elaborate further on this statement, Russell continued:

> I think there are schools in some neighborhoods where students are really prepared to get jobs, but those schools are not in poor neighborhoods like this one [Grand Boulevard]. You must leave this neighborhood to find a job, and you must leave this neighborhood to get the skills to get a job.

These perceptions created a kind of "push-pull" tension that often resulted in an illogical analytical framework for understanding the relationship between work preparation and employment. These young men were often unsophisticated in their understanding of how their current skill sets (or lack thereof) will affect their future employment opportunities. They either failed to take full advantage of the available public educational and career-preparation opportunities or they felt that such opportunities would not bring the expected return. It is, however, important to recognize that lack of such critical thinking skills is commonplace during adolescence. That some of the younger fathers have not taken full advantage of the educational opportunities available to them is generally consistent with adolescent behavior. The unfortunate distinction between these young men and their peers who reside in families with stronger social supports lies in the familial reinforcement and guidance that supported behavior directed toward their best interests (Lee 1994). In addition, as the education offered in the community schools in which these young fathers reside becomes increasingly obsolete (and its decreasing value is widely recognized by the students and neighborhood adults alike), there is little incentive for students to fully engage in educational pursuits within the schools. Nor will parents and adults necessarily continue to stress the need to complete high school among students attending these neighborhood schools.

The younger fathers acknowledged that education is the key but that other factors like age and racial discrimination also kept them locked out of the job arena (Ellwood 1986; Kirschenman and Neckerman 1991). Todd was not optimistic about his chances to get a job:

> The deck is really stacked against us. I mean, young black men don't have a chance. A lot of businessmen feel that young black men cannot be trusted—that we are only thieves and violent. We can't get a fair shake.

John was not as pessimistic as Todd, but he did not offer much more hope that young men who found themselves in his position would fare better in the labor market if they completed school:

> I know that it will be hard to get a good job and finish school at the same time. I believe that my chances are slim, but I don't know if having a [high school] diploma makes a big difference if you're a black man. What do they say, "last hired, first fired"? I'm still trying to get to first base.

Older Fathers' High School Experiences

Comparison between the younger and older fathers' experience is instructive. Hershey and Keith had similar experiences with school. Hershey dropped out of school after the eleventh grade, while Keith graduated from high school but felt the diploma had little value. But both Hershey and Keith acquired full-time jobs as teenagers. Hershey said that he did not complete high school because jobs were plentiful and did not require a diploma when he entered the labor market during the late 1960s and early 1970s.

> I quit high school in the eleventh grade because you did not need a high school diploma to get a job in the steel mills. They were booming and all you needed was to be referred by someone already working there. My father was working in the mills. He felt that I was not very serious about school (which is probably true) so he pushed me to go to work. At first, I was working the evening shift after school, but it got to be too much. I couldn't keep up in school, so I just dropped out. The money was good, so I just dropped out.

Hershey's decision to drop out of school did not appear to have any negative consequences at the time. It enabled him to support himself and help out his parents. Hershey, like several other fathers in the study, said that he felt pressure as an African-American adolescent male to get a job so he could help out his parents financially or, at minimum, to support himself. This perception reflects a larger community expectation in which African-American males are encouraged to enter the labor force as young as preadolescence. During this period of economic opportunity, the expectation placed on Hershey and his peers to provide immediate financial support to their families of origin potentially competed with school completion. The available jobs, especially jobs in the factories and mills, were relatively secure as they had been for his parents and older family members. There was no evidence that a full-scale economic downturn was imminent and that all of these workers would be adversely affected.

Keith stated that many of his male peers also dropped out of high school to get full-time, blue-collar jobs for reasons similar to Hershey's. He stated that he, too, was tempted to drop out of high school:

> I was not [a] smart [student] in high school. I got a part-time job and wanted to drop out [of high school] like all my homeys [male peers]. But my mother wasn't hearing [in support of] that. She always said "all of my children will get a high school diploma." She [insisted] that I stay in school. I did just enough to get by so [that] I could graduate.

Keith stayed in school and graduated, but he distrusted the school curriculum and his teachers:

There was nothing [in the curriculum or no one of the faculty] to keep me interested in staying in school. We were not learning the things that helped us to get jobs. I knew lots of people in my neighborhood who graduated from that high school but could not get jobs that really paid [substantial jobs]. The teachers were not serious about the students— they were just there to get a paycheck. I felt like I was wasting my time going to school every day when I could have been out making money.

Keith had no faith that his high school education would land him a job. He knew countless men and women in his neighborhood who held high school diplomas but could not get jobs. In contrast, he knew people like Hershey who got jobs without a high school diploma. He did not see himself going on to college or vocational/technical school, so he questioned why he should devote his time and energy to the seemingly futile effort of completing high school. But he did. He completed high school and as he predicted, it did not improve his job prospects.

Keith's employment record was rather unimpressive. He described himself as being "laid back" throughout his work career. Because he continued to live with his parents and did not have any children, he worked a variety of jobs for relatively short periods of time. If he became dissatisfied with the work environment or wages, he promptly quit and moved onto the next job. He would also take hiatuses between these jobs. The jobs he landed varied, usually hourly or day work. He now recognizes that he failed to build a solid work career. Instead, he held a series of unrelated jobs that enabled him to meet his basic needs but offered little or no economic security. In addition to his spotty job record, Keith was involved in a series of petty criminal offenses throughout his twenties. His criminal record has disqualified him for a number of jobs.

But the distinction between Keith's work experience and that of the younger fathers lies in his ability to remain connected to the labor force over time despite his personal problems. Personal networks and job training opportunities once buffered these workers and provided a second, third, and sometimes many more chances for young men in poor communities to stay in the labor force even if their academic performance was marginal or, even worse, if they had dropped out of school.

Work Preparation among Younger and Older Fathers

Similar opportunities are not available for the younger men today. As Keith explained:

I was a teenager when CETA [Comprehensive Education and Training Act] and the Summer Job Corps was still available. I think these programs helped young people to get some job training so when they finished high school, they could get better jobs. Today, CETA and Summer Jobs are not available and a lot of young people have lost hope of ever getting a good job. That's why so many of them drop out of high school and turn to the streets.

Hershey echoed Keith's sentiments as he reflected back to the days when job training opportunities were plentiful:

> Job training programs are hard to come by these days. The ones [that exist] are tied to jobs instead of helping people to get jobs. You need more training nowadays to get a job and when you get the job, you still have to go through training to keep it.

In contrast to the older fathers in the study, the labor market experiences of the five youngest fathers in the 1996 Chicago pilot are indeed weak. Three of these fathers have never held ongoing employment, part-time, or afterschool work. Only two of the younger fathers could boast of having held at least one summer job. These jobs, especially those with the [Chicago] Mayor's Summer Employment Program, were often the only summer employment opportunity for many inner-city youths. Todd, however, discussed his experience as an employee in this program in rather negative terms:

> I remember going through the whole process to get that summer job with the City [of Chicago]. I had to go to the area office to be certified [as an eligible applicant]. The lines were very long. When I finally got a job, I was so happy because the money was going to pay for my school clothes and help out at home. I was pissed when I got paid because they [city/state administrators] cut my mother's [Public] Aid check in order to pay me. My mother was pissed, too. You just can't get ahead being honest.

The entire experience embittered him. The following summer he decided to work in the informal economy. He performed odd jobs for neighbors and a series of businesses for which he was paid in cash. He added:

> I was not going to do anything illegal, like sell drugs or stolen merchandise. I am not that kind of person. Yet, I see how people come to be like that. It's a trip out here. There are few honest people out here and even fewer work for the government.

Job training and summer youth employment programs provide pathways to inclusion in the formal labor force. Russell, one of Todd's many peers who was unable to land one of those summer jobs as a high school student, made the following remark:

> People talk about how bad things are today for young males seeking a job but things were just as bad ten to fifteen years ago. I beat the streets trying to get after school and summer work, but I had no luck at all. I feel that if I had had an opportunity early on, I would be further along in my work (career) now. As a corporate messenger, I make "ok" pay, but where do I go from here? How do I move up?

Russell landed his current job after graduating from high school. He credited a friend for helping him to get this job that he has held for the past seven years:

> I found out about the job from a friend who works for another messenger service. He said that these jobs are seldom in the want ads. You need to be referred by someone already within the system. I have seen more and more blacks get these jobs, but when I started with this company seven years ago, there was only one other black working here—and he referred me.

This raises an important issue regarding the job networks available to these young fathers. As Russell suggests, corporate messenger jobs represent only "the tip of the iceberg" in terms of the kind of jobs that are not advertised in the newspapers' classified listings and related sources, but instead are circulated through employee and friend networks. Referral to many of these jobs is limited by the racial, ethnic, and employment status of those within the job network. In addition, access to other jobs is restricted by union status, education, and training. Union jobs, which often require an apprentice period, would provide the sustaining salary needed by these young fathers but acquiring those jobs is very difficult. The number of union jobs is diminishing due to the weakening of labor unions in America. African-Americans are especially underrepresented in the union contingent of skilled workers. Given that these positions are vanishing from the labor market, African-American men will continue to experience great difficulty in gaining entry to these job slots as well as sustaining them.

Even within the informal economy, opportunities for these young men have declined. Keith and Hershey's depiction of work situations in the informal economy suggest that such opportunities are disappearing because of what they perceive as competition with "illegal Mexicans for cheaper pay," legal efforts mounted to make employers pay employment taxes and FICA, and the constant relocation of jobs out of the African-American community and the urban core into suburban communities where public transportation is limited. African-American male job networks have been decimated, partially due to white employers' perceptions of African-American males, especially young males, as unreliable and undesirable workers (Kirschenman and Neckerman 1991; Taub 1991). Finally, male informal work networks in the African-American community are increasingly associated with crime and drugs. As Keith stated: "It is very dangerous today to even be involved in 'legitimate hustles' because they can put you at odds with drug lords and others fighting for turf." As Keith disclosed earlier, his employment record contains a number of "legitimate hustles":

> I did odd jobs for neighbors and relatives in between regular jobs for a long time. Today, I still do odd jobs off the books, but now I do them after work. I use the money I make from these jobs to help make ends meet.

Hershey said that the opportunity to make "an honest buck off the books" is coming his way far less than it did in the past:

> That's a bitch 'cause I need the money more today than I did when I was younger and just blowin' the money on foolishness. People have less money to pay you to do chores and jobs. People also are less trusting today so if they really don't know you, they won't hire you. Things are bad all the way round.

Willie concurred:

> Things are really bad. Money is tight for everyone and when money is tight, it don't flow like it should. The only definite hustle going on today is dealin' drugs and it is dangerous.

Russell agreed that selling drugs is the way most young men make some money, but he felt that a lot of them do it out of necessity:

> Like I said earlier, getting a stable job like mine is not easy for black men. We don't know anyone who can help us to get these jobs, so we settle for what we can get. For a lot of friends, that means doing illegal things. But these guys are not criminals. At least, they don't set out to be criminals. They are just tryin' to make it in the world.

The lack of job preparation and opportunities hits these young men at a time of growing economic pressures to not only support their new families but also their families of origin. In the 1996 Chicago pilot study, whether the father resided in the household or outside, his family of origin often lived in the shadows of poverty. As sons, these young fathers were encouraged to help out or contribute to the household income. The "push" seemed especially intense in the households largely dependent on public assistance. Several of the fathers said that peer and parental pressure had forced them to choose between work and school. Legitimate demands for income seemed to come from all sides, yet as adolescent and young adult fathers, they were ill-equipped to meet them. These young fathers often responded by making decisions about parenting behavior that did not satisfy their parents, the mothers of their children, or themselves.

How Far Can a Brother Push a Quarter?
The Competing Demands of Paternal Presence
and Financial Support

Although nonresident young fathers are often viewed as uninvolved and uncommitted parents, systematic research examining the link between paternal presence, involvement, and child support expectations and provisions among these young fathers suggests otherwise (Danziger and Radin 1990; D. Johnson 1996). This deficit perspective is due, in part, to the continuing practice of assessing paternal involvement almost exclusively in terms of financial support to and residential status with the child (D. Johnson 1996). Other forms of paternal support, in-kind gifts and services, and nurturing and child care during visitation are often overlooked. In addition, the degree to which residential status and marital status affect the provision of support (financial, in-kind, nurturing) is unclear in these assessments, especially in examining paternal involvement among poor, nonresident fathers. Finally, the sources of influence that affect paternal role development and subsequent functioning as fathers require further study. Early socialization to the rights, obligations, and expectations of fatherhood learned in childhood appear crucial to an adolescent father's subsequent paternal development (W. Johnson 1998).

The fathers in this study vary in their financial commitment to their children, ranging from the weekly child support provided by Hershey to his newborn daughter, the regular but not quite weekly child support payments made by both Russell and Willie to their newborns, and the sporadic child support provided by Todd and John. Because both Russell and Willie obtained child support orders for their other children, the regularity with which they felt they could make child support to their newborns was reduced to twice monthly. Damon was employed and made child support payments "under the table" to the mother of his daughter at the insistence of his own mother. She felt strongly that he should provide financial support to his daughter. Keith's commitment to supporting his newborn daughter and his older son is predicated on his finding paid work. Given his unemployed status, he depended on his family for money and other forms of support for his daughter.

Commitments to the Family of Origin

As sons, siblings, and members of their families of origin, these fathers felt intense pressure to provide support to those households as well. Many of these fathers resided with their families of origin. They often moved back and forth between the residences of their mothers, grandmothers, and siblings. This was especially true for those who were unemployed or worked intermittently. While they also resided with their families of procreation for periods of time, these stays were usually temporary and often short in duration.

There is far more competition for these fathers' meager income than one might imagine. The jobs they obtained were often temporary, seasonal, or curtailed due to interpersonal problems between themselves and their employers, usually during the probationary period. As a result, their income did not easily lend itself to systematic or regular distribution. In addition, many of these fathers, even as legally adult men, depended on household income from their families of origin to sustain them or at minimum, "tide them over." If and when they were able to get a job or even a time-limited hustle, they were expected to contribute to the financial expenses of the household. Any amount of money dispensed outside the home might be viewed by the other household residents as lost income.

The father's partner (or mother of his child) may welcome any financial support (even irregular), but this form of support is usually insufficient to justify an invitation to the father to reside with his child in the mother's household. Such an arrangement is seldom an option for adolescent fathers. Nor may the older father desire to establish residence with his child and her mother. The provisions of PRWORA require adolescent mothers receiving Temporary Assistance to Needy Families (TANF) to reside with their families of origin instead of setting up separate households.

One employed father's dilemma illustrates this problem. In the household of Hershey's family of origin, which was composed of family members working outside the home as well as receiving Public Aid and Social Security benefits, the residents maintained a tightly managed interdependent relationship. Although Hershey did not reside with his family of origin, he gave money to his mother regularly to meet the household expenses.

Subsequent to his daughter's birth, his modest but fairly consistent child support payments, paid "under the table," actually siphoned off money that was equally needed by his family of origin. His announcement that he would be contributing less money to the household income was met with resistance and criticism:

> My mother was angry with me for fathering a second child. She reminded me that I could not afford to support my older child, otherwise I would be living with that child. I agree that my wages are not totally sufficient to support my children, now that I will be giving money to three households, but my older child's mother and me do not get along. That's why I do not live with that child. I would like to move in with my new baby and her mother, but I am afraid that money will become a problem and destroy our good relationship. My mother really does not want me to move in with my newborn and her mother because I would not be able to help her [my mother] out.

Intergenerational poverty is a common thread in the lives of all these fathers. Keith contended that his poverty status has heightened since he moved out on his own:

> I can hardly make ends meet. I was laid off from my job two months ago, and I have very little money saved. I didn't know I would be laid off, otherwise I would not have moved out of my grandmother's house. I probably would not have had this new baby either. I am looking for another job right now. I know that I must get some money coming in and in a hurry. With all the things that I got to do and people to take care of, I got to get myself a job.

Commitments to the Family of Procreation

Whether via the formal legal system or informal social paternity arrangements, visitation is typically negotiated by providing ongoing financial or child support. Tangible evidence of financial support serves to ensure paternal access. This has created an enormous barrier to low-income, nonresident fathers' involvement with their children.

Labor economists have long contended that the low wages of young men who experience difficulty gaining entry into the labor force will eventually increase as their labor force participation matures. Unfortunately, many of these men experience chronic difficulty in gaining entry into the labor force. This problem lengthens the period in which they must work for lower wages before they are able to see the accelerated fruits of their labor. And this is particularly disadvantageous for young men whose financial obligations include providing child support for their families of procreation as well as assuming other financial responsibilities for their families of origin.

The fathers in this study acknowledged their responsibility to provide various forms of instrumental support (e.g., money, milk, diapers for their newborns) and complementary support for their older children, but provision of financial support was contingent on their success in obtaining and sustaining employment. To date, the efforts of several of the fathers have proven futile. Keith offered the following:

> I am trying to work out arrangements with my son's mother so I can see him on weekends. I know that it would help her out, but she's so mad with me because I can't give her child support that she would rather inconvenience herself than let me see my son.

Hershey, who has a daughter from a previous marriage, said that he had problems with his former wife in gaining visitation rights when he was unable to contribute money to the household:

> When I was younger and unemployed, my daughter's mother would not let me or my family keep my daughter. I now realize that she [my daughter's mother] wanted me to give money, but I had no money to give. My mother gave money and gifts to my daughter from time to time, and, finally, my daughter's mother would let my mother keep her, but not me.

Hershey felt that his daughter's mother was unfair because "she knew I was unemployed from the jump [beginning]" and her change in attitude "came out of nowhere." He currently views her expectations differently:

> I was eighteen years old at the time, and I hardly had any commitment to myself. I just wasn't into taking care of someone else, not even my daughter that I truly love. I now understand that having a child means taking care of her and for me, that means working to take care of her. I do not have those crazy ideas now. I know what I must do for my newborn.

Such experiences have contributed to the fathers' skepticism about their ability to negotiate child visitation rights with the mothers of their newborns because of their underemployed or unemployed status.

The Other Side of the Story: Mothers Weigh In

Interviews with the mothers confirm that their expectations of paternal support were largely financial. When asked about their expectations regarding a father's financial commitment to his children, all sixteen mothers indicated that fathers should provide at least 50 percent of the financial support, and the majority of these mothers felt fathers should provide at least 75 percent of the financial support for their children. The mothers stated that they typically expected the father to assume the primary responsibility for supporting their children and often made this expectation a condition for child visitation and relationship-building with both their children and their partners.

Only one mother in this study stated that she really did not expect the father of her newborn to provide financial support because of his age and the limited opportunities available to him to earn money. But this perspective was offered by an adolescent mother immediately following the birth of the baby. She believed that her parents would support her and the baby. Efforts to conduct a follow-up interview with this mother were unsuccessful. It is questionable that she would maintain this position over time.

When asked about their child visitation dilemmas, most of the fathers acknowledged that they should be providing financial support to their children. John made the following statement:

> It's really like part of the agreement. If she [the mother] has to take care of the baby every day, I can see how she believes that I should give money to help out. That's the way it's always been. My mother agrees, and she told me that I should help out with the baby's expenses. She says that's what a real man do.

Willie also believed that providing child support should be his responsibility, but he felt that his extenuating circumstances should be given some consideration:

> I think a father should support his children and that's what I am trying to do, but it seems that no one cares about all the father has to go through to do that. It is hard trying to make ends meet, especially in two places [households].

Russell shared Willie's concern that his efforts, although not always successful, are not recognized and fully valued:

> No one helps fathers who want to do the right thing. I know men who do not care about their children. But fathers like me do not get any

props [recognition] or help. The government only wants us for what money we can give and that's not much. I would like to be the one who supports my children—not the government—but I need help to get to that point. I don't see no help on the horizon.

These fathers are not proud of their past and emerging track records of supporting their children. Clearly, they feel that their efforts to provide financial support could be improved. Todd expressed embarrassment that he has only twice earned money for his newborn:

I have to depend on my mother to give me money for my child. I would like to earn the money myself, but I am still looking for a job. But the baby need things every day.

During the survey interview, John requested assistance in finding a job. When told that he could possibly be referred to a community-based organization that works with young nonresident fathers to connect them with their children, he seemed more than enthusiastic. Before initial contact with the agency could be made, John called fourteen times (within six days, which included only three working days) to inquire about the contact. During a follow-up interview with John, he shared the following information:

I did not visit the baby in the hospital because I did not have anything to take. I wanted to give my girlfriend some money, but I didn't have none. I asked my mother to help me out, but she started "sweating me" [giving him a lecture]. She finally gave me the money but not before she let me have it [gave him a lecture]. I felt kinda bad.

The poor socioeconomic status of John and the mother of his child further dramatizes the need for these fathers to assume some financial support for their children. Only three of the sixteen young mothers held jobs. Only one young mother stated that her parents planned to support her and her child. If the remaining mothers were dependent on public assistance to support their children, they all probably recognized that those financial allotments would be insufficient to fully support them and their newborns. Therefore, financial support from the fathers, however meager, is not only appreciated: it is crucial.

It is important to point out that, like the mothers of their children, the young fathers in the study do not disagree with the assumption that their breadwinner role is a prerequisite for their other parental responsibilities. They describe fatherhood as a multidimensional undertaking, involving the following roles: provider, nurturer, protector, disciplinarian, friend, and confidant. However, they contend that while each of these roles is important, the provider role is tantamount. Cazenave (1979) viewed the provider or instrumental role as an "interface phenomenon" that makes the execution of other paternal and male familial roles possible. He further believes that the provider role is so intricately tied to other socially approved roles and activities that the father's failure as a financial provider weakens his ability to successfully undertake other critical paternal roles.

The disclosures of the fathers in the study support Cazenave's contention. These nonresident fathers, younger and older alike, viewed the provision of instrumental support to the family as a prerequisite to other paternal roles. Given their overall labor market statuses, their levels of commitment to this paternal obligation are compromised by their inability to uphold it. Although five of these young fathers stated that they were willing to endure significant hardship in order to maintain their financial commitment to their children, only two fathers felt that they could fully take on the "breadwinner" role.

For the younger fathers, the impact of their inability to sustain themselves in the labor force and support their families of procreation made the adolescent-to-adult transition far more difficult (Bowman 1990). It posed a special psychosocial challenge to these young men that has far-reaching developmental implications, which include an enfeebled sense of personal empowerment and efficacy in coping with role barrier in subsequent stages (Bandura 1986). The costs of defining fatherhood primarily or solely in terms of a provider role, therefore, are suffered not only by children whose fathers fail to perform other crucial parental roles but also by the fathers themselves, who often view themselves as parental failures, as well as failures in their work and work preparation roles. More than thirty years ago, Liebow (1967, 73) poignantly described "fathers without children" as "some who are not always absent and some who are less 'absent' than others." He continued:

> Moreover, the same father may have relationships of different intensity with his different children at the same time. The spectrum of father-child relationships is a broad one, ranging from complete ignorance of the child's existence to continuous, day-by-day contact between father and child. The emotional content of the relationships ranges from what, to the outside observer, may seem on the father's part callous indifference or worse, all the way to hinted private intimacies whose intensity can only be guessed at.

In a recent research study of low-income, nonresident fathers in the Parents Fair Share Demonstration conducted by the Manpower Demonstration Research Corporation, ethnographer Earl Johnson eloquently described contemporary men who are also "fathers without children." Johnson's portrait was strikingly similar to Liebow's. It is chilling to think that thirty years later, so little has been done, given recent social science findings about the importance of paternal involvement for improving child well-being (E. Johnson and F. Doolittle 1998).

Contextual Research on Nonresident Fathers: A Basis for Public Policy Strategies and Intervention Practice

The findings of the 1996 Chicago pilot form the basis for the subsequent field-based research examination of circumstances, behaviors, and attitudes of unmarried parenthood and the effects on child well-being. As the largest research study to date that includes nonresident fathers, the Fragile Families and Child Well-Being Study explores the dimensions of out-of-wedlock paternity and applies innovative research approaches to fathers as well as mothers. The proposed use of in-depth interviews with fathers in between survey collections offers a more-detailed understanding of parenting activities and family processes for examining what otherwise might be viewed as dysfunctional paternal role and family functioning.

Research Strategies and Approaches to Examining Nonresident Fathers: Missteps in Understanding the Context of Fatherhood in Fragile Families

Patriarchal responsibility and obligation are valued in American society. Paternal presence and involvement are among the strongest indicators of improved child well-being outcomes. An important issue of public concern is the seeming disenchantment among fathers in general toward supporting their children. National, state, and local legislative bodies have responded by enacting legislation to galvanize public concern. This theme is implicit in major portions of the 1996 PRWORA. Family and neighborhood mores also dictate acceptable behavior and behavioral responses for which strong sanctions may be otherwise imposed.

The perception of fathers as "mainly breadwinners" is persistent throughout the United States. Men themselves view their identity and self-respect as integrally tied to their work (Gaylin 1992). Many fathers take on painstaking and personally unfulfilling jobs to support their families. Societal changes, however, have contributed to changes in relationship patterns and family formation as well as in the labor force. In this broader context, fatherhood is being reconsidered and traditionally reaffirmed simultaneously

(Blankenhorn 1995; Marsiglio 1995a, 1995b). These "push/pull" factors have created enormous tension in the public discourse as professionals and lay-persons alike grapple with the attendant issues.

The designation of "deadbeat dads," men who do not support their children, has been assigned to a broad range of nonresident fathers who do not provide a sufficient level of child support. Most efforts to identify dead-beat dads fail to distinguish between those nonsupporting fathers whose earnings enable them to financially support their children ("deadbeats") and those financially unable to do so ("turnips," as in "you can't get blood from . . .") (Mincy and Sorenson 1998). A disproportionate number of the fathers portrayed in the preceding sections are turnips. The designation deadbeat only serves to create monstrous public reaction toward poor fathers by citizens, judges, policymakers, and mothers alike. It fails to illuminate the context, that is, the individual and structural circumstances that lead to lack of support from these young fathers, and it also does little to encourage the creation of realistic interventions designed to ameliorate this national problem.

A Call for Innovation and Improvement in Research Endeavors Aimed at Nonresident Fathers

The population of fathers under examination needs to be better defined. The terms "teen," "adolescent" and "young" father have been used inter-changeably for identifying and describing a group of fathers whose paternal role functioning, among other things, is socially inept. Early attempts to identify the partners of adolescent mothers reflect a mixed bag of re-search approaches: the inclusion (Lerman 1986) and exclusion (Marsiglio 1987) of fathers who are in their early twenties without taking into account the mother's age at birth; a definition of the sample in terms of the mother's age irrespective of the fathers' age (Furstenberg and Harris 1993); as well as those who restrict their research to adolescent pregnancy/childbearing issues specifically relevant to teenage parents or hypothetical teen parents (Marsiglio 1988, 1989; Marsiglio and Menaghan 1990). The fact that young men are often three (or more) years older than their adolescent female part-ners (Males and Chew 1996) further complicates efforts to properly iden-tify young fathers.

Improvements in data collected on fathers continue to evolve. Social science and policy researchers, however, still know far less about these young fathers than they are willing to admit. Large survey studies based on U.S. Census data as well as national study samples yield relatively little infor-mation on the activities of the jobless men, particularly those out of the labor force. Poor, young African-American fathers are most heavily concentrated among the jobless and the underemployed. The Current Population Survey (CPS), for example, lacks information on certain alternatives to work that may be quite important to youth. It is widely recognized that crime (broadly defined to include working in the "underground economy" as well as violent crime) is a major alternative to employment for youth, yet the CPS contains no questions on such activities (Freeman and Holzer 1986). Finally, because most of these large national samples focus on households rather than individuals, nonresident dads will continue to be "missing and unaccounted for" (Greene and Moore 1996).

Conclusion

Although self-sufficiency is a frequently articulated goal for poor, young fathers, this is far more difficult to achieve than they often realize. The absence of a systematic plan to acquire employment that supports them and their children generally renders them powerless to achieve this goal. Without educational and vocational skills necessary for entry into the labor market, many young nonresident fathers must reside with their families of origin and depend on household income to meet their personal obligations. As fathers, sporadic support to their children is often derived from their parents and families of origin (W. Johnson 1993).

This examination of urban, poor nonresident fatherhood has yielded important information about the partners of young unmarried mothers and their propensity to become self-sufficient as well as to support their children. Although the age range of fathers in this study is rather broad, these men are strikingly similar in terms of their labor force participation and in other areas impacted by their employment status. For all of the fathers under study, the equation of fatherhood with financial support was desired yet problematic because the luckier ones were among the working poor, often with more financial commitments that they could possibly meet, and the rest were unemployed. This primary focus on financial provision was equally problematic for their children because it supports a parenting system in which expectations are generally inflexible and unrealistic, causing conflict between the parents and, ultimately, depriving the children of an ongoing relationship with their fathers. For children, this also results in the loss of future income that might otherwise be provided them if their fathers' economic situation were to improve.

Involvement with fathers who cannot provide a steady stream of income is nonetheless critical to children's future functioning and well-being. Even when fathers believe that fatherhood is a multidimensional undertaking, the embarrassment they may feel about not providing for their children may lead them to withdraw emotional support from their children as well. Previous studies have suggested that the families of origin and extended families from which adolescent and young nonresident African-American fathers emerge often have marginalized work experiences, marginalized paternal involvement, or both (W. Johnson 1993; Miller 1994; Sullivan 1985). The neighborhoods and communities in which they reside often have limited visible examples on which they might model paternal behavior that reflects broader societal parental expectations (W. Johnson 1993). The areas of family, neighborhood, and community socialization are regarded as strong predictors (Anderson 1990; Christmon 1990; Miller 1994) of future paternal responsibility and obligation. Thus, encouraging fathers to remain committed to their children and to fulfill the multiple dimensions of their paternal role is crucial to their children's willingness and ability to parent their own future children.

When the fathers are young in chronological age, there are additional costs associated with an early withdrawal from the parenting role. The equation of paternal responsibility with income provision is generally unrealistic for these young fathers, given their lack of developmental preparation needed for entry into the labor force. It also contributes to the established cycle of "lack of efficacy" in socially approved roles, creating an "all or nothing" framework that does not offer fathers a way to assume increasing responsibility. Further research should examine adolescent fatherhood, fully considering the developmental trajectories that poor, young males face growing up in poor inner-city environments and the various supports that could enhance their chances of successfully meeting the challenges of paternal obligations (W. Johnson 1995; Lee 1994; Marsiglio 1989).

Current statistics suggest that adolescent males are the biological fathers of children born to adolescent mothers in roughly one out of four such pregnancies (Males and Chew 1996). As adolescents, they are educationally unprepared to assume the financial responsibilities associated with paternity. In fact, marginal and/or poor academic achievement, truancy, and dropping out of school are associated with early sexual engagement, teen pregnancy, and parenting (Crane 1991; Ku, Sonenstein, and Pleck 1994). Adolescent fathers are unlikely to have completed high school or obtained a GED certificate at the point of paternity. For African-Americans, differences in skill, geographic location, and family background explain some of their disadvantages in the job market relative to whites, but a large part of the observed differential is attributed to discrimination (Freeman and Holzer 1986). The extent to which racial differences in gaining access to job market success affects paternal obligation and support has not been fully explored.

Antecedents to labor force participation include formal education and training. While high school completion remains a minimum criterion for many entry-level jobs that lead to possible career options, postsecondary education and job training have become increasingly important prerequisites. Without sufficient education and training, these adolescent fathers are unable to gain employment that will support themselves and their families. Public policies must address the limited availability of jobs once formal training has been obtained. Many of the jobs in the urban labor markets in which these young fathers reside are temporary in duration, pay less than self-sustaining salaries, or offer benefits that do not adequately support these young men or their families. Pilot urban projects such as the Annie E. Casey Foundation's Jobs Initiative now recognize that job seekers must be linked to the larger regional labor market. Of particular significance to young fathers is the pilot project's attempt to build and strengthen connections between jobs projects and human service systems (Annie E. Casey Foundation, 1995).

However, in addition to better preparing fathers for the labor market and to linking all fathers to better jobs, the public discourse regarding poor nonresident fathers must also be reexamined. In the context of welfare reform, issues of paternity establishment and child support enforcement must be explored in a broader, more inclusive context. Establishing paternity and providing financial support are important components of paternal support. It is reasonable to expect fathers who can financially support their children to do so, and public policy should focus on strategies to make these fathers assume responsibility. Urban, poor, young fathers who are unable to support their children due to weak labor market participation should also be encouraged to provide whatever instrumental support they can, whenever possible, and society should willingly supplement their support to ensure that all children are protected from poverty (Garfinkel 1992). However, when these fathers are adolescents or young adults whose developmental stage may preclude assumption of this role and whose transition into fatherhood lacks the human/social capital base to help them properly assume this role, the economic provider role should not be the absolute barometer of paternal role functioning.

The paternal role is ideally facilitated when related issues do not impinge on the nonresident father's willingness to provide financial and nurturing support, both of which are critical to his children's orderly growth and development. But these young fathers live in a world that is far from ideal, and societal perceptions of this problem require reshaping. New system approaches that employ law, economics, education, medicine, social work, and other disciplines are crucial to developing paternal responsibility and raising the standard of living for young fathers and their families to a level at which they can meet their obligations. They cannot do this alone.

NOTES

1. The Fragile Families and Child Well-Being Study is funded by National Institute for Child Health and Human Development (NICHD) and a consortium of foundations including the Ford, Robert Wood Johnson, W. T. Grant, St. David's Hospital, and Hogg Foundations, the Public Policy Institute of California, the Healthcare Fund of New Jersey, the Fund for New Jersey, and the Commonwealth Fund and will include more than 4,700 families in twenty U.S. cities. The research study was designed to gain more insight into nonresident fatherhood in "fragile families" (Mincy 1994), which are characterized as unmarried relationships involving low to unskilled parents who are often unemployed and to whom children are born out of wedlock. It explores several domains of personal functioning among non-resident fathers previously unexamined in any systematic analysis—social capital, human capital, antisocial behavior, mental health, attitudes toward paternity, and fathering behavior—in order to understand these domains' developmental relationships with paternal role perception and functioning. Eight junior research scholars (including six African-Americans and one Latina) are investigators in the study under the direction of principal investigators Irwin Garfinkel of the Columbia University School of Social Work and Sara McLanahan of Princeton University.

2. Contact with most of these fathers was made during the young mother's hospital stay. It was anticipated that the fathers could be interviewed at the hospital when they came to see their newborn and the baby's mother. Unfortunately, I was unable to conduct any of the fathers' interviews at the hospital. Not all the fathers visited the mothers and children in the hospital. Some mothers indicated in their interviews that their partners had not been informed of their children's births and the mothers and children were dismissed from the hospital prior to his visits. Among those fathers who visited the hospital, their visits did not necessarily coincide with visiting hours and in a few instances, due to the status of the couple's current relationship, the fathers may have visited the baby but not the baby's mother. As a result, I made provisions to conduct the interviews in the father's neighborhood. While conducting an in-home interview may seem ideal, I realized that it might create some discomfort, not only for the young father but for other residents in the household. Thus when contact was made, the interview was scheduled at a neighborhood McDonald's or Burger King, since at least one of these fast-food restaurants are located in virtually every neighborhood. The fathers' responses to these locations were generally positive.

REFERENCES

Anderson, E. 1990. *Streetwise: Race, Class and Change in an Urban Community.* Chicago: University of Chicago Press.

Bandura, A. 1986. *Social Foundations of Thought and Action: A Social-Cognitive Theory.* Englewood Cliffs, NJ: Prentice-Hall.

Blankenhorn, D. 1995. *Fatherless America: Confronting Our Most Urgent Social Problem.* New York: Basic Books.

Bowman, P. 1989. "Research Perspectives on Black Men: Role Strain and Adaptation Across the Adult Life Cycle." In *Black Adult Development and Aging,* ed. R. Jones, 117–50. Berkeley, CA: Cobbs and Henry.

———. 1990. "The Adolescent-to-Adult Transition: Discouragement Among Jobless Black Youth." *New Directions in Child Development* 46:87–106.

Bowman, P., M. Callahan, J. Davis, T. Forman, K. Harris, A. Hunter, and W. Johnson. 1996. "African American Men Across the Life Span: Social Identities, Family Role Meaning(s) and Function—Theory, Research and Policy Considerations." Symposium presentation at the 58th Annual Conference of the National Council on Family Relations, Kansas City, Missouri.

Bozett, F., and S. Hanson. 1991. *Fatherhood and Families in a Cultural Context.* New York: Springer.

Annie E. Casey Foundation. 1995. *Annie E. Casey Jobs Initiative: Making Connections Initiative Summary.* Baltimore, MD: Annie E. Casey Foundation.

Cazenave, N. 1979. "Middle-Income Black Fathers: An Analysis of the Provider Role." *Family Coordinator* 28 (4): 583–93.

Cherlin, A. 1978. "Remarriage as an Incomplete Institution." *American Journal of Sociology* 84:634–50.

Christmon, K. 1990. "Parental Responsibility of African American Unwed Adolescent Fathers." *Adolescence* 25:645–53.

Crane, J. 1991. "The Effects of Neighborhoods on Dropping Out of School and Teenage Childbearing." In *The Urban Underclass,* ed. C. Jencks and P. Peterson, 299–320. Washington, DC: The Brookings Institution.

Danziger, S., and N. Radin. 1990. "Absence Does Not Equal Uninvolved: Predictors of Fathering in Teen Mother Families." *Journal of Marriage and the Family* 52:636–42.

Ellwood, D. 1986. "The Spatial Mismatch Hypothesis: Are There Teenage Jobs Missing in the Ghetto?" In *The Black Youth Employment Crisis,* ed. R. Freeman and H. Holzer, 147–90. Chicago: University of Chicago Press.

Forman, T. 1995. "Black Family Poverty, Children and Social Policy. The Role of Fathers." Unpublished manuscript, Department of Sociology, University of Michigan.

Freeman, R., and H. Holzer. (1986). "The Black Youth Employment Crisis: Summary of Findings." In *The Black Youth Employment Crisis,* ed. R. Freeman and H. Holzer, 3–20. Chicago: University of Chicago Press.

Furstenberg, F. 1976. *Unplanned Parenthood: The Social Consequences of Teenage Childbearing.* New York: Free Press.

Furstenberg, F., and K. Harris. 1993. "When and Why Fathers Matter: Impacts of Father Involvement on the Children of Adolescent Mothers." In *Young Unwed Fathers: Changing Roles and Emerging Policies,* ed. R. Lerman and T. Ooms, 117–238. Philadelphia: Temple University Press.

Garfinkel, I. 1992. *Assuring Child Support.* New York: Russell Sage Foundation.

Gaylin, W. 1992. *The Male Ego.* New York: Viking.

Greene, A., and K. Moore. 1996. "Non-resident Father Involvement and Child Outcomes Among Young Children in Families on Welfare." Paper presented at the Conference on Father Involvement, 10–11 October, National Institutes of Health, Bethesda, Maryland.

Grief, G. 1985. *Single Fathers.* Lexington, MA: Lexington Books.

Grubb, W. 1989. "Preparing Youth for Work: The Dilemmas of Education and Training Programs." In *Adolescent and Work: Influences of Social Structure, Markets and Culture,* ed. D. Stern and D. Eichorn, 13–41. Hillsdale, NJ: Erlbaum.

Henly, J. 1993. "The Significance of Social Context: The Case of Adolescent Childbearing in the African American Community." *Journal of Black Psychology* 19 (4): 461–77.

Johnson, D. 1996. "Father Presence Matters: A Review of the Literature." A commissioned paper of the National Center on Fathers and Families, University of Pennsylvania, Philadelphia.

Johnson, E., and F. Doolittle. 1998. "Low-Income Parents and the Parents' Fair Share Program: An Early Qualitative Look at Improving the Ability and Desire of Low-Income Non-Custodial Parents to Pay Child Support." In *Fathers Under Fire: The Revolution in Child Support Enforcement,* ed. I. Garfinkel, S. McLanahan, D. Meyer, and J. Seltzer, 220–52. New York: Russell Sage Foundation.

Johnson, E., A. Levine, F. Doolittle. 1997. *Father's Fair Share: Helping Poor Men Manage Child Support and Fatherhood.* New York: Russell Sage Foundation.

Johnson, W. 1993. "Perceptions and Patterns of Paternal Role Functioning Among Urban, Lower Socioeconomic Status, Adolescent and Young Adult African American Males: A Social Choice/Social Norms Perspective." Ph.D. diss., University of Chicago.

———. 1995. "Paternal Identity Among Urban Adolescent Males." *African American Research Perspectives* 2 (2): 82–86.

———. 1998. "Paternal Involvement in Fragile, African American Families: Implications for Clinical Social Work Practice." *Smith College Studies in Social Work* 68 (2): 215–32.

Kirschenman, J., and Neckerman, K. 1991. "'We'd Love to Hire Them but . . .': The Meaning of Race for Employers." In *The Urban Underclass,* ed. C. Jencks and P. Peterson, 203–34. Washington, DC: The Brookings Institution.

Ku, L., F. Sonenstein, and J. Pleck. 1994. "Neighborhood, Family and Work: Influences on the Premarital Behaviors of Adolescent Males." *Social Forces* 7 (2): 479–503.

Lee, C. 1994. "Adolescent Development." In *Nurturing Young Black Males,* ed. R. Mincy, 33–44. Washington, DC: Urban Institute Press.

Liebow, E. 1967. *Tally's Corner: A Study of Negro Streetcorner Men.* Boston: Little, Brown.

Lerman, R. 1986. "Who Are the Young Absent Fathers?" *Youth and Society* 18:3–27.

Males, M., and K. Chew. 1996. "The Ages of Fathers in California Adolescent Births." *American Journal of Public Health* 86 (4): 565–68.

Marsiglio, W. 1987. "Adolescent Fathers in the United States: Their Initial Living Arrangements, Marital Experience and Educational Outcomes." *Family Planning Perspectives* 19:240–51.

————. 1988. "Commitment to Social Fatherhood: Predicting Adolescent Males' Intentions to Live with Their Child and Partner." *Journal of Marriage and the Family* 50:427–41.

————. 1989. "Adolescent Males' Pregnancy Resolution Preferences and Family Formation Intentions: Does Family Background Make a Difference for Blacks and Whites?" *Journal of Adolescent Research* 4:214–37.

————. 1995a. "Young Non-resident Biological Fathers." In *Single Parent Families: Diversity, Myths and Realities,* ed. S. Hanson, M. Heims, D. Julian, and J. Sussman, 325–48. Binghamton, NY: Haworth Press.

————. 1995b. "Fathers' Diverse Life Course Patterns: Theory and Social Interventions." In *Fatherhood: Contemporary Theory, Research and Social Policy,* ed. W. Marsiglio, 78–101. Thousand Oaks, CA: Sage.

Marsiglio, W., and E. Menaghan. 1990. "Pregnancy Resolution and Family Formation: Understanding Gender Differences in Adolescents' Preferences and Beliefs." *Journal of Family Issues* 11:313–33.

Miller, D. 1994. "Influences on Paternal Involvement of African American Adolescent Fathers." *Child and Adolescent Social Work* 2 (5): 363–78.

Mincy, R. 1994. "Strengthening Fragile Families. A Proposed Strategy for the Ford Foundation Urban Poverty Program." Unpublished paper.

Mincy, R., and E. Sorenson. 1998. "Deadbeats and Turnips in Child Support Reform." *Journal of Policy Analysis and Management* 17 (1): 44–51.

Moss, P., and C. Tilly. 1991. *Why Black Men Are Doing Worse in the Labor Market: A Review of Supply-side and Demand-side Explanations.* Prepared for the Social Science Research Council Committee for Research on Urban Underclass Working Group on Labor Market Research. New York: Social Science Research Council.

Salter, W. 1997. "Paternal Involvement Among Poor Non-Resident Fathers: National Concern, Local Solution." Invited presentation at the School of Social Service Administration, Friends' Luncheon, University of Chicago, Chicago, Illinois, April.

Sullivan, M. 1985. *Teen Fathers in the Inner City: An Exploratory Ethnographic Study.* New York: Ford Foundation Report, Urban Poverty Programs.

————. 1986. *Ethnographic Research on Young Black Fathers and Parenting: Implications for Public Policy.* New York: Vera Institute of Justice.

Taub, R. 1991. "Differing Conceptions of Honor and Orientations Toward Work and Marriage among Low-Income African Americans and Mexican Americans." Paper presented at the Chicago Urban Poverty and Family Life Conference. Chicago, Illinois, October 1–12.

Wallerstein, J., and S. Corbin. 1986. "Father-Child Relationships After Divorce: Child Support and Educational Opportunity." *Family Law Quarterly* 20:109–28.

Williams, C. 1991. "The Role of Fathers in the Socialization of Moral Attitudes and Behavior in African American Children and Adolescents." Unpublished paper.

Wilson, W. 1987. *The Truly Disadvantaged: The Inner City, the Underclass, and Public Policy.* Chicago: University of Chicago Press.

————. 1996. *When Work Disappears: The World of the New Urban Poor.* New York: Knopf.

CHAPTER 10

Social Contexts in the Making
of Public Policy

Ann Chih Lin

In the analytical models used by policymakers and policy analysts, individuals act rationally in response to a variety of incentives. Set taxes too high, and work effort will drop as people realize that their work is worth less relative to leisure; reduce penalties for drug possession, and more people will use drugs more flagrantly. This causal model of behavior is simple to understand: who can argue with the proposition that people generally try to do the best they can for themselves, that they are rational enough to weigh different alternatives and choose the most favorable? The model also allows for recurrent optimism in the face of seemingly intractable social problems: find the right lever, as Archimedes asserted, and one can move the world.

Yet the simplicity of this model overlooks many complexities of the ways in which people live their lives. People certainly try to make choices that will benefit them; they certainly act with forethought and reason. But they do not make choices in isolation from their life circumstances, their understanding of history, their beliefs about the world, or their networks of relationships. The context in which incentives operate can make them more or less important, alter their meaning, or set off a chain of unforeseen circumstances. Thus, carefully targeted interventions introduced amid fanfare and welcomed as "bold" and "daring" often turn out, months and years later, to have few effects, or effects quite different from those anticipated. Proponents of an incentive-based model of policy-making, however, tend to view such negative findings as indicating only that the wrong incentive was chosen, or perhaps that the incentive was not properly implemented. The assumption itself—that behavior will respond to the right incentive—is rarely questioned.

By contrast, some scholars, including those represented in this volume, challenge not only the incentives that policymakers have offered to change behavior, but the behavioral model of policy-making as well. They do not dispute the importance or the utility of finding the right incentives. But they focus their attention on the social contexts in which incentives operate, seeking to understand how the contexts of neighborhood, workplace, and family strengthen, weaken, or divert attention from specific incentives. Some of the authors, including Gina Barclay-McLaughlin, Carla O'Connor, and Andrew Reaves, examine prerequisites for action, explaining that opportunities and incentives need to be offered by those one trusts and against a background of social support. Many, including Mary Pattillo-McCoy, Sharon Hicks-Bartlett, Ariel Kalil et al., and Waldo E. Johnson Jr., analyze competing motivations, explaining why inducements that seem powerful in isolation can become peripheral in context. Others, like Alford A. Young Jr., look at differences in worldviews, which can skew or even reformulate the meaning of incentives. And some, including Sharon Hicks-Bartlett, Ariel Kalil et al., and Waldo E. Johnson Jr., emphasize the downstream effects of incentives, particularly the ways in which they can reverberate through kin, friendship, and neighborhood networks.

The policy recommendations that can be developed from this kind of interpretive research often differ from those produced by behavioral models. It is impossible to design a change in social context in the way that one might design a tax credit: social environments are discovered, not created. But this kind of research can help policymakers to evaluate proposals with respect to the social contexts in which they are going to operate, so that they can better anticipate obstacles and predict consequences. This kind of research can also help in designing policies that take advantage of traits within a particular social context, so that they can work in tandem with habitual practices and derive reinforcement from existing beliefs and relationships.

Research into the social context of policy thus leads to two kinds of recommendations. The first is a set of recommendations about what to consider and what to avoid. What factors, apart from the direct effect of an incentive on individual behavior, are relevant in determining whether a policy might be successful? In essence, such recommendations serve as a form of preimplementation evaluation; they map the possible consequences of a policy prior to implementation. The second is a set of recommendations about building policy upon salient contextual characteristics: what expectations, practices, relationships, or strengths in the social context can be incorporated into the motivational structure of an incentive or into the prerequisites for its success? Recommendations like these replace abstract, general models of human motivation with specific, grounded information about the group and area that a policy seeks to affect.

The chapters in this volume on the social contexts of African-American poverty reinforce the advantages of this approach. The essays cover a wide range of experiences and age/gender groups, but they all document the centrality of relationships, the priority that people attach to maintaining them, the resources they provide, and the obligations they impose. The salience of relationships suggests that policies should be evaluated for their effects on people other than those targeted, and they should attempt to target family and peer groups rather than individuals. A second, related theme is the critical role of social support in transferring knowledge and enabling action. The chapters show that the availability, the credibility, and even the will to use information is often determined by social support and reinforcement, rather than by the qualities of the information itself. Put another way, for policy incentives or mandates to have the desired effect, they must be mediated through social and familial networks that validate individuals, and that individuals trust. A third set of issues highlights the importance of non-material motivations, such as safety and respect, to the decisions people make. This suggests that policies should be evaluated for the ways in which such motivations might clash with the incentives a policy offers, and it predicts that policies that appeal to these motivations are more likely to be successful than those that ignore them.

Building Policy around Relationships

Listen to current policy debates on poverty, and one hears words like *responsibility, opportunity, work,* and *accountability.* Listen to the writers in this volume, and one hears the word *relationship* instead. The relationships the authors discuss vary with the individuals they study. For Kalil et al., Johnson, and Hicks-Bartlett, it is the relationship of parents, often young parents, to their families of origin. For Reaves, in the context of staying in jobs or accepting promotions, and Pattillo-McCoy, in the context of choosing schools and extracurricular activities, it is the desire not to abandon one's peers. What binds these accounts together is the level of effort, both individual and social, it takes to maintain these relationships, and the level of importance placed on maintaining them. When poverty combined with racial disadvantage means that financial resources, supportive services, and social esteem are all scarce in these neighborhoods, reliance on family, friends, and neighbors enables people to better meet both their physical and emotional needs.

The centrality of relationships to the coping strategies of the African-American urban poor implies that policy initiatives that focus only on the individual will face predictable problems. For instance, as Hicks-Bartlett shows, policies that require all welfare recipients to work can create dilemmas for the relatives and neighbors who depend on them for informal, but necessary, care. Bringing some women into the workforce might thus make it harder for other workers to keep their jobs. In other cases, as Kalil et al. and Johnson document, work and child support mandates for young parents, which may be good policies in themselves, may create more dependence on parents and relatives and upset informal financial and child-rearing agreements between unwed parents. In a different policy area, as Reaves and Pattillo-McCoy illustrate, even necessary and valuable reforms— opportunities for promotion or for better schooling—may be perceived as unattractive or as imposing high psychic and social costs, when weighed against solidarity with one's peer group. In such cases, opportunities might go un- or underutilized, and policymakers might mistakenly conclude that either the opportunities were unnecessary, or that those who were targeted were unwilling to take advantage of them.

Taking social contexts into account during the policy-making process would enrich policy debates. Even if it does not lead to different policy proposals, knowledge about social contexts could guide implementation and assist in policy evaluations. In the cases cited previously, for instance, knowledge of the ancillary effects of policy might lead policymakers to think not only about child-care subsidies but also about child-care options: what can be done to ensure not just the affordability of child care, but also the flexibility, the trustworthiness, and the availability that family-provided child care offers? Conversely, what can be done to help families cope better with the strains that mutual obligation places on relationships? Similarly, awareness of competing motivations might lead to more-informed evaluations when incentives, such as a better education, a better job, or court-ordered child support payments, fail to achieve desired ends.

In addition to informing the content of specific policies, however, a knowledge of social context could actually lead to different kinds of policy. Policymakers might consider models in which groups in relationship, rather than individuals, are the relevant units. For instance, microcredit programs, unlike asset development programs targeted on individuals, are based on the power of social relationships. Their basic unit is a group of neighbors that administers loans to members, uses ties of mutual trust and obligation to enforce repayment, passes on information and expertise, and provides mutual aid. Innovative programs aimed at raising the well-being of children born out of wedlock bring not only the unmarried parents, but also the parents' families of origin, into decision making about child support and parenting. Some foster care agencies are creating programs that bring a panoply of involved participants—aunts, grandparents, and teachers as well as the parents and the social worker—to the table to make decisions about a child's placement and future.

Taking relationships seriously as an aspect of social context that affects policy does not mean that all relationships are beneficial. The authors give examples of both useful and harmful relationships and show that even socially important relationships may have negative, as well as positive, aspects. Johnson's discussion of mothers who do not wish their sons to pay child support because it diverts money from their own households, Kalil et al.'s account of a young mother who felt the need to move out of her parents' home and into a situation of greater independence, and Hicks-Bartlett's example of a student who puts her college plans on hold to help her mother demonstrate that even the bond between parents and children may not always foster positive outcomes. This information does not negate the importance of relationships. Rather, it underscores the importance of critical research. Too often when policymakers incorporate relationships into the service of policy aims, they assume, as in the requirement for teen mothers to live with a parent or guardian, that parental or community supervision is always good. They do not empirically assess the trade-offs or the possible consequences of these proposals. Taking social context seriously as a necessary aspect of policy-making, by contrast, pushes social phenomena like relationships into the foreground. The results could enhance the policy tools we currently have, while displacing some of the stereotypes that stand in the way of both good policy and good analysis.

The Social Dimensions of Information

For many, a distinctive feature of the last decade is the explosion of information, through the Internet, multiple media outlets, and self-styled experts. Yet as information sources become more and more numerous, questions of credibility—what or whom can one believe?—fit—how does this compare to what I already know?—and utility—what do I need to act upon information?—become more pressing. The chapters by O'Connor, Young, and Barclay-McLaughlin highlight these questions. Many residents of inner-city neighborhoods are isolated from information sources available to those in more affluent areas: O'Connor's students do not use the Web to look for scholarship information, Young's younger men do not hear about job opportunities from their peers, and Barclay-McLaughlin's housing project residents find their worlds getting smaller as the fear of crime and of their neighbors forces them to limit their social circles. What is most striking about these chapters is their insistence on the social dimensions of information: the dependence on family, neighbors, and peers for information and guidance in a context of reliability or trust.

Each author explores a different dimension of this issue. For O'Connor's ambitious young women, information about how to prepare, how to apply, and how to afford college is critical for them to have any hope of fulfilling their dreams. But information must also be delivered by people who care about them: teachers who encourage and push them, relatives who visualize their graduations and who expect them to succeed. This social and emotional support is not separate from information: it is required to make the information usable. For the young men in Young's chapter, information makes sense or is discounted because of its fit with their particular world-view. Because their notion of "good jobs" is based on the last good jobs held by men they know, they are unable to perceive available options as stepping-stones to a better life, albeit of a different kind. And the longer they are absent from the workforce, the less they are likely to understand how to translate what they can do into something that an employer would need. Simply providing information would not help them: without a context in which to understand that information, they distort it—as they do information about a world in which computers are increasingly important—into something that makes sense within their social context. The neighborhood perspective offered by Barclay-McLaughlin puts O'Connor's and Young's chapters into context: the change, from a community in which one's ties to other people were extensive and deep to a place where people fear their neighbors and are afraid to leave home, limits the opportunity for meaningful relationships. Along with other negative implications, this change in neighborhood context limits both the possible sources of information, and the reinforcement and support that make acting on information possible.

Efforts to increase the flow of information into poor neighborhoods should improve opportunities. These chapters show, however, that making data available is not enough. Telling students about available scholarships is not enough to generate applications: encouragement to apply must come from people who know them and can help them to write an application that is convincing to people who give out scholarships. Students also need to know that others like them have won and used those scholarships successfully. Telling people that companies have job openings does not help them to visualize what the job requires, what they would be doing, and why they might be valuable. Nor does it help them to present themselves in ways that attract potential employers. Most important, information provided by outsiders is limited in reach and utility if a trusting relationship is absent. When new information from an unfamiliar source does not complement what people think they already know, it is likely to be discounted. The chapters imply that people depend on the sources they trust to deliver information, even if those sources do not have access to accurate or updated information. The provision of better information does not guarantee that people will believe or use it.

Thus, policies to increase opportunity or to change behavior should pay attention to how information is conveyed, received, and understood. They should also incorporate these observations about the social dimensions of information into policy delivery. Many of the methodological sections in the chapters describe how the authors became conduits of information as they conducted their research. Their interest in, concern for, and identification with their respondents allowed them to be seen as reliable sources of information. This underscores the importance of expecting those who administer programs to be visible in the community and to develop informal ties to residents. The resources they provide cannot be separated from who they are. People also need to know how others with similar problems and challenges solved them, and they need to be able to imagine themselves in the same position. Developing plans for disseminating information that include the use of realistic models would be an important policy innovation. A third approach suggested by these findings is to remember that information is a social phenomenon. Developing policies that utilize existing friendship groups or social institutions, or that develop social entities to accompany new programs, can reinforce policy messages in ways that repetition or expert authority would not.

Policy analysts, entranced by the possibilities of an information age, often believe that their most important challenge is to collect information and make it available. Responsibility for using information belongs to individuals, who are assumed to show their motivation and their willingness to help themselves by taking advantage of what has been provided. But if information is influenced by its social context, such models could create new hierarchies of haves and have nots: hierarchies based not on individual motivation and will, but on being part of social networks where those around you normalize the process of searching for information, convince you that the information is reliable, and give you the background knowledge you need to use it. Taking the social dimensions of information seriously would instead bring existing networks of people into available information networks. It would fulfill the democratic possibilities of new mediums, rather than allow them to reproduce existing hierarchies.

Safety, Respect, and Incentives

Whether due to the fungibility of money or the influence of economists, policy incentives are usually monetary. Consider the Earned Income Tax Credit (EITC), which encourages employment by supplementing the wages of low-income families; or conversely the "family cap," which prevents welfare grants from rising when a welfare recipient bears additional children. Neither policy necessarily assumes that the marginal increase in income is the only reason low-income workers work or welfare recipients bear children. In fact, defenders of these policies often make their case on moral grounds ("People who work should be able to support their families" or "If workers don't get a raise when they have children, why should welfare recipients?"). Monetary incentives, however, may be used even when the underlying policy goal is moral: they are easy to administer and measure, and their value can be standardized.

But although money clearly matters to the African-American urban poor, the authors in this volume caution against a singular reliance on monetary incentives to produce desired behavior. Whether the subject is Young's account of unemployed men turning down work that would bring in at least a little pay, or Reaves's discussion of a young man who leaves "good" jobs with promotion potential because he feels isolated by his race and gender, money recedes into the background when compared with "respect." Hicks-Bartlett and Kalil et al. both explain how the desire to keep their children safe leads some low-income mothers to be overprotective, to cling to bad jobs that provide health insurance for their kids, and to reject better employment that would require them to leave their children unattended or with strangers. It may not be economically wise for these respondents to prioritize "respect" or "safety" over employment that might eventually get them the respect and the safe environments they crave. But the impulse is no different than that of a professional who decides to leave his job because his supervisor consistently denigrates him and his co-workers, or that of middle-class parents who flex their work schedules so that one can be home when school lets out for the afternoon. Such impulses are not less strong for the poor, even though acting on them has more serious economic consequences. Attention to nonmonetary motivations can help explain the seeming failure of some monetary incentives to change behavior.

The implications for the implementation and evaluation of policy are significant. According to current rhetoric, a "good" job is one that pays a living wage, offers benefits, and has a promotion track. Analysts often debate whether policies should strive to provide "good" jobs as opposed to "any job." The respondents in Reaves's and Young's chapters, and in many of the other chapters to a lesser degree, also talk about wages and benefits. They are also concerned, however, about workplaces where they are treated with dignity, where their co-workers are friendly, where they have some control over their time, where they feel they can contribute, and where their efforts are rewarded. There is some correlation between low-skilled, low-paying jobs where the managers are less likely to retain workers, and uncongenial work environments, but the association is not necessary: the workers who talked to Reaves and Hicks-Bartlett remember fast-food establishments and home health care as good jobs. Conversely, while jobs that pay more and that have promotion potential invest more in their workers and thus may do more to retain them, they may not be congenial workplaces. This is especially true when racial or class stereotyping enters the picture: when managers are afraid that workers of a different race or class background might not be as competent or as professional, and thus must be monitored more carefully or even "tested" for fitness. Thus, some low-income workers flourish in "bad jobs" and conversely have trouble in "good jobs," not because money is unimportant, but because the social context of the workplace is also essential.

Debates over child-care subsidies provide another example. It is commonplace to speak of child-care subsidies as a necessary component of welfare reform, and to realize that high-quality child care costs money—whether in subsidies for grandmothers or other family-provided child care, funding for early education programs, or other alternatives. For many parents, however, safety may be just as important as cost. They want to do their best to protect their children by choosing caretakers and peers for them. They want to be present for emergencies even when children no longer need constant supervision. In dangerous neighborhoods, they want to keep their children within known boundaries. As Hicks-Bartlett and Kalil et al. show most vividly in their discussions with mothers, and Pattillo-McCoy and Barclay-McLaughlin allude to in their discussion about community supervision of older children and teenagers, such concerns are not always alleviated with subsidy checks. They point out that in the most vulnerable environments, personal supervision is highly valued even when it may not be the best child care from an objective standpoint, because it is the form of care that makes mothers feel as if they have the most control.

An analysis of the nonmonetary dimensions of good jobs and good child care can help policy analysts understand the obstacles that employment programs or child-care subsidies may face in these communities. It also raises questions about new models of policy-making. For instance, antidiscrimination laws must be enforced. But the adversarial nature of making a claim, and the resources of time, money, and energy it takes to sustain one through investigation, limit the usefulness of the complaint process for improving ordinary work environments. This is especially true when the harassment is severe enough to affect workers' decisions but does not constitute a legally enforceable claim. If workplaces are to become truly respectful of African-American workers, and of all workers in general, different approaches are required. Although much maligned, sensitivity training, especially when focused on multiple kinds of diversity, may be one approach; Sharon Hicks-Bartlett has developed models of such programs. Another might be the establishment of support networks for workers, to share skills for confronting and coping with discrimination, short of leaving one's job. Government cannot always mandate these activities, but it can recognize and promote good models for them.

Government could take a more active role in helping working mothers to evaluate the safety of various child-care options and to have more personal control over their children's care. Whether it is report cards for child-care facilities, afterschool programs that ensure the safety of older children, pagers that allow parents to have easier contact with their children, or ways to make child-care cooperatives more viable, local governments and school systems could provide children with the safe and appropriate care that wealthier parents are able to purchase on their own.

On a broader scale, government is responsible for the safety of neighborhoods—both for the prevention of crime and for the development of trust between residents and police. Bringing parents into contact with the police, with local government, and with schools to design acceptable alternatives is a first step toward creating policy that addresses problems that the poor themselves consider important.

In general, policymakers can promote and support values as a conscious task rather than as a symbolic gesture. Conservatives have often been more aware of the didactic power of government policies than liberals. But both find it easy to assume that the use of the bully pulpit and the passage of regulations—prayer in schools or the condemnation of entertainers—will inculcate values. Both also often assume that values are for government to teach and the people to learn. Taking nonmonetary incentives for behavior more seriously suggests a change in the approach: away from "values" as a code word for the beliefs of politicians, and toward "values" as an instrument of policy. We may not want to create public policy that supports workers who quit when they are harassed or parents who forgo employment to watch their children. But we can find multiple policy instruments to create "respect" and "safety," or learn to use these as incentives that make other policy goals more acceptable to the poor.

Conclusion

All of the chapter authors recognize that most of the problems in urban African-American communities are structural in origin and need structural solutions. A technologically advanced economy, the deterioration of industrial cities, changing patterns of work and family life for men and women—all have profoundly affected the character of American life in ways that harm the most disadvantaged. These changes cannot be reversed; instead, they have created a new economy and a new society to which the poor and the country at large must adapt. Traditional policy solutions—economic growth, public or private job creation, better schools, changes in tax structures, social assistance—have an important role to play as part of that adaptation.

But just as it was once innovative for government to influence growth, create jobs, improve schools, impose an income tax, or create a system of social provision, it is also important to adopt different, but complementary, policy strategies to deal with economic and social inequality. The complexities of a modern world, the fact that society is at once more diverse and more interdependent, may also make us more willing to accept more complex policy models. The behavioral model of policy-making, with its focus on monetary incentives and rational decision making, needs to adapt by incorporating human relationships, the social nature of information, and non-monetary incentives. More generally, models of policy-making must work with and within social contexts: to adapt policy goals and policy tools for particular circumstances, habitual practices, and places.

The analysis of social contexts lacks the simple elegance of economic models. Because its strength is in the details it provides, the number of cases it can examine is necessarily limited. Used in conjunction with more traditional methods, however, the analysis of social contexts adds understanding to prediction and flexibility to mechanistic solutions. The result can be the creation of multidimensional policy approaches, more appropriate for a multidimensional world.

Contributors

Gina Barclay-McLaughlin is a researcher with GBMC International, a global research and development center. She is currently conducting a study entitled "Dreams, Aspirations, and Pathways for Goal Attainment," funded by the Kellogg Foundation. Her work on the chapter for this volume was undertaken while she was a senior research associate for the Chapin Hall Center for Children at the University of Chicago.

Ashli Breen received an M.S.W. and an M.P.H. from the University of Michigan and worked as a research assistant for the Poverty Research and Training Center. She now lives and works in New York City.

Marijata Daniel-Echols is a Ph.D. candidate in the Department of Political Science at the University of Michigan. She is writing a dissertation on the impact of welfare reform on the political beliefs and activity of welfare clients.

Sheldon Danziger is Henry J. Meyer Collegiate Professor of Social Work and Public Policy, Director of the Center for Poverty, Risk and Mental Health, and Director of the Research and Training Program on Poverty, the Underclass and Public Policy at the University of Michigan. He is the coauthor of *America Unequal* (1995), and the coeditor of *Confronting Poverty: Prescriptions for Change* (1994) and numerous other volumes.

Sharon Hicks-Bartlett is the president of Terrapin Training Strategies, Inc., a training and consulting company that helps institutions and organizations manage workplace diversity. She holds a Ph.D. in sociology from the University of Chicago and is currently working on a book about Meadow View, entitled *Kin of Mine*.

Waldo E. Johnson Jr. is Assistant Professor of Social Work at the University of Chicago. He writes on low-income fathers and is a coprincipal investigator on the Fragile Families and Child Well-Being Study, a national longitudinal study on more than 4,700 low-income families in twenty U.S. cities.

Ariel Kalil is Assistant Professor of Public Policy at the University of Chicago. She writes on teenage pregnancy and parenting, the effects of welfare reform on child development, and transitions from school to work for low-income youth.

Ann Chih Lin is Assistant Professor of Public Policy and Political Science at the University of Michigan. She is the author of *Reform in the Making: The Implementation of Social Policy in Prison* (2000) and of articles on qualitative methodology, policy implementation, crime, and immigrant political socialization.

Carla O'Connor is Assistant Professor of Education at the University of Michigan. Her fields of interest are sociology of education and urban education. She is currently exploring the influence of time on the process of educational resilience by examining the life stories of African-American women who are first-generation college graduates and grew up in low-income and working-class households.

Mary Pattillo-McCoy is Assistant Professor of Sociology and African-American Studies at Northwestern University, and a Faculty Fellow with the Institute for Policy Research. She is the author of *Black Picket Fences: Privilege and Peril among the Black Middle Class* (1999) and articles on black urban geography, the black church, and inequality among African-Americans.

Andrew L. Reaves received his Ph.D. in psychology from the University of Michigan and was a postdoctoral fellow in the Program on Poverty, the Underclass, and Public Policy. At the time of his death in November 1999, he was Assistant Professor of Psychology at the University of Alabama. He studied homicide among poor and minority populations and was working on a project on rural teen pregnancy.

Heidi Schweingruber is Director of Research for the Rice University School Mathematics Project and a lecturer in psychology at Rice University. Her current work focuses on elementary and secondary education in urban settings.

Alford A. Young Jr. is Assistant Professor of Sociology and Afro-American and African Studies at the University of Michigan. He is working on a book about African-American men in the inner city, entitled *The Minds of Black Men: Making Sense of Mobility, Opportunity, and Future Life Chances.* He also writes on urban poverty and on African-American intellectuals and intellectual thought.

Index